CHANGING PRIORITIES IN TEACHER EDUCATION

Also Published for the British Comparative
Education Society:

POLITICS AND EDUCATIONAL CHANGE: An International Survey
Edited by Patricia Broadfoot, Colin Brock and Witold Tulasiewicz

Changing Priorities in Teacher Education

Edited by Richard Goodings, Michael Byram
and Michael McPartland

Published on Behalf of
The British Comparative Education Society

CROOM HELM
London & Canberra

NICHOLS PUBLISHING COMPANY
New York

© 1982 The British Comparative Education Society
Croom Helm Ltd, 2-10 St John's Road, London SW11

British Library Cataloguing in Publication Data

Changing priorities in teacher education.
   1. Teacher's, Training of
   I. Goodings, Richard   II. Byram, Michael
   III. McPartland, Michael
   370'.7'1   LB1715

   ISBN 0-7099-1130-0

First published in the United States of America in 1982
by Nichols Publishing Company, Post Office Box 96, New York, NY 10024

Library of Congress Cataloging in Publication Data

Main entry under title:

Changing priorities in teacher education.
   1. Teachers — Training of — Addresses, essays, lectures.
I. Goodings, Richard. II. Byram, Michael. III. McPartland, Michael.
LB1715.C52 1982   370'.7'1   82-10574
ISBN 0-89397-141-3

The British Comparative Education Society exists for the fostering
of an international dimension to educational study. It holds conferences,
publishes proceedings - as this volume - and operates an academic
journal, *Compare.*
Initial contact: The Secretary, British Comparative Education
Society, Brighton Polytechnic, Welkin House, Carlisle Road,
Eastbourne, Sussex.

Printed and bound in Great Britain

CONTENTS

370.71
G652

INTRODUCTION

Michael Byram, Richard Goodings and Michael McPartland

The Secretary of State for Education for England and Wales
in a recent speech, suggested that the difference between
good schools and bad schools could be wholly explained in
terms of the quality of the teachers. He concluded that all
could be brought to a common standard of excellence if some
method could be devised of preventing the recruitment of the
unsuitable and purging the profession of the incompetent.
As his critics were quick to point out, it is not quite as
simple as that. The efficiency of a school is a function of
many, complex factors. Though some system of 'payment of
results' is perennially attractive to politicians, agreed
criteria for assessing the efficiency of teachers, are in
fact, extraordinarily difficult of definition. Nor, indeed,
are even teachers generally acknowledged to be inefficient,
at all easy to get rid of. Legal protection and the less
precise but no less powerful notions of academic freedom,
combine in most countries, to afford members of the teaching
profession an unusually high degree of security.

All these are valid points, but at the same time nobody would deny that teachers constitute the crucial educational resource. Good teaching can compensate for many
other deficiencies in a school; poor teaching can render
nugatory almost any other advantages. The simplest model
of the process of education is the pupil on one end of a log
and the teacher on the other. There is no conceivable model
which does not include a teacher. Consequently, in every
educational system, the selection and training of those who
are to teach in it, is of paramount importance.

In these circumstances, it is surprising that systematic thought was given to the appropriate professional
preparation of teachers only relatively late in the evolution
of most educational systems. In England, throughout
virtually the whole of the nineteenth century, at a time
when very substantial public funds were devoted to the
provision of schools, it continued to be assumed that

1

teachers of young children could be adequately prepared by a crude extension of the apprenticeship system then obtaining in industry and that secondary school teachers were sufficiently equipped by sound moral character and a good knowledge of their subject. In the earlier part of the century, Dr. Arnold had summarised the qualities he looked for in making appointments to the staff of Rugby, "I want a man who is a Christian and a gentleman; an active man and one who has common sense and understands boys". Professional preparation was not included in this specification, but most other secondary heads of the time would have subscribed to his views. Indeed, the major problem for the early advocates of secondary training was to say just precisely what it was that was missing from Arnold's definition. It was even more difficult for them to show that this missing element could be supplied by what they had to offer. The debate rumbled on throughout most of the century and it has to be admitted that the case for training finally triumphed more through administrative sanction than through intellectual conviction. As late as 1905, Dr. William Garnett, the educational advisor to the London County Council, and a firm advocate of training, still had doubts whether it was appropriate for all or only for those lacking abundant natural aptitude. "I can believe," he wrote, "that there are persons born with a genius for teaching, whose originality would be destroyed and whose energy would be cramped by the ordinary course of the training college". It is doubtful if there are many who continue to believe that the natural teacher would be positively harmed by a training course but there are certainly still some who are far from convinced that he or she is necessarily much benefitted by it. Beyond this, the very limitations of the early training courses, the considerable emphasis on the elementary knowledge they would need to teach, the childish discipline exacted in most training institutions and the lowly social status of the elementary teachers who were its chief recipients, all acted as powerful brakes on the extension of the system to the secondary schools.

Those who advocated training were further not helped by their frequent failure to distinguish sufficiently clearly between their demand for professional preparation and their desire for professional status. To the defenders of the status quo there was consequently joined the substantial body of those wholly opposed to the notion that teachers should be encouraged to entertain social or financial aspirations beyond that of their existing modest condition. Universal training would unquestionably strengthen the teachers' claim to professional status, a development widely regarded with deep apprehension both as permitting the teachers to escape in some measure from their

2

servant status and consequently from the close control of managers, ministers and local authorities and also as making it more difficult to resist demands for a salary structure commensurate with that of other professional people. This latter concern was all the greater in that, in most countries, the demand for training arose at a time of substantial expansion of educational provision. Teaching was clearly on its way to becoming a mass occupation and no society could contemplate paying its teachers at a rate comparable to that of small occupational groups.

The outcome of all this was that, by the end of the nineteenth century, very few secondary teachers had any training at all and even the limited preparation of element- ary teachers was far from universal. In England, for example, a substantial proportion of the women teachers continued to be recognised under Article 68 of the education code for which the sole qualifications were a willingness to confess themselves females over the age of eighteen who could display satisfactory proof of vaccination.

The need for training courses is now universally accepted, though not yet universally adopted. But, arguably, like the camel in Kipling's "Just So Story", teacher training has never quite caught up the time it lost in the beginning. Much of what is provided continues to exemplify to a striking degree that time-lag which is endemic in the education service as a whole. That is to say, the knowledge of a generation ago is offered to children who will be called upon to live their adult lives in a world a generation in the future. The content of training courses remains remarkably similar to the programme proposed by the earliest advocates nearly a century ago. In defence of this situation it might be urged that the way in which children learn has not changed in that time and that a basic under- standing of this process is as essential now as it was then. In that time, however, considerable advances have been made in the development of traditional methods and materials. Even so, such a view might conceivably have remained tenable up to the middle of the present century, but it cannot possibly remain so in the context of the technological revolution of the last few decades. So many of the skills which were formerly essential to the teacher can now be automated or computerised. This situation raises fundamental questions concerning the content of courses. Do we really believe that a modestly competent teacher in the flesh is better than a brilliant teacher on video-tape? If we do, and we continue to behave as if we do, for the technology is available and the costs are not dissimilar, then should we not attempt to define precisely in what the superiority of the live teacher resides and direct the training accordingly? Even at a time when children are increasingly accustomed to assimilating information from tapes and television and when disorder in schools is practically everywhere a matter of mounting concern, few would suppose that a teacher on television and a policeman in front of the class would be the ideal arrangement. But just what it is that the mature and experienced adult can contribute to children's development which the mass media cannot, is a question which deserves more careful analysis than it has so far received. The new technology raises questions not only of how to teach but also of what to teach. With the proliferation of communication systems, the amount of knowledge and information of all sorts which is provided by the school is a diminishing proportion of any person's mental furniture. We need to ask if there is something that the school and the school alone can provide and, if so, what that something is. In recent years considerable attention has indeed been given to this question, but the tentative conclusions of the curriculum developers have, so far, had relatively little impact on the courses of teacher training.

This points to a further factor which has retarded the sufficiently rapid adaptation of teacher training to radically changed circumstances. Research in teacher training has been conducted with rather little regard to developments in other aspects of educational enquiry. Partly this is a function of a preoccupation with the context rather than with the content of training. Much of the literature of teacher training is concerned with the evolution of institutions rather than of ideas. Many current studies continue to be addressed to such questions as should the professional preparation be separated from the general education of the students; should it be consecutive or concurrent; should it be in mono-technic or multi-technic institutions; should those institutions be publicly controlled, and so on. These questions are not unimportant, but a very considerable concern with them has diverted attention and effort from almost all other issues.

An equally deleterious separation has been the almost total absence from the debate of the schoolteachers themselves. The result has been at least a potential dichotomy between the needs of the profession as perceived in the training institutions and as actually experienced in the classrooms. If the teachers have shown a marked disinclination to dance to the piping of the reformers, it cannot in fairness be wholly ascribed to conservatism or self-protectiveness but must be partly due to the fact that they had little share in the discussions that preceded the proposals. There are hopeful signs in many countries that this situation is changing and that the barrier between the training institutions and the schools is being eroded, both personally by encouraging teachers to participate in research

4

and researchers to teach, and institutionally by siting more courses, particularly in-service courses, in the schools rather than in colleges or universities. But much of the barrier still remains substantially intact. The quite indefensible refusal of the majority of training institutions to admit the schools to any real responsibility for the assessment of the practical competence of students on initial training courses, is a striking example of its continued resilience.

The present time affords a peculiar opportunity to seek solutions to many of these problems. In fourteen European countries, the birthrate is currently below replacement level. Falling rolls in the schools everywhere pose formidable difficulties. But at least the unremitting pressure of continual expansion is relaxed. Time and space is created for a radical reappraisal and a response to the situation which is limited to a simple demand for smaller classes, is plainly inadequate. Decisions concerning entry to the profession can be more carefully made. With the passing of the years of desperate shortage, the greatly increased sophistication of occupational selection techniques can be applied to teaching. More attention can be given to the special needs both of those who are in their first years of teaching and also of those who are coming to the end of their careers. Courses can be lengthened and their content carefully scrutinised. In contrast to most professions, teaching is likely to become less rather than more special-ised. The vocational function of the school will persist but, as leisure increases, its responsibilities for the moral, social and individual development of its pupils will become relatively more important. Life-long and adult education everywhere comprise a steadily increasing propor-tion of educational provision. With the population explosion over there is a chance to re-orientate courses to take account of all these developments as well as the challenge of the new technology.

In the Third World countries the times are perhaps equally propitious, though for very different reasons. For all of them expansion continues. The fifteen Asian countries, meeting in Karachi in 1960, estimated that to provide seven years' education for all their children would require an increase in the teaching force from the existing 1.8 million to 6.7 million by 1980. In other countries a growth of similar magnitude was required. In many places the initial response to this situation was to provide courses which adhered closely to the traditional models of the industrialised countries. The teacher training programmes which were established tended to accord high value to the skills of verbalisation, to the authority of the text-book and to the reliability of examinations. Training institu-

5

tions were concentrated in the urban areas and the teachers, not unnaturally, showed a marked reluctance to return to their villages when they had qualified. The experience of the last few decades has prompted an increasing number of departures from this pattern. Experience of alternative solutions is steadily accumulating and a new confidence and willingness to experiment is widely manifest. The present situation in many Third World countries conveys very forcibly the impression of greater detachment from established norms and a willingness to test pioneer programmes which are more closely related to their economic and social needs.

In all countries the need for new priorities in teacher education is clear. Though the inertia of established forms and institutions is formidable there are refreshing signs that both the desirability and the urgency of change are widely appreciated. One such sign was the conference for which the following papers were written, and from which this volume takes its title. Some authors followed closely the theme of the conference and consequently expounded their views from that particular perspective. Others took a more liberal interpretation of the conference title and provide insights which are derived from their current research.

The framework for the papers has to be imposed retrospectively but it genuinely reflects the character of the conference and the range of papers submitted. The first section entitled 'Problems and Perspectives' is characterised by the exploration of the theme within three general categories: the industrialised world, the communist world, with specific reference to the U.S.S.R. and Eastern Europe, and the developing world. This follows upon a general survey of the changing priorities in teacher education unlinked to any politico-geographical category. These papers allow us to perceive one overriding theme: the need to prepare teachers for a world of accelerating change and uncertainty, the need to free teachers from the notion that a fixed period of training equips them for all future eventualities. The concept of 'lifelong learning' has now moved beyond an educational cliché and demands practical realisation. Yet these large politico-geographical categories in section 1 reflect a diversity of cultures and traditions and thereby, inevitably, difference in emphasis of priorities in teacher education. Should one rationalise the institutional structure of teacher education to eradicate class differences within the profession, or should one expand the system such that those who demand to be educated are not frustrated by a shortage of teachers? It is thus quite appropriate that William Taylor warns us in the first article that comparative education and, in particular, a comparative view of the education of teachers is only meaningful when the analysis includes a deeper understanding of the culture of the country or region within which the educational system, and the education of teachers, functions. It is for this reason that any discussion of the education of teachers within or between countries and regions must ultimately be grounded in a theory of culture. This is a massive challenge in a world of increasingly complex societies.

Though none of the articles which follow can fully answer the challenge, the cultural context within which changing priorities in teacher education are discussed is never forgotten. Indeed in King's article broad societal changes, whether they be of rapid urbanization, increasing unemployment for the young, or technological change, are described in detail. They provide a backcloth against which the question of a teacher's role, and the form and content of his or her education is examined.

Other views articulated by Taylor find an echo in the papers which follow. He vividly descibes two profiles of students in the process of being educated as teachers, clearly demonstrating both the contrasts that exist between the developed and less developed realms as well as the consequences of such resource disparities. This is more fully explored in the paper by Farrant. After rightly warning us against crude generalisations regarding the geographical, economic and social conditions of the less developed countries, Farrant asserts that "what these countries need are not more imported solutions but help with developing their own innovations by being involved at all levels in the planning and implementation process". The danger of making judgements about teacher education divorced from the cultural framework in which this process is taking place, which Taylor warns us against, is thus underlined. Farrant further asserts that wholesale transplantation of innovations between different cultures frequently leads to disillusionment as they fail to live up to expectation.

Similarly, Taylor's description of the eventful changes in teacher education in the United Kingdom since 1977, changes now weighed in the balance as future demographic trends are pondered, is sharply focussed on the impact of social changes in teacher education in the United Kingdom. These are precisely the changes which King elaborates upon, in a larger context, in his paper. Taylor explores the problems of a contracting teacher education system; the most appropriate balance between different forms of training; the role of in-service training; and the relationship between theory and practice in teacher education. These issues clearly demonstrate the validity of one of King's central assertions, encapsulated in the phrase "a world of headlong change". Headlong change requires 'lifelong learning and re-learning' and this is no less true for teachers than for

7

others in the community. Indeed one could argue that
teachers above all must respond to that challenge by accepting that there is no disgrace in acknowledging that one's
knowledge and skills require updating or that one's values
need re-assessing. Teachers above all must not be
"imprisoned in a technological/educational pattern established for different purposes and a very different range of
population in the vastly different context of nearly two
centuries ago".

This process of "headlong change" transcends the East-
West Divide and the North-South Divide. Grant's paper
explores the broad patterns of development in teacher
education as they relate to the U.S.S.R. and Eastern Europe.
Farrant's paper examines the problems affecting national
systems of education in the developing world and the new
priorities in teacher education which must reflect changing
circumstances. In spite of the enormous cultural differences,
the similarities are striking. Two are worth noting.
Firstly, there is the need to re-shape and rationalise the
institutional structures within which the education of
teachers takes place. In the case of the Communist world
this is to make the structure accord more with the prevailing
ideology. In the case of the less developed countries, the
structure must respond to the accelerating social demand for
education while attempting to attain this within strong
financial constraints. Secondly, there are similar problems
in overcoming the contrast between the urban and rural areas
with respect to the quality of education provision. The
difficulty of overcoming this imbalance, even in the U.S.S.R.
with its centralised decision-making apparatus, only serves
to remind us that, as in most countries, there is a gap
between educational reality and the educational and political
rhetoric.

It is debatable whether Taylor's claim that a way of
coping with the oversupply of teachers within the U.K. would
be to encourage teachers to accept short-term employment
overseas and thereby relieve the problem of teacher shortage
within the less developed world. Certainly only those
teachers would be suitable who are aware of the needs of the
developing countries, knowledgeable about their cultural
traditions and sensitive to the fact that educational
strategies have to be geared towards their particular
circumstances. It may be that out of the pressure of scarce
resources, population growth and an insatiable demand for
educational opportunity, new, more relevant models for
coping with the problem of the education of teachers will
evolve in the developing world. We, in the West, might well
investigate such models to our advantage. Farrant's paper
sketches out a number of these innovative approaches to the
problems of teacher education. In many developing countries

8

the needs of the rural population have dictated a number of innovations which involve strengthening the school's links with the community. The experiment in Sri-Lanka in which the Hinguiakgoda Teachers' College was instrumental in constructing strong relationships with village communities in close proximity, and sensitising their students to the needs of the village communities. It led not only to a curriculum more relevant to the educational and health needs of the village children, but also helped to promote the whole process of rural development.

The papers by Burns and Dove in section 2 take up some of these issues, and describe some of the initiatives which education must adopt if meaningful change is to take place. Hence the title of the section. What is the most appropriate curriculum for teacher education, especially at a time of increasing and more accessible knowledge when the simple transmission of knowledge is regarded as inappropriate to the world of the late twentieth century and beyond? What are the inherent role conflicts in the education of teachers which inevitably emerge when teachers are involved in the entire process of forging closer links between the community and the school system? Burns begins with the issue of knowledge, the process of generating, transmitting and applying knowledge. In examining this issue, she makes the assertion that the prevailing paradigm is now deficient. It is this paradigm which dictates what is worthwhile knowledge and how it ought to be organised, which dictates the most appropriate methodological approaches for the generation of this knowledge and which dictates the most appropriate ways of applying knowledge - all distinctive hallmarks of the traditional disciplines. It is this paradigm which is now found to be deficient. As the dominant paradigm, with its emphasis on a value-free search for empirically testable explanations, has become institutionalised, then other more radical questions tend to be ignored, questions about the nature of knowledge, about new and valid ways to discover and apply it. The question therefore is simultaneously an epistemological and political one. This is of crucial importance for education and, in particular, the education of teachers. If a comparative perspective reveals that the malaise to which she refers transcends different socio-cultural systems, and has arisen as a result of our failure to find adequate answers to the questions which are posed, then teacher education should be at the forefront not only of the analysis. As Burns says, teacher education must contribute "to both the debate about and quest for knowledge, and the trying out of new frameworks and practical solutions". This involves bringing about a rapprochement between research and training within teacher education establishments by emphasising the role of the teacher as a researcher. Teaching becomes a

focus of research by the teacher for the teacher. Teachers
then must be equipped to apply the appropriate research
techniques for the investigation and evaluation of their own
teaching so that they bring a greater degree of critical
awareness to both the knowledge they teach, the methods they
teach by and the relevance of their work to the 'outside
world' or community at large. And yet a paradox lies at the
heart of this endeavour, a paradox more fully explored by
Dove in her examination of the community schooling. The
challenge laid down by Burns demands a re-assessment of the
role of the teacher. This re-assessment may lead teachers
to the conclusion that the selection of the curriculum is
much more than a technical problem. Fundamental questions
of value are involved and with them a radical re-examination
of urgent global problems. It may lead teachers to the
conclusion that they must act in a more positive way as
"representatives of socio-cultural change". And yet the
established order is inherently conservative in that it
demands stability and continuity and is fearful of approaches
which may precipitate change and dissonance. This tension
is the focus of Dove's analysis of community schooling within
the context of the developing countries. If teachers in the
developing countries are to serve the needs of the disadvantaged communities within which they live and work they must
align themselves with the pursuit of radical transformational
goals rather than reformist ones adopted by the government-
financed community schooling schemes. Teachers then interpret
their role differently depending upon whether they seek to
serve the community or the government which finances their
work. Teacher education which is government-financed
reflects a conservative ideology which, Dove feels, is
incompatible with the needs of the communities served by the
teachers. The central paradox remains. Schools need
teachers who act as radical agents of change; governments
cannot accept this role as it would undoubtedly threaten the
social order which they wish to maintain.

Dove maintains that a decentralised approach to the
training of teachers for work in community schools, the
application of wider criteria for selection of teacher
trainees, the demonstration of a real commitment to teaching
within a community by the applicants, remain the most valid
criteria for the selection of teachers and the organisation
of the training system. Above all the teachers, once
trained, would bring the kind of critical awareness, which
Burns advocates, to bear upon the educational activities of
the school and evaluate their contribution to community
development. What is fundamentally required is "a very
thorough knowledge, critical understanding and sympathy for
the community on the part of the teacher trainees". In the
final analysis Dove feels that no government would reject

10

the notion that what its communities need are young teachers who are adaptable, flexible and capable of "creative and independent thinking". This inevitably leads to clamour for change in terms of a more appropriate curriculum, methods and systems of evaluation within the school as well as clamour for change in terms of the social and economic system within which the schools function. Governments then take the view that teachers are potentially subversive agents of change. For this reason the political will is frequently lacking.

In fact, the important pre-requisites for a teacher education system which is responsive to the needs of the community: maturity of the nation-state; decentralisation of organisation; an acceptance of lay involvement in the selection and training of teachers and a radical acceptance of new roles by the teacher, can all be examined within the context of the developed world. It is there that these important conditions are likely to exist earlier than in the less developed countries. Indeed much of what she has to say is of great relevance within that context. Thus, Denmark's tradition of providing financial support for non-state schooling and teacher education has led, in recent years, to the financing of Tvind schools and training colleges. Although the extent of their commitment to trans-formational goals is debatable, the schools and the teachers within them are concerned to establish alternative values, economic systems and community responsibilities to those generally found in the nation as a whole. Although, initially, there was much debate about these schools and the extent to which they might undermine the social fabric of the nation, they are now an accepted part of the educa-tional scene, though catering only for a minority. Perhaps these schools and their teachers testify that education need not always be merely re-active to change but can offer new models which Burns and Dove might find acceptable.

One of the advantages of the case studies which follow in section 3, is that they illustrate in detail some of the general and theoretical discussions of the previous papers. Each paper has, of course, its own character and purposes and the degree to which they provide illustrations of the previous general points is, in original conception, purely coincidental. Yet this coincidence is a sign of general agreement about existent or pending change which is forcing itself into our awareness and of which this collection of articles is no more than a symptom. Nonetheless, a detailed case study clarifies the need for modification of general statements, of which the earlier authors are very conscious. John Owen claims for Belgium many of the features of an industrialised country which King outlines. It is also worth noting that Owen suggests Belgium is already entering the "Third Wave" of civilisation, which includes the breaking down of the mass entity of the nation-state and with it the notion of a unitary education system. In this sense it accords closely to the ideals laid down by Dove in which schools reflect to a large degree the needs and aspirations of the community in which they are located. The active participation of parents in running schools - known as associative management - is an important feature in this respect.

Owen takes us succinctly through the fundamental philosophy of Belgian education, tracing the gradual evolution of answers to questions about the aims and methods of education. It is encouraging in the context of these papers to discover that Belgian Government policy statements incorporate an approach to knowledge which reveals an awareness of paradigm shifts, as Burns discussed them, and an awareness of "headlong change" in the world, to use again King's phrase. The teacher is no longer expected to reveal "a world regarded as given"; he is to facilitate learning and the child's capacity to explore, conquer and make his own world. This requires nothing less than a teacher committed to flexible, open approaches, respecting the autonomy of the pupil, and capable of bringing a wider perception of the world. As Owen himself says, there is an element of pious but unfulfilled hope and a familiar ring about these views, but it is in the struggle to give practical realisation of these views within the context of Belgian education that one sees even more the relevance and validity of these attempts. Thus a variety of paths is being explored through which teacher education becomes continuing education and begins to meet the challenge issued by King. In the final analysis, the gauntlet must be picked up by all involved in the process of education: teacher educators, inspectors and advisers cannot escape the responsibility to effect change and be changed by it. Moreover, the strategy of involving practising teachers deeply in the process of evolving new approaches is crucial, since it not only makes the subsequent changes more acceptable to the practitioner but also enhances the relevance of the change because it has emerged as a consequence of their deliberations.

It is a similar element of variety and flexibility which is particularly striking in MacLaughlin and Murphy's paper. They describe how one university is seeking to prepare teachers for a diversity of schools and teaching tasks. There is here something of our common theme, in so far as the programmes described are intended to take into account the inevitability of changing demands on teachers in schools of the future. There is, too, a reminder that each country or region, even local community, has its peculiar needs. The content of education in remote rural communities in British Columbia demands a special response, just as densely but diversely populated Belgium seeks its own particular educational solution.

In his account of developing countries, Farrant stressed the importance of each country finding its own way in education and preparation of teachers. Aguilar and Retamal support this view by pointing out the dangers of cultural invasion brought about covertly by the importation of apparently purely technical innovation. In the Latin American context, they show how a tradition of 'normal school' education for teachers had, until recent decades, produced a type of teacher committed to the communities he served. We see here how the conflict of interests between nation-state and community become openly politicised, much as Linda Dove suggests in her paper. For Aguilar and Retamal, however, it is the presence of international agencies and foreign countries, particularly the U.S.A., which brought the conflict into focus. They document this by reference to a U.S. Senate paper which alleged that no 'normal school' was free from communist infiltration. They suggest that one of the devices which, as Farrant tells us, are commonly used to improve educational provision - namely the up-grading to university status of teacher education - was in the case of Latin America a means of rooting out the tradition of a teacher training system geared to serving the needs of the community. The school and the teacher were to serve a dual function: one of imparting basic instruction as well as promoting the notion of general social and political reform. The nation-states in question, according to Dove's criteria, did not have the political maturity to allow and support teacher education programmes which challenge the existing social and political norms. They lacked the political will. The teacher as an agent of transformational change is more likely to be accepted in the pluralistic, industrialised countries, such as Belgium, than in the developing countries of Latin America where the perception of education as an important factor in the process of change is clearly accepted. It is with sadness that Aguilar and Retamal conclude that in Latin America, attempts to alter the priorities in teacher education towards making the teacher "a technician" insensitive to the wider needs of society - a trend which reflects the drive towards modern-isation - is undeniably an adverse trend, with ominous consequences.

The last three articles consider particular aspects of teacher education, and the consequent changes in role and identity of teachers. In a comprehensive and wide-ranging article, Mawer discusses the training of teachers of physical education. His article demonstrates how insistently we must take into consideration the political and cultural context, even in an apparently highly specialised matter such

13

as this. For he shows how the familiar interaction of
politics and sport leads to change in status of the institutions preparing physical education teachers and even to the
change of title in some cases: 'sports teacher' carries more
weight than 'physical education teacher'. Clearly the
consequences for the individual in his understanding of the
expectations placed on him are major. The consequences for
the institutions are no less so. Mawer documents the
improvements in facilities, the introduction of professional,
academic research into institutions and the increased
funding involved which are the symptoms of changes in
political and social attitudes. For those countries which
are generous in the funding allocated to physical education
a reflection of the importance they attach to this area of
the curriculum - a basic truth becomes manifest: physical
education sensitively and imaginatively taught and with an
array of resources, can accomplish a great deal in nourishing
the self-image of children.

A group of teachers which has been in the midst of
change for some time is the modern linguists. Language
teaching could have a vital role to play in a world dominated
by the communications boom, by the imminent possibility of
receiving television programmes from many countries. Yet
language learning is notoriously difficult, and language
teaching no less so. Weil's article takes its inspiration
from the acknowledged problems in language teaching in two
countries which both have a long and powerful colonial
history, and a consequent egocentric view of language. Both
England and France, Weil suggests, need to review fundamentally the training of their language teachers and the
aims of language teaching if the potential contribution to
education for a changing, and shrinking, polyglot world is
to be fulfilled.

At several points in this book, the reader will notice
a 'meta-discourse'. Not only do we have teacher educators
discussing the nature of teacher education, but also
Comparative Educationists, as a sub-group of teacher
educators, discussing the nature and role of Comparative
Education in teacher education. Taylor raised the question
of the role of Comparative Education in decision-making in
all aspects of education. King and others have, sometimes
explicitly, reminded us of the need for widened horizons in
all education especially in the realm of teacher education.
Comparative Education has a crucial task in widening these
horizons. It is therefore particularly appropriate to have
Watson's survey of Comparative Education in teacher training
in the United Kingdom. Unfortunately, the results of that
survey are not encouraging and indeed demonstrate that
priorities are changing in this respect too. In essence,
Watson reports a decline in Comparative Education as a

14

component in teacher training. By giving a brief intro-
ductory account of the development of Comparative Education,
and by reporting the responses to questions about multi-
cultural and development education, Watson presents the
conceptual context to his statistical results. He suggests
that Comparative Education has a role to play despite the
changed priorities caused by financial stringency. Yet he
also proposes changes in the emphases within Comparative
Education. In a situation where the requirement for
practical help with classroom activities is uppermost, in
both initial and in-service training, Comparative Education
needs to consider what it can offer. It is evident from
responses he quotes that many people are acutely aware of
the need for comparative studies, because of the growing
interdependence across national boundaries and because of
the multiplicity of contrasts and dependencies within any
nation-state. As is clear from other articles here, the
received wisdom, the fixed paradigms, the traditional roles
and identities of teachers are on the threshold of change.
If the change is felt as a threat, the prospects are poor.
In his final line, however, Watson presents a challenge. An
affirmation of a willingness to meet the challenge of change
is what we must hope for not only from Comparative Educators,
not only from future teachers in training, but also from the
teacher educators themselves.

CHANGING PRIORITIES IN TEACHER EDUCATION

William Taylor

"Changing priorities" necessarily involves making decisions. I begin with a consideration of those voluntary professional and disciplinary bodies which in my view do more than almost any other kind of organisation to improve the quality of our thinking and understanding about education, the existence and the activities of which help to ensure that decisions are less wrong and less damaging than otherwise they would be.

Co-ordination between and within institutions of higher education critically depends upon access to information generated by networks that cut across institutional boundaries. Such networks may have a formal or quasi formal character, but they also operate informally, transmitting, sieving and sorting facts, interpretations, judgments, reputations, gossip and rumour.

It seems to me that there are six networks, which can be labelled political, administrative, managerial, employee, professional and disciplinary. The columns of THES and of the newspapers carry a great deal of material generated by the political, administrative, managerial and employee networks. They have less to say, understandably enough, about what circulates within professional and disciplinary networks. Yet it is just this kind of information that is crucial to effective decision-making.

In most subjects there exist networks of information and influence, contributed to by the existence of scholarly associations, by the holding of conferences and meetings, by the activities of external examiners and through the journals and publications of the trade. I do not think it is fanciful to identify these with what Hayek[1] calls a 'spontaneous order', such as a market, within which is generated far more information than could possibly be produced by the administrative process. It is the judgments of quality and promise that are made within such networks, according to such informal rules and procedures as they develop, through such mechanisms as the referee system, that help shape the biography of

16

individuals, that colour the responses that funding bodies make to requests for research support. And, let it not be forgotten, which also now influence the decisions of grant allocation bodies such as the University Grants Committee!

If decisions about closing departments, merging institutions and rationalising teaching are to give due weight to all the relevant considerations, including academic quality, they must reflect the full range of information that circulates within the networks, and avoid giving undue prominence to the views of the better organised political, administrative, managerial and employee interest groups. We may deplore the degree of specialisation that characterises our world, not least our academic world. Many of the more significant advances in our knowledge and understanding, the really significant paradigm shifts that will influence the pattern of future teaching and research, are likely to be inter-disciplinary or multi-disciplinary in character. Nonetheless, it is only those with an intimate knowledge of the literature and methodology of their own subject, who know its practitioners and the institutions within which they work, who are really equipped to make judgments about quality, performance and promise.

Our rhetoric demands allegiance to openness, the abolition of 'old boy networks', to the universalisation of discourse, and the breaking down of those insider/outsider distinctions that exert a powerful conservative influence on the development of any subject or discipline. Our reality inevitably includes judgments, differences, distinctions that, without such facilitating networks, would be infinitely more crude and dangerous, that would lack that lubricating and emollient subtlety of nuance and meaning that is one of the most precious possessions of any group of personal or professional intimates, and denied which we would be hard put to avoid that world of impersonal committee-based relationships so feared by Eliot and many others before and since.

As in most human affairs, there is a balance to be struck. On the one side the claims of openness and universality. On the other those of the group where membership has to be earned by more or less public demonstration of relevant knowledge, and within which the absence of the need for high levels of redundancy of discourse, the presence of understanding based upon consensus on meanings, can effectively sharpen the depth and quality of scholarship.

The specialisation that brings such groups into being and sustains their identities also embodies risks. It is much to be welcomed that teacher education should be approached with a cross-national perspective, particularly when such an approach is not commonplace. Yet even here, we must be cautious. Some years ago Merle Borrowman[2] wrote about the inclusion of comparative studies in teacher

17

education programmes in the following terms:

> Let us assume that a major portion of teacher education
> candidates ... approach their training with little or
> no experience in non-American culture and with little
> or no cross-cultural studies. In most cases they will
> not even have learned, at more than a superficial
> propositional level, that the meaning of a cultural
> pattern inheres in its relationship to other patterns
> in that culture. For such students a datum about the
> educational choices made by fourteen year old males
> in Tanzania might be highly revealing in the context
> of other data concerning life in Tanzania. Isolated
> from that data, compared with other data about similar
> choices in other countries, the selected item becomes
> worse than meaningless. It becomes in a fundamental
> way untrue because of the response it evokes.

The discussion of teacher education in different countries
runs these risks at several levels.

One cannot understand the way in which a country tackles
teacher education, and the priorities it attaches to various
aspects of that process, unless the data are placed in the
context of schooling within the educational system concerned.
But the educational system itself owes much to a cultural
context, torn from which it loses much of its meaning. Most
cross national studies of teacher education are descriptive
in character. There is nothing wrong with that, especially
if the descriptions are accurate and up-to-date, and some
attempt is made to use the comparative method to enhance our
understanding of observed similarities and differences.
Inventories are invaluable sources of information, but they
do not themselves add much to our understanding of the
purposes, processes and outcomes that generate the items that
form the basis of the inventory or description. Our ability
to achieve a level of understanding adequate to support any
kind of systematic evaluation is dependent upon the introduction of theory.

Few good theorists are really interested in teacher
education, treating it as something of an epiphenomenon of
its ambient system of schooling. Few students of teacher
education have much interest in the development of theory.
In the gap thus created it has been easy for some vulgar
kinds of neo-Marxism on the one hand, and some rather hastily
adapted notions of socialisation on the other, to secure
niches of their own, from which, at least in the case of the
Marxists, claims are then made upon the whole territory.

A life-time is too short for any one individual to
achieve an adequate grasp of more than a very small number of
cultures, especially since this usually requires substantial

18

periods of personal participation. No funding body has yet seen fit to finance a major cross-national study of teacher education that goes beyond the description of institutions, pedagogies, curricula and modes of assessment. Thus any attempt to look at teacher education in cross national perspective demands a principle of selectivity by means of which relevant data can be identified and that which, for this purpose, is irrelevant set aside. Neither economic determination, nor individual socialisation serve this purpose well. The first soon deteriorates into political polemic. The second ignores the social and economic contexts that are crucial to an understanding of the business of teacher preparation. Clearly, something more is needed.

If we are to avoid the kinds of single dimensional error to which Borrowman refers, to eschew the polemical suppression of data that a politically biased doctrine requires, and at the same time to give due weight to historical, social and institutional contexts, we must examine teacher education in terms of a theory or theories of culture which are broad and inclusive enough to accommodate a diversity of levels of economic development and types of political organisation.

Yet we are concerned not simply with cross national comparisons, but also with changes in teacher education priorities. It is in this respect that contrasts in levels of development between systems are so glaring. To personalise this a little, let me sketch two student profiles, illustrative of the gaps that now exist between the developed and the less developed world, a contrast in relation to which the metaphors of 'North' and 'South' (a usage ripe for cultural analysis) has achieved common currency.[3]

John Smith is white, twenty three years old, and lives in a country with a per capita g.n.p.equivalent to $US 15,000. He has completed thirteen years of pre-primary, elementary and secondary school before entering university five years ago at the age of eighteen. He took his Bachelor of Arts degree twelve months ago, majoring in English and Education, and obtained high grades. He is currently pursuing a twelve month programme in the professional aspects of education practice.

During two thirds of his course he studied in College, spending four days each week in the lecture room and teaching laboratory, and the other day working in a neighbouring school with a small group of fellow students under a supervising teacher and a Professor who had himself taught ten years before obtaining his doctoral degree for research on children's classroom behaviour. During the remaining third of his course John teaches classes in an ordinary school, again with the help of a teacher who has been trained in supervisory techniques. He is visited regularly by his

College Professors, who videotape his lessons with portable equipment they carry with them for this purpose. These lessons are analysed during the one day per week that he spends back in College during these block teaching periods.

In preparing his teaching material John has access to a resources collection that includes 35 mm film, slides and film strips, audio and video tapes, charts, booklets, pamphlets and hard copy editions, overhead projector transparencies, prepared worksheets, computer software and a variety of recently introduced electronic devices. He also makes frequent use of a library which contains a quarter of a million volumes on education, and which annually acquires some two thousand serials. In preparing bibliographies for his essays and projects he employs computer search facilities linked with ERIC and some 130 other data bases in Europe and the United States.

When in a short while John begins actively to seek employment (which he confidently expects to obtain) in the school system he will utilise a telephone link computerised job information and vocational advice service provided through the Post Office computer. In his first post he will teach for only four days each week for the first year, and will be enrolled in a systematic induction programme linked to his initial training. As part of this induction sequence he will engage in micro-teaching, classroom simulation, curriculum and lesson analysis, the trial and evaluation of innovative assessment techniques, and basic school administration.

John is still committed to his chosen career, but has found some of the classes that he takes during block practice unreceptive, and a disturbing rate of truancy among older pupils. He finds some of the educational ideas he is called upon to study a bit irrelevant to the tasks he feels he will be asked to undertake as a qualified teacher, but he is interested in the psychology of child development and in the work of those thinkers who are highly critical of the social and educational arrangements that for a long time he has himself taken for granted. He would like in due course to obtain a position as Head of Department or Principal.

Let us switch from John Smith to John Fulani. John Fulani is eighteen years old, and is completing his training in one of the three primary training colleges located in the capital of his country, which has a g.n.p.of about $US 300 per head. He started school in a village three hundred miles from the capital at the age of seven and progressed rapidly with only one repeat to the age of fifteen. He learned to write on a slate and to read from one of the twenty-five books which were all the village school had for its two hundred pupils. At fifteen, having failed to win one of the few places offered in the region's secondary school, he

applied for entry to the training college, where he has
continued to study the whole range of primary school subjects,
largely by means of notes dictated to him in a language that
is not his mother tongue and different from the one used as a
medium of instruction in his primary school. If he is
successful in the final examination, he will obtain his grade
C certificate and is likely to be appointed as the only
qualified and paid teacher in a village similar to that in
which he was brought up. The college library has a limited
number of books, is woefully short of recent editions and
takes very few journals. A good deal of lecture time is
spent on those official school texts that have so far appeared
as a result of a UNESCO sponsored programme of curriculum
renewal in his country that began three years ago.

John's brother, who qualified six years ago and is now
teaching in a provincial town, warned in his last letter
against paying too much attention to the ideas of the college
lecturers. He listed some of the shortcomings of his own
school, such as the almost complete absence of books and the
radio set that has been out of operation since just after the
last visit of the technician four months ago. Even when
working it is often useless because batteries cannot be
obtained. A Supervisor from the Education Office in the
provincial capital came some months ago to offer advice and
took away a list of orders for books and equipment. Neither
Supervisor nor orders have been heard of since. Meanwhile,
John's brother has applied to the Ministry for transfer to a
larger school, and also for an upgrading course in the
University. Again, he has heard nothing. He continues to
cope with pupils in large classes who for the most part are
eager to learn, and especially eager to qualify for one of
the very limited number of places available in the regional
secondary school. He co-operates as best he can with the
town community, whose help he tries to enlist in reducing the
very high rate of drop-out in his school, especially among
the girls. Less than half of his pupils complete their
primary education.

In the case of the very slow progress that his country
is making in universalising primary schooling, John has of
late begun to wonder if any real change will take place in
his life time without a radical transformation of political
and economic structure. Such ideas have become a frequent
theme of discussion among fellow students.

I do not want to labour these extremes, which will be
familiar enough. At a certain level of abstraction, the
teacher education priorities of the systems in which John
Smith and John Fulani are being trained are identical. They
include the need for facilities to train a number of teachers
adequate in quantity and quality for the nation's schools; a
student body recruited and selected from among the ablest

21

members of their respective age cohorts, comparable in ability and motivation to those who plan to enter a traditional high status occupation; staff responsible for teaching, supervising and assessing students with relevant and up-to-date experience in the types of schools and educational institutions for which their programmes prepare, together with a commitment to keeping such experience fresh by regular participation in classroom and school work; close and positive relations between teacher educators, teachers and administrators; curricula which reflect the most recent and well founded knowledge in the disciplines of educational studies, are based upon carefully thought-through principles of coherence relevant to the successful induction of neophyte teachers, and are likely to encourage a permanent commitment to personal learning and professional development; a genuine commitment to the improvement of teacher education in the schools where students undertake their practice, consistent with the objectives and procedures of the college-based elements of the course.

Such a specification is familiar enough in the rhetoric of teacher education, and in those aspirational - but not always inspirational - documents produced by the international agencies for the purpose of cross national discussion. It may be useful to have lists of such objectives and priorities, although not when they get in the way of realistic appraisal of what is actually happening on the ground, and what is possible within the social, political, cultural, geographical and other constraints in relation to which teacher education, like anything else, has to be pursued.

When such constraints are reckoned with, consensus on priorities soon breaks down. Increasing plant, capacity and output; raising standards of entry to training; lengthening courses of professional preparation; securing degree status qualifications for all new entrants; remedying shortages of teachers in particular subjects; making induction to the profession more effective and humane; enhancing in-service study opportunities; offering training for managerial and supervisory roles - all these are merely a sample of the items that might feature in any list of priorities from the last thirty or forty years.

And today?

As we all now know, the minimum system of teacher education that we in the United Kingdom thought was settled in 1977 has turned out to be not minimum enough. The Advisory Committee for the Education and Training of Teachers (ACSET) has advised the Secretary of State on how further reductions in teacher supply might be brought about, in order to reduce the very high level of unemployment among the newly qualified that threatens to provide some of the shock horror headlines for the educational press in 1982 and for some years thereafter.

There was understandable reluctance on the part of the interests represented on ACSET - the employing authorities, the training institutions, the staff associations and teachers' unions - to appear to acquiesce in a further round of contractions. Yet short of a direct challenge to the Government's current spending proposals, which it is not the Committee's task or responsibility to make, it is difficult to see how further cuts could have been avoided.

The reasons for them are obvious enough. Despite cries of a new baby boom every time the quarterly birth rate figures show a small rise, the overall trend has been closer to the Department of Education and Science's lower rather than upper demographic projection. With fewer jobs available elsewhere, wastage from the existing teaching force has remained low. The size of the pool of inactive teachers, now unglamorously known as the PIT, from which schools and authorities draw a substantial percentage of their annual needs for new teachers, is likely to remain large. Rolls in secondary schools are declining, and will go on doing so for some years, only partially compensated for by the rise in the number of younger pupils until the late 'eighties. Public expenditure restrictions mean that authorities are unable to employ as many teachers as they would wish. Although recruitment to three and four year BEd courses is well below original targets - if it was not, our current problems would be much worse than they are - institutions have over-shot in recruiting graduates to Postgraduate Certificate in Education (PGCE) courses, in some cases by considerable margins. To overshoot targets on a one-year course has obviously greater short-run affects on supply than in the case of the longer programmes.

Every item in the litany will be entirely familiar. Taken together, they constitute an overwhelming case for making both short-term and medium-term reductions - of somewhat differing magnitude - in the output of the newly qualified. The 1982/83 and 1983/84 output is likely to exceed demand by many thousands. The BEd students who will qualify in those years are already on course. Only by cutting PGCE can any impact be made on the output.

On such simple indices as class of degree, there is no doubt about the improvement that has taken place. In 1973/74 just under a quarter of the graduates entering my own Institute for training had a first or upper second honours degree. In 1980 it was thirty-four per cent. At the other end of the scale, a parallel fall has taken place in the numbers with only pass or third class degrees. Many course innovations have been introduced, and there is now a wide variety of school-based and other options available.

On the BEd side, the picture is less clear cut. There are many candidates with excellent A-levels. Many institutions are able to pick and choose among well qualified

applicants, who compare well with those entering other
Faculties and working for BA and BSc degrees. This is not,
however, uniformly so. Many of the better candidates choose,
understandably enough, to keep open their options by taking
a science or arts degree, followed by PGCE, rather than
electing the BEd route at the outset.

Bearing these and other considerations in mind, the
question of consecutive versus concurrent, degree plus PGCE,
against three or four years of BEd training is by no means
simple and straightforward.

The consensus seems to be that both routes should be
retained. Although many excellent primary teachers come
through PGCE channels, professional opinion - there's little
hard evidence - favours extended professional socialisation,
possible over a three or four year course, for most teachers
of young children. In many of the practical subjects, there
are few suitable degree plus PGCE combinations available,
and the BEd supply is essential. There are no clear cut
rules of thumb which enable, in terms of improvement criteria,
a once for all balance to be struck between PGCE and BEd.
This is one of the tasks to which the Advisory Committee and
other bodies will need to give continuing attention.

Yet it is not just initial training that is facing
reduction. Much of the in-service training effort, which has
had such high priority in discussion of teacher education for
the past ten years, is also threatened. That effort, is not,
of course, a monopoly of colleges, polytechnics and universities. A great deal is done by school staff themselves, by
inspectors and advisers, and by a multitude of other agencies,
few of which are themselves exempt from the funding pressures
which apply within the teacher training sphere.

During the run down in teacher education in the 1970s,
there was constant stress on the importance of building up in-
service provision, not simply to sugar a pill that teacher
educators were themselves being forced to swallow, but in
recognition of the fact that, for example, three quarters of
the teachers who will be standing in front of classes in the
year 2000 are already employed in schools. Teachers will
have to acquire knowledge about computers, how to cope with
the special needs of the handicapped, the encouragement of
entrepreneurial attitudes and so on, during their service,
rather than before they begin in the classroom. For years
and years we have been saying just how impossible it is for
initial training, whether of one, three or four years'
duration or even longer, to provide the fuel and supplies
that a teacher needs for a life-long journey. Indeed, we
seem in some cases willing to settle for the idea that
initial training provides little more than a survival kit for
the first two years or so in the classroom.

24

The simple answer to improving in-service training in the 1980s is to call for more resources, improved teacher/pupil ratios, a more systematic development of school-based, school-focussed, job-embedded, job-related and other modes of in-service training that are neither courses nor conferences, that stress on-site experience with the people with whom one will have to work to implement the knowledge acquired and skills learned, rather than a dozen or a hundred miles away in the ivory tower of college or university.

It is now nearly ten years since the James Committee proposed an initial three per cent level of release, to be increased to five per cent as resources permitted. The latest figures we have suggest that the current figure is in the order of 1.5 per cent. To argue that school-focussed, school-based, job-related, job-embedded approaches have now put the whole thing on a new footing, and that we have no need to worry about our failure to achieve the targets of a decade ago convinces few beyond the circles of those trying to sell this convenient excuse. For excuse it is.

Of course a great deal can be done on site. Of course heads and advisers are capable of providing some of the necessary expertise. Of course there should be partnership between schools and specialist individuals and institutions in the provision of an appropriate mix of programmes and events. Of course. But the yeast in that mix of ideas is provided by the theories, the new findings, the original techniques and all the other elements, from diverse sources, without which the most carefully planned employer-provided and school-based provision is likely soon to become flaccid and tired. It is in the production and dissemination of those theories, ideas, findings and techniques that colleges, polytechnics and universities have such a vital role to play.

To give priority to the more fashionable, participatory kinds of educational development work and in-service training threatens an intellectual and professional impoverishment that will be felt for many years to come, and which will do little to carry forward the improvements that have been made in standards of entry, duration and design of courses, and in the disciplinary foundations of teacher education over the past twenty-five years.

The loss of faith in Education as a panacea for economic growth, social mobility, a harmonious policy and more integrated society has left its mark on the rhetoric, and to a more limited extent the reality, of curriculum and pedagogy. In the middle of the last decade, Sixten Marklund[4] was speaking about the way in which traditional terms were changing their meaning in the context of educational advance. For school, read system of school unit. For class, flexible grouping of pupils. Lessons were becoming systems of shorter time modules. Subjects were reclassified as study units.

For teacher, substitute teacher team, for text book, educational materials system. Others of us were talking about how the instructional role of the teacher was turning into that of a manager of learning resources.

From the mid 'sixties onwards, official and much professional opinion favoured a pedagogic brew into which, alongside some traditional ingredients, there had been poured generous measures of self-paced learning, mixed ability grouping, high level questioning and pupil initiated activity. All this had its implications for the content and organisation of teacher training courses and programmes. Indeed, some of it may have been a product of the values and practices embedded in such programmes.

The last seven years or so have seen a considerable shift in teaching priorities. It is not just a matter of 'back to the basics'. We never left them. The Inspectorate in England and Scotland, and numerous groups of independent investigators have shown pretty conclusively that too much teaching is still narrowly conceived in an out-dated mould of basic skills, that there is too little variety, not enough imagination, and a great deal of boredom, all of which students and teachers alike tolerate to a surprising degree. Brian Simon and his team from Leicester[5] spent over one thousand days in primary classrooms in connection with their ORACLE project, and found that 'teaching basics took up nearly two thirds of class time, with pupils working silently on their own for most of this period'.

What we now have to reckon with are the implications for teacher education of findings on teacher effectiveness which, for example, underline the importance of academic contact time as a variable, which stress the importance of teacher direction of activity, whole class teaching, fewer small group activities, less independent seat work, a higher proportion of teacher initiated activity and reduced opportunities for feed back.[6] We find references in the recent research literature on what Rosenshine[7] calls 'direct instruction':

> ... teaching activities where goals are clear to students, time allocated for instruction is sufficient and continuous, coverage of context is extensive, the performance of students is monitored, questions are at a low cognitive level so that the students can produce many correct responses, and feed back to students is immediate and academically oriented. In direct instruction the teacher controls instructional goals, chooses materials appropriate for the student's ability, and paces the instructional episode.

The above statements are not, I believe, untypical of much current and recent work in the United States and the UK. It would be premature, if not foolish, to draw any conclusions

26

from them for priorities in content and methodology of teacher
education programmes. The only point I would wish to make at
this stage concerns the danger of referring to 'change' in
teacher education and its priorities in an undifferentiated
and aggregated manner, of neglecting the disjunctions between
changes in governance, institutional framework, academic
organisation, programme design and course content. It is the
last two of these that are most likely to be significant so
far as student learning is concerned. Yet it is inevitably
structural and processural factors that get the lion's share
of attention, at the expense of content and learning outcomes.

All this generates questions about priorities that are
very different to those which exist in other systems. Is it
better to spend such money as we have on more and better in-
service training, or in lengthening the course of initial
training? What proportion of in-service training resources
should be used to sustain the on-site (and usually cheaper
and apparently more cost-effective) activities, and how much
should go to the costlier (because they involve replacements)
college or university-based programmes? What are the implications for courses and programmes of recent findings of Her
Majesty's Inspectorate concerning the inadequate subject
knowledge of many teachers?

Priority issues of this nature have little meaning for
countries that are still struggling to produce enough teachers
of any kind to provide basic education for semi-literate
populations, which are striving to universalise primary
schooling, which lack adequate supplies of text books and even
writing materials.

Faced with contrasts of this kind, any consideration of
changing priorities demands both practical and theoretical
responses. As far as theory is concerned, we are still short
of adequate descriptions and taxonomies of national teacher
education provision. In the five level model of teacher
education outlined in my article on this subject in the
current edition of Encyclopedia Brittanica, I distinguish
between normal school A, which students enter prior to the
first certificate stage of secondary education; normal school
B, with entry at sixteen or thereabouts; college, where
candidates for training have a full secondary education; and
university, offering degree level qualifications to candidates
with normal university entry requirements by means of either
concurrent or consecutive courses. There are also many
alternative courses, which do not fit these categories.

I have reclassified the college and the university
levels into four sub-types. In the United States, most parts
of Canada and in some other countries, where the term
university embraces institutions which vary greatly in size,
quality of programme, status and scholarly output, and which
offer courses oriented to many vocations and professions,

27

teacher education is provided through colleges, schools and faculties subject to overall governance by the appropriate academic bodies, and by staff employed by the university and paid on its normal scales. This I call the integrated university type. In countries which have a binary system of education, with both university and non-university institutions offering degree level work, as in England and in Australia, initial teacher education is provided in both 'sectors', although it is common for the bulk of primary teachers to be prepared outside the universities, and for all or most of advanced study and research to be a university responsibility. This I call the binary type.

In many parts of Europe, and in other countries outside the English speaking world where there are long-standing differences in the status and rewards of primary and secondary teachers, the pre-service education and training of the former is undertaken in specialist non-university institutions, while preparation for secondary teaching is the university's task. Advanced in-service work for primary teachers may also be undertaken outside the university, as well as a certain amount of pedagogical research. For the most part, however, advanced training and fundamental research are the responsibility of university staff or of specialised agencies and personnel with status equivalent of a university. This I call the European type. In a few countries, all initial teacher preparation is done by non-university colleges, for both primary and secondary teachers. University Departments, Faculties or Schools of Education restrict themselves to advanced studies and research. Such arrangements can be found in, for example, Scotland and New Zealand. This, for want of a better term, I call the Scottish type.

Taxonomy is an elementary, but nonetheless very important stage towards the development of theory. The one I have outlined is very crude, and can stand considerable refinement. There is need for amplification of such models, which identify the historical, social and other conditions to which the system of teacher training is a response, and offer a variety of bench marks in relation to which the desirability and feasibility of particular reforms can be examined.

The framework I have outlined is by no means exclusive. Some of the alternative programmes of teacher education, such as was employed in Tanzania to universalise primary schooling, would clearly need separate consideration. Such crash training is, however, a temporary expedient, and not intended as a long term solution.

We also need to make a practical response to gaps that we can readily identify in the teacher education priorities of developed and less developed countries. There are a number of schemes whereby teachers qualified in the UK can be encouraged and helped to accept short-term employment overseas. It has been suggested from time to time that by sending large numbers of British teachers to those countries which still have shortages, we should be rendering a valuable form of overseas aid, and at the same time relieving our own unemployment problems. Many countries have set their sights on the education and training of an indigenous teaching force, and opportunities for work overseas, especially on a permanent basis, are less good than they were. Nonetheless, a number of countries still welcome British teachers for shorter or longer periods of service, and devices such as salary supplements, bridging the gap between UK and local remuneration, travel grants, and protected UK pension rights and service credits are all greatly to be welcomed as a small, but significant contribution to helping countries with a continuing teacher shortage.

In conclusion, let me again urge the importance of describing, categorizing, and evaluating the ways in which countries meet their needs for teacher education in a cross-cultural rather than cross-national perspective, which recognises the manner in which the preparation of teachers is embedded, not just in an educational context, but also in complex and overlapping sets of cultural assumptions and practices. Currently, the possibilities of the cross-cultural comparisons I have in mind are diminished by the theoretical poverty of each country's research and literature on teacher education. Whatever the inadequacies of data and theory, there are bound to be large differences in the priorities that systems attach to particular reforms and improvement in teacher education, having to do with what each country identifies as its most pressing social, political, economic and educational problems.

NOTES

1.   F.A. Von Hayek, Law, Legislation and Liberty Vol. 2 The Mirage of Social Justice, London, Routledge and Kegan Paul, 1976.
2.   M.L. Borrowman, 'Comparative Education in Teacher Education Programmes', Comparative Education Review, Volume 19, number 3.
3.   I have adapted these profiles from my paper to the XVth Annual Conference of the International Council for Education in Teaching.
4.   S. Marklund, 'Towards a New Professionalism' in, D. Lomax (ed) European Perspectives in Teacher Education, London, Wiley, 1976.
5.   M. Galton and B. Simon (eds), Progress and Performance in the Primary Classroom, London, Routledge and Kegan Paul, 1980.

6.   D.M. Medley, 'The Effectiveness of Teachers' in
P.L. Peterson and J.H. Walberg Research on Teaching, Berkeley,
California, McCutchan Publishing Co., 1979.
7.   B.V. Rosenshine, 'Content, Time and Direct Instruction', in Peterson and Walberg, op. cit., p. 38.

INDUSTRIALISED COUNTRIES

Edmund King

The term 'industrialised countries' covers a large and varied area, yet we can assume wide agreement on its meaning. We think of those countries most marked by heavy industrialisation and urbanisation during at least the past century and a half. We recognise too how many urban centres in less industrialised countries have followed the "Western" lead, and know that some of these centres have the most galloping urbanisation of all at a time when the oldest industrialised countries have long been talking of a third technological revolution leading to a "post-industrial" society (to use Daniel Bell's phrase).

It is worthwhile remembering how recent our industrialised urbanisation is. Not long ago Scientific American published a special issue on "Cities", later re-published as an impressive book. It pointed out that at the beginning of this century only one country (Britain) could be called predominantly urbanised, and that at the outbreak of the first World War the number of cities with more than a million population anywhere was still very small. Now industrialised urbanisation is the characteristic of life in most of Western Europe, North America, Japan, Australia and so on; but there is a world shift in its distribution as South Korea, the Philippines, Mexico and other recently "less-developed countries" outstrip the earlier homelands of industrialisation in the production of textiles, ships, and even electronics. Meanwhile, life in the old industrialised world is internally challenged not only by outside competition but by qualitative changes in occupational expectation, in social relationships responding to technological changes of a far-reaching nature, and - not least, for us - in the relationships of learning to teaching, and between school, work prospects, and living and learning around and after school.

How does all this affect teachers and their education? And what do we mean by "teachers", anyway? We are not thinking of Locke's or Rousseau's tutors, or any other text-

book figure. In saying "teacher", we are thinking of a
publicly paid employee in schools or similar institutions.
In saying "teacher education" now, unfortunately, we are
perforce thinking of many who will never find jobs in schools.
Dr. William Taylor's recent article in Educational Review[1]
reminds us that by the mid-1980s the output of teachers will
annually exceed likely demand by several thousand - on top of
the present unemployed and those who have sought jobs or
careers elsewhere. There is an evident implication here for
those engaged in "teacher education". What future are we
preparing people for?

If we can momentarily forget unemployment and career
uncertainty in the teaching profession itself, we may focus
on associated implications of a more directly educational
kind. A serving career of some forty to fifty years was the
normal expectation for most stable professions not long ago,
with competences and commitments much the same throughout a
successful career. The rewards of schooling and examination
success were founded on such prospects; they were the
incentive to learning in school; they regulated priorities
and objectives; they established the hierarchy of "subjects"
and of topics within the subjects; and the pyramid of schools
and awards was consequentially structured not only at the
initial stages but in any return to educational opportunity
later. People felt certain, and even experts imagined they
could predict. That situation was logically finished by the
mid-1950s in industrialised countries; by the mid-1960s
rebellious students knew it, and even some top planners and
researchers. But the "teacher education" establishment and
most of the teachers did not. Hence the shock caused by
dismantling or dismembering colleges of education and indeed
teachers' courses in the 1970s. Hence the need to look at
changed priorities in teacher education in the 1980s -
especially when we acknowledge the need for revolutionary
change in our whole attitude to teaching and learning because
our charges are already living in a revolutionised world.

CONSTRAINTS FROM THE PAST

It has long been clear to any educator familiar with Africans,
for example, that many students of today live in a world
quite alien to that of their parents. Indeed, I live in a
world largely alien to that of my own grandparents -
especially when they were young. It is a commonplace to say
that every decade now telescopes the scale and scope of
discovery, ingenuity and change associated with previous
centuries.

Elsewhere[2] I have shown the close connection between
the way formal education takes place (or shapes its priorities) and the technologies of production, distribution and

32

communication. There should be nothing alarming today in recognising a technological/educational linkage, or indeed in expecting today's methods and commitments in education to be at the <u>forefront</u> of technological advance. Yet in some ways we are imprisoned in a technological/educational pattern established for different purposes and a very different range of population in the vastly different context of nearly two centuries ago. Since we are already some way along the path of a microelectronic revolution's progress towards a "communications society"[3], we surely need to alter our practices (and, still more, our <u>perspectives</u>) from those of a pre-railway age. Education seems to be the one department of public life where such anachronisms so widely persist.

I strongly agree with Dr. Taylor in saying we need a "theory of culture" (or of cultural change) addressed to the perspectives of teacher education. That is why I have tried to provide one in several articles and a book[4], or at least to apply directly to education and its priorities the theories of Daniel Bell and others about technological and cultural change which have persuasively surrounded us since at least the early 1970s.

Without speculating, we plainly see one central educational need of our times if we recognise that almost everyone over the age of about 30 is in some sense a survivor from an earlier technological epoch, not to say a school experience which logically antedates much of that. Our own anachronisms may be serious; but they are not as perilous as perpetuating those anachronisms into the education of tomorrow's adults especially the growing percentage who stay on in full-time education or training when they are socially and legally adults. I consider them especially because of extensive researches into their case[5]; but that case is pivotal to changing many educational attitudes before the adult frontier is reached in <u>post-compulsory</u> education, and it also affects every decision about learning and careers afterwards. We may still be constraining the future to fit the mould of the past, whereas the real task is to release energies and potentialities so far unused, and then develop them for new commitments and a different order of questions.

As we look back on the 19th century phase of industrialising formal education (when a contemporary could say: "The grand principle of Dr. Bell's system is the division of labour applied to intellectual purposes ... The principle in manufactories and schools is the same"), we observe several inherited but persistent features often overlooked - most of them being aspects of <u>control</u> and <u>convergence</u>:

(a) industrialisation of the process and the personnel was most marked in elementary schooling - and perhaps confined to it at first;

33

(b)   standardisation and the interchangeability of parts (an essential feature of industrialisation) was most marked where industrialisation came later (France, Germany and the USA), and particularly where teachers are civil servants (i.e. nearly everywhere except the UK and the USA);

(c)   teachers and their education were (are) classified in broad strata, these in turn subdivided into specific bands or categories licensed to teach this subject or that age-group; and pupils were categorised to match these;

(d)   teachers were expected to be "your obedient servant" of the state (note the Danish word Inspektør for a headmaster), or of the local community (note the "selectmen" in the USA and New Zealand), or of the Church (as in Sweden), or of the parents (in the USA);

(e)   by contrast, teachers in secondary schools on the continent and in "Public Schools" in the UK until recently, and most recently in mathematics and science teaching in our really public (l.e.a.) schools, have not been required to train;   (No training is necessary now for teaching in "further" or "higher" education, even though a growing percentage of "16 to 19"s are in "tertiary colleges" or "further education").

(f)   consequently, the whole question of whether higher education should train teachers (or, for that matter, anybody) is still unresolved in many places - so much so that Frank Bowles in Access to Higher Education (1963) used that as a criterion for distinguishing between old and modern higher education systems.

Patterns of teacher control persist now - even in the USA, where grading, specific licensing and short-term contracts are common. Elsewhere the "civil service" tradition standardises teachers and their roles in specific, controlled strata. This is the production-line inheritance surrounding teachers (as "super-monitors") and much of their preparation. It is no wonder that schools still retaining the "second technological/educational idiom"[6] as their norm impose similar blinkers on their pupils' expectations and on teachers' perceptions of their own roles.

These are some starting points for our present survey of changing priorities in teacher education.

LEARNERS LIVE IN A WORLD OF HEADLONG CHANGE

In almost total contrast to the context and assumptions which shaped the patterns of teacher (and pupil) control just described, today's circumstances call for divergence and creative growth - not just in and around school, but through-out life and across all its ramifications. "Lifelong learning and relearning" is no empty phrase; it is the very condition of any school's relevance to those who leave it.

In two other places[7] I have shown (with hard statistics and illustrative diagrams) how necessary it is to think of a "provisional" school, a "conditional" curriculum - especially for young adults from the age of 16 upwards, but earlier too in anticipation of that stage during the years preceding it. The "relevance" of school and what it offers does not depend only on content, or skills, or "within school" efforts to build character and commitment. This truism is reinforced when we consider the well-documented boredom, frustration and downright antipathy to school fare shown by a large proportion of school leavers. There is indeed impatience with "schooly" norms and expectations among many who stay on in the fold or who return to it later - even if we limit attention to narrowly cognitive aspects of teaching and learning. Within that field itself we teachers cannot know the outcome of school's curricula and disciplines, or the future context of their application, or our young people's experience and motivation in the years ahead. Of one thing we are certain: that all proper education today is education for uncertainty.[8]

Today's context of uncertainty for all who look out from school is painfully obvious. That outer change comes right into school. Let us take a few reminders, starting first with population shifts. I quote from France, since French statistics are thorough, but the figures are widely relevant to other countries, though the categories may be different. Since 1945 France has had an immigration of 4,147,978 (including 850,000 Portuguese - more than Lisbon's population, 850,000 Algerians, 400,000 each of Italians, Spaniards, and Moroccans, and 106,000 from Francophone Africa). Meanwhile, in 1981, France has an unemployment figure of 1,800,000. Consequential problems of schooling and acculturation are obvious. One-sixth of West Germany's "blue collar" workers are foreign, and about one-eighth of Sweden's. More than a quarter of Australia's population has gone there or been born of immigrants since 1945; between 1970 and 1980 alone there was a marked shift in the youthfulness of the Australian population as a whole - both chronologically and in such things as the staffing of higher education and business enterprises. No doubt in consequence, within the same decade, Australian preferences in food, wine consumption, music, theatre and art have altered greatly - becoming much more "continental-European". Expectations of higher education and diligence in scholarship have grown in due measure - despite massive cuts there (as elsewhere) from 1980 onwards. These remarks show that educational providers cannot claim to "know" permanently their "consumer" population, or the circumstances of their self-fulfilment.

When youth unemployment first hit the headlines after
1973 it was fashionable to blame it all on the "energy crisis"
and the fivefold increase in petroleum prices; and when this
in turn was followed by spiralling inflation, a ready-made
scapegoat became available for the misfit between school-
based job expectations and the job market outside. However,
we know now that the problem is widespread in all industrial
countries, is increasingly long-term in nature, and will
persist. In the United Kingdom between 10% and 11% of the
labour force was unemployed in 1981 (OECD Observer No. 111,
July 1981); in the OECD area the total of unemployed was
expected to grow from 23 million in 1981 to 25.5 million by
mid-1982, and to be increasingly long-term - especially among
youth (OECD Observer No. 108, January 1981). This same issue
of OECD Observer showed a UK forecast of youth unemployment
rising from 16½% of the youth labour force (under 25) rising
to 20¼% in 1982.[9] Figures from other sources show that 42%
of all French unemployed are under the age of 25, and that
indeed some 47% of all the unemployed in the European Economic
Community are between 16 and 25 years of age. The average
duration of completed employment between the ages of 16 and
20 was 6 months, while average unemployment lasted 5 months
at that age.

These, of course, are large-scale regional or national
averages. When we get down to localities and particular
groups the situation is much worse. For example, 63% of black
youth in New York City is unemployed, and a disproportionate
figure for black or other disadvantaged unemployment is
characteristic of conurbations in Britain too. But the
familiar, traditional population of industrial countries is
also hit. Ship-building, mining, textile industries have
migrated to Korea, the Philippines, Mexico and so on. Car
manufacture, aeronautic construction and traffic, optics,
precision instrument making are internationally dominated -
and now precarious careers. Yearly, innovations in the
microprocessor industry make obsolete not merely the instrumentation of communications, manufacturing controls or
processes, and the very locations of industry and commerce,
but also the whole range of many formerly comfortable service
occupations - from being a clerk to managing many an enterprise. The entire occupational prospect is in slippage.
When such remarks were made in the late 1960s and early 1970s
they were considered to be scaremongering; now they are not
merely the subject of many thoughtful surveys but the actual
experience of many middle-range, middle-class, middle-aged
people who have had the "good education" which once promised
lifelong security and perhaps success.[10]

Young adults leaving school know this harsh reality
only too well. For years they have been bombarded with the
evidence on TV, or through contact with friends. They have

36

seen the self-same frustration credited with being the cause
of riots - if not indeed a justification for them. They know
only too well the shortcomings of Youth Opportunity Programmes
of brief duration, of no certain outcome, and often of
questionable relevance - apart from masking the endemic and
perennial perils of "the transition from school to work"
which has been the theme of so many conferences right round
the world.[11]

Since the early 1960s, but with enhanced publicity since
the "events of May" in 1968 in France (and other countries),
young adults still at school have questioned as never before
the whole structure of "authority" and values. Older people
looking in on youth forget that TV programmes for adults (like
"That Was The Week That Was") likewise brought into question
not only human foibles but much that had seemed sacred in
politics, religion, the socio-economic order, the "Protestant
ethic", the family - or, as academics would have it, the
values of "structural functionalism". Since 1955 the rapid
acceptance of the contraceptive pill, alongside women's
liberation movements, black power, "alternative communities",
and a now frequent pattern of "dropping in and out" - not to
mention associated problems of one-parent families, divorce,
and so on - have all helped to shatter the "end-on" prospect
of school/work/family relationships settled for life. And
looming over everything (and undermining it) is the frightful
mockery of possible nuclear war. These things are in the very
fabric of young people's minds - not just the youngest adults
on the threshold of life, but of many young teachers and
students who might teach.

Until fairly recently - in progressive countries and
schools at least - the "school context" was more nearly the
real context of outside actuality than it often is now -
especially in terms of employment prospects. But many surveys
since the mid-1960s have shown a hiatus between the teachers'
"view from inside" and the "view from inside" experienced by
upper-secondary students.[12] Not too long ago, teachers "knew"
their prescribed population, the "future" of their particular
curricular slices, the socio-economic processes which would
"digest" their output of students and knowledge or skills in
after life; and thus they could hand on relevant received
wisdom. No longer is that the case in any completeness.
Teachers must be more than ever learners - learners lifelong
and learners indeed from those whom they teach.

It is impossible to repeat too often the truism that
education does not even begin until the learner accepts
whatever is taught, builds it into himself after ensuring
that it tallies with other knowledge and experience, and then
takes it further. Taking it further implies personal,
critical involvement, as well as a vital ingredient of exper-
iential feedback. (Of course, my remarks apply principally

37

to students over 16; but all post-adolescence competence in
these respects requires a gradual pre-adult apprenticeship in
the process). Most young adults' forward view of the world
now includes keen awareness of "alternative educators",
alternative criteria, and also of alternating phases of reappraisal - whether after work/unemployment on the one hand,
or at points of crisis in personal, family, or public life.

In contrast to most present teacher-trainers or indeed
sensitive teacher-educators, whose formative years may have
been in the expansively confident 1960s - with modernisation
and social engineering, if not "prediction" - young people
now mature in a world marred by calculations of contraction,
decline, and the rough passage from high industrialisation's
"second technological/educational idiom" to post-industrial-
isation's "third technological/educational idiom"[13] where
remote control by "telematics" is becoming normal and where
"communications" means something more electronic than human.
More obviously, governments make calculations of destruction.
The 1960s' ruthless politics of growth and ambition are
replaced by no less harsh politics entailing unemployment,
third world hunger, and much wastage of human potential.
Teacher-preparation and in-service development must surely
come to terms with this real world which is the context of
all learning and re-learning today.

NEW POPULATIONS AND NEEDS CALL FOR REORIENTATION OF ALL
TEACHING AND LEARNING

So far my emphasis has been on far-reaching and pervasive
changes in our context, and in the changes of concept (or
orientation) demanded by them. Let us telescope many other
considerations and think in particular about the young adult
population in our schools or colleges (not exclusively, of
course, but because young adults make or mar our system, and
communicate very effectively indeed with their juniors).
What happens at 16-plus is always on the front doorstep of
anyone aged 14-15; and sometimes it is right in the home or
the school because younger pupils bring it in from brothers,
sisters, or friends.

Many of our scholastic institutions (indeed, whole
systems) have been overwhelmed by the doubling and trebling
of post-compulsory enrolments since the early 1960s. Though
some teachers seem to suppose that this massive shift is
peripheral or "just one more thing", I believe it marks a
fundamental challenge to previously accepted "end on"
relationships between school and whatever follows.[14] Consequently it is a challenge to all teachers directly concerned
with the lead-up to the frontier at 16, and it poses questions
about altering teaching/learning relationships (and emphases
on content) throughout the secondary phase - at least.

Indeed, because enrolled full-time percentages bring such pressure on school systems (more than half enrolled to the age of 17-18 in many continental countries, and with over 70% in Norway, well over 80% in Sweden, and about 95% in Japan) many young adults still at school over the age of about 16 find themselves in greatly altered upper-secondary institutions. Sometimes they are quite separate new-style establishments, like British "sixth form colleges", "tertiary colleges" and their counterparts on the continent. Britain has scarcely felt the full impact of this change yet, since our full-time enrolments to nearly 18 years of age amount to little over 30% of the age-group - itself a trebling within about two decades.

Numbers are far from being the whole story. Far more important is the change of style: a fresh start is given over a wider field of learning to a much wider range of students than ever before, often coming in through "open access" to courses for which they would at one time have been considered unsuitable material, unsuitably motivated. Yet they succeed in numbers unprecedented; and (despite unemployment) they go out into a wider range of occupations or studies than ever before. That is exactly what is called for by the "third technological/educational idiom" and its widening variety of service occupations, despite the present shortfall in the gross number of jobs available for individuals. It may well be that with time-sharing at work, and paid educational leave (already established by right of law in some continental countries), and in consequence of increased worker-participation in industry, a much wider range of "returners" to post-compulsory education will have to be accommodated at the level of upper-secondary schooling though not at the normal age. Even as things stand now in our educationally conservative country, at this level all students are new in important respects - even in apparently traditional institutions.

When we consider "young adult" levels of learning by all these people - often moving at different paces, and with differing profiles of attainment even in one and the same person - and the different worlds of "relevance" and motivation or experience which give them momentum, problems of "management" and partnership assail any educator. If teachers are not ready to cope, be sure that someone else will. Alternatives to teachers have long penetrated every home where children spend as long before the "box" or with transistor radios as in school. Now with microprocessors - of the kind that even small children now hold in their hands to play electronic games - computer-assisted delivery systems for instruction and comment (sometimes with feedback) are already a supplement to whatever schools or teachers can offer. That is especially true for unfamiliar subjects ("fringe" languages, interdisciplinary courses from CSE upwards, and rapidly changing knowledge in science). An old problem in every secondary school has been how to combine provision for "the average" with opportunities for "the special", "the gifted" or the simply unusual. The USSR nearly solved that with its "circles" for recreation, supplementary studies, and near-genius requirements - without destroying the common school or strong socialisation. Now parallel electronic agencies or activities in support make it possible for a very large percentage of ordinary people to learn, and indeed to contribute to learning, in ways never envisaged when the "school-factory" formula was spelt out in the early nineteenth century. Today's (or tomorrow's) "communications society" requires appropriate educational instrumentation, with at least a nation-wide system of supply and support in an electronic network.

IMPLICATIONS FOR TEACHER EDUCATION

My remarks are by no means a full catalogue of obvious implications, or even representative; they deal with aspects which strike me most. Other aspects are discussed in the papers and books to which reference is made in the notes.

It has long been said that the best teacher is a life-long learner. The very condition of being alive and alert today places this obligation on every educated person, especially on teachers and parents. No teacher preparation lacking commitment to the opening of opportunities for a quite altered population in a quite altered world, deserves the name "education". It is a latterday "treason of the clerks" - a retreat into sterile scholasticism or the "tricks of the trade".

Teachers must first and foremost know the world context of headlong change - especially the world as it most affects those who leave school. By that I mean both those who leave school at 16 (or 18, or 21, or whenever) and those who leave school every day to go home or meet their friends. In my team's survey of post-compulsory education, a recurring complaint in every type of school in all five countries was that "our teachers don't know us"; and indeed the hard evidence shows that even good teachers very often do not know the whole "scholastic self" of the student, let alone all the other "selves" that Professor W.D. Wall once described.

Then teachers must know the changes in school and schooling far beyond their usual purview. Teaching is by its nature often a lonely profession. Few really know exactly what goes on in other classrooms, let alone other schools and other places. The study - the comparative and analytical study - of world-wide, lifelong changes in the conditions and commitments of formal education is another prime essential.

40

A collateral essential is the study of those alternative educators who work with or against the teacher in the school; and this study should be operational as well as cognitive, so that teachers can work with, or compensate for, those alternatives.

Quite rightly, much of the change in teacher preparation since 1945 has integrated many kinds of higher education previously separated; but that should not make us think that all teacher preparation (or all teacher competence, knowledge, or responsibility) is of equal worth, or equally demanding. Manifestly it is not; and it does terrible harm to the teaching profession (and education's prospects) to pretend that it is. Of course we need a fresh, up-to-date concept of the teaching profession and its commitments. At a fundamental, generalised level these are much the same on every plane of the teaching profession. But there is no such generic animal as "the teacher". Rejecting the rigid, permanent status categories of earlier educational history (still very much alive in some other places) according to the level of school taught in, the social class of the learners, and their expected destinations, does not mean we should deny the very different attainment levels, performance, or perspicacity of individual teachers or groups of them. What it does mean is that in the teaching profession (as in business or medicine) some practitioners' responsibilities can be <u>initially</u> discharged with a modest degree of specialisation, after the common requirements of initiation to that profession are adequately ensured. Thereafter, specialisation or advancement or deeper-and-wider education for teachers (and others) can and should be developed in a series of tiers.

Two- or three-tier qualifications are now accepted as the norm in some other occupations, and doubtless will be in more. Why nurses, medical auxiliaries, or dieticians should be prevented from self-improvement and self-advancement in the medical profession (under proper educational and professional control), I have never been able to see. The same is true of the teaching profession. In any case, the special needs of migrants, backward children, the gifted, the adolescent, and the young adult in education, obviously require teacher preparation around or after the acquisition of basic professional competence; and the responsibilities associated with these special commitments merit special professional recompense. Not everyone can undertake them properly.

This is of course an argument for permanent in-service updating of knowledge, attitudes, and skills as school systems evolve, populations change, or needs express themselves. Institutional restructuring of school systems, operational innovations, new locations and personnel for the learning process, the whole electronic network - all these challenges demand fresh responses. The essential reform, none

41

the less, is a change of commitment implicit in the very
phrase "teacher education"[15] - a concept of partnership in
other people's learning to cope lifelong with their re-
learning by every available means in every fresh commitment
or new learning circumstances. We do not - cannot - know
where they will be going. We cannot know precisely where
teachers and teaching will proceed; but we can open our own
and others' windows on what today's most careful evidence
suggests may happen, fearlessly using every possible means
to that end.

NOTES

1.   'Teacher Education - into the 1990s', Educational
Review Volume 33, number 2, 1981.
2.   Other Schools and Ours, 5th edition (1979), pp. 36
ff. Also in the European Journal of Education, Volume 15,
number 2, 1980.
3.   See 'Education for a communications society' in
E.J. King (ed), Reorganising Education: Management and
Participation for Change, London, Sage, 1977.
4.   As in Note 2.
5.   Research findings are given in E.J. King, C.H. Moor
and J.A. Mundy, Post-Compulsory Education I: A new analysis
in Western Europe, London, Sage, 1974. Further evidence and
conclusions from the research are given in Post-Compulsory
Education II: The way ahead, London, Sage 1975, by the same
authors.
6.   As Note 1.
7.   See Appendix 1 to Other Schools and Ours, op. cit.,
and p. 42 ibid.
8.   See E.J. King (ed), Education for Uncertainty,
London, Sage, 1978.
9.   See also the OECD booklets Youth Unemployment - The
causes and the consequences, Paris, 1980, and Youth Without
Work - Three countries approach the problem, Paris, 1981.
10.   See E.J. King (ed), 'Education's approach to
computer-assisted learning', European Journal of Education,
Volume 15, number 2, 1980, pp. 132-133.
11.   One such conference is reported in G. Neave (ed),
Research perspectives on the transition from school to work,
Strasbourg, Council of Europe and Swets and Zeitlinger, 1978.
A collection of studies connected with a conference in
Melbourne in 1980 is contained in D.S. Anderson and C.
Blakers (eds), Youth, Transition and Social Research,
Canberra, Australian National University Press, 1981.
12.   Shown vividly in the histograms in Post-Compulsory
Education I, op. cit., pp. 225 ff.
13.   Other Schools and Ours, op. cit., p. 42.

14.   See Post-Compulsory Education II: The way ahead, op. cit., and "Post-Compulsory Education - the frontier of uncertainty" in Education for Uncertainty, op. cit.

15.   Well brought out in G. Fragnière, "Teacher education in higher education systems - A new conception of education for the coming decade", European Journal of Education, Volume 15, number 1, 1980.

Nigel Grant

Although under close Soviet tutelage at a period of crucial change, and still under varying degrees of Soviet influence, the Eastern European school systems - and, therefore, their teacher training systems - were never a monolithic bloc, and are even less so now. All have their own characteristics and peculiarities, and even when implementing a broadly similar policy have, perforce, done so in their own ways. (This is true not only of deviants like Yugoslavia and Albania, but full members of the bloc as well). Obviously, it would be quite impossible to attempt a detailed survey of the whole area and the USSR in the space available here. It is therefore proposed to deal with the broad patterns of development over the entire area - with specific reference to the Soviet Union in particular, but also with reference to other systems where appropriate, lest general patterns be taken for uniformity in what is an intriguingly diverse area.

It is, nonetheless, convenient to begin with a quick look at the situation following the second World War, when the Soviet Union was engaged in educational reconstruction and then expansion, and the other countries were also undertaking basic structural reform, for these developments had implications for teacher training that are still being worked through. The post-war communist regimes inherited school systems that were not only backward in most cases, but divided (as had the USSR after the Revolution). Details varied enormously, but broadly they were systems organised in two tiers, the elementary and the secondary, quite separate except for a limited common primary base (see Fig. 1). For a minority, the primary school was a preparatory stage before entry to the Gymnasium or lycée, the academic secondary school, which admitted perhaps ten per cent or so of 10- or 11-year-olds and prepared them for higher education. For the majority, the continuation of primary into terminal elementary schooling up to the age of 14 or so was all they could expect - if that, for the laws on compulsory

Fig. 1:   Eastern Europe - Pre-Reform School Systems

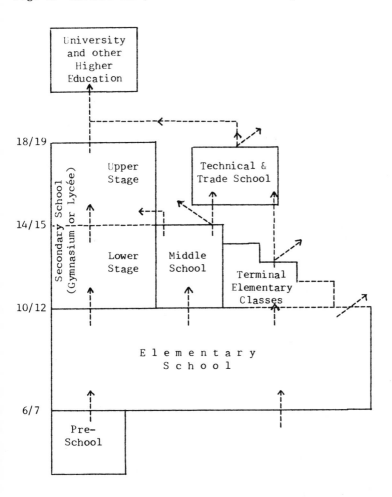

schooling were unevenly enforced. In some countries, there
were intermediate schools that made some contribution to
filling the gap - the German Mittelschulen and their
imitators, like the Yugoslav narodne škole or "people's
schools". Some of these, like the "civic school" (měst'
anská škola) in Czechoslovakia, even provided a second chance
for entry to secondary school, but generally their impact was
slight. Secondary schooling, of any kind, was a minority
experience; after the common primary base, there were totally
separate schools serving totally different clientèles.

Not surprisingly, the teaching professions were divided
also - so much so that there was usually a quite different
nomenclature, reflecting the differences between the
instituteur or Lehrer and the professeur or Studienrat which
have survived in the West (and in some eastern countries
too, for that matter). Teachers for the secondary schools
went to secondary school themselves, thence to university,
and thence (often with no professional training at all) back
into the secondary schools. Elementary school teachers did
not go to secondary school at all, let alone into higher
education; they finished elementary school, then went to a
normal or pedagogic school (parallel to but separate from
the secondary, though perhaps following a largely similar
curriculum), and then went back to the elementary school to
teach, having had no contact with the secondary-higher
academic system at all. This was the position in Eastern
Europe (where the systems had been modelled on German or
French originals). In the USSR, they had gone past the
stage of vertical division of this kind, but still retained
a horizontal division - higher education (or something close
to it) for the upper or secondary classes, and pedagogic
schools (at the upper secondary stage) for the pre-school
and primary classes.

Even before communist governments were installed in
some cases, popular front governments, determined to break
down what they saw as a class-bound and divisive system, set
themselves to reform the structure, generally along lines
already being pursued in the Soviet Union. This usually
took the form of a basic school, a comprehensive unit
embracing the primary classes and the lower secondary stage -
the first half of the secondary school, the intermediate
school (if any) and the terminal elementary classes all
combined - thus embracing the whole compulsory stage in one
institution up to age 14 (later extended to 15 or 16). The
upper classes of the Gymnasium or lycée, the trade training
schools, and a new category of upper secondary schools with
a professional bias, remained as separate entities after the
basic school. Some systems tried to homogenise the primary
and lower secondary stages, others to reorganise them (like
East Germany) into three steps instead of two, but most kept
the primary-secondary division as an internal point of
demarcation, with all-purpose teachers before it, subject
specialists after. (See Fig. 2).

Naturally, this meant that the old two-cycle system of
teacher training would no longer fit. If the reforms had
not unified the school systems, they had at least blurred
the distinctions by introducing a new category, the lower
secondary stage, largely modelled on the lower half of the
old Gymnasium or lycée but now spread across the entire age-
group; and there was thus a need for teachers for that

46

Fig. 2: Eastern Europe – Reformed School Systems (c. 1960)

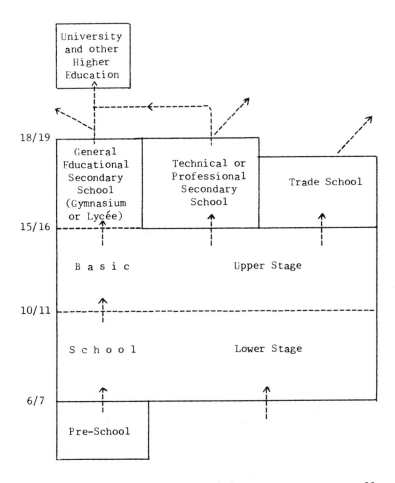

stage – something the higher training system was too small to cope with, and the "normal" system not advanced enough. Nor was this all; attempts to raise the level of teacher training, both in expertise and esteem, went along with the general attempts to improve the educational systems. This in turn meant at least the intention to move the training institutions into the higher sector if possible, or at least nearer to it.

Response varied from country to country, according to resources and demand. Some converted the secondary teachers' schools into post-secondary institutions, but still short of higher educational status. In East Germany, the outcome of this process was the Teacher Training Institute (Institut für Lehrerbildung) or the Bulgarian colleges known as "semi-higher institutes" (poluvisši instituti). In some, new institutions were created essentially for the lower secondary stage - teachers' institutes in the USSR, teachers' studiums (studia nauczycielskie) in Poland, pedagogic institutes (pedagógiai intézetek) in Hungary, higher pedagogical schools (visše pedagoške škole) in Yugoslavia - while retaining the secondary teachers' schools for most of the supply of primary teachers.

As for the attempts to raise teacher training (or at least part of it) to higher educational status, the main difference between the countries lay in the role of the universities. In some cases, the universities virtually absorbed all teacher training for secondary classes as in East Germany, Romania and to an extent in Poland; and in Czechoslovakia, the conversion of the pedagogic institutes into pedagogic faculties brought all training (apart from pre-school) into the universities. Others placed the emphasis on building up alternative structures as the equivalent of university training - the pedagogic institutes (pedagogicheskie instituty or pedvuzy) in the USSR, the Higher Pedagogic School (Wyższa Szkóła Pedagogiczna) in Poland, the Pädagogische Hochschule in East Germany, the high school (visoka škola) in Yugoslavia. Most of them kept some university involvement as well, notably the USSR, as we shall see presently.

Where secondary training schools still existed, attempts were made to promote them into the post-secondary level, to replace them with higher courses, or to restrict their role. As sources of primary teachers, they have now virtually disappeared, with the signal exception of the USSR and (within Yugoslavia) Serbia. They were retained in Czechoslovakia, but for pre-school training only. In the USSR, the development of four-year pedagogic institute courses for primary teachers was intended to replace the pedagogical schools, but even now this process is still far from complete, for reasons that will be examined shortly. There have been also one or two oddities, like Romania's introduction of pedagogic lycées in 1966, but generally primary training at the secondary level has gone out, or has been confined to kindergarten training. (The assumption that teachers of the very young need less general education and a shorter training seems to be a hangover from the pre-reform systems, and does not appear to have been widely questioned - interestingly enough, in view of the political and social value placed on pre-school education in all communist countries. This could be yet another example of the training system limping behind the realities of the

48

educational system itself).[1]

In sum, then, reform and expansion of the school systems stimulated demand for a raising of the general level of teacher training into, or at least towards, the post-secondary and higher sector, and was carried through with varying degrees of success. Commonly, this was seen as a move towards the eventual unification of all training under the higher system; but, commonly, in the short term at any rate, it often meant the proliferation of institutions, often with overlaps, to cope with the new categories required. (One is reminded of the Highland village with three churches before two of them amalgamated, and four afterwards). We can now look more closely at the structure of teacher training in some particular systems in more detail.

In some respects, East Germany would seem to have gone furthest along the road of consolidation of the training system (except for Czechoslovakia, as already remarked). But the integration is not complete, nor is there a totally post-secondary structure - rather surprisingly, in view of that country's tendency to be well ahead in East European developments generally. The basic school in this case is one of ten years, the Ten-Class General Educational Poly-technical School (Zehnklassige Allgemeinbildende Poly-technische Oberschule, conveniently contracted to ZAPO or POS), from age 6 to 16. Thereafter, a minority proceed to two further years of general education in the Extended Secondary School (Erweiterte Oberschule or EOS), the normal route for preparation for higher education, though some vocational schools also offer similar facilities (Berufs-schulen mit Abitur). Teachers for the upper classes of the POS, and for the EOS, are given a higher education at a PH (Padagogische Hochschule), a college of university status with a four-year course following the Abitur. But teachers for the lower classes (1-4) of the POS (Unterstufenlehrer) go immediately from the 10th class of the POS at age 16 to the Teacher Training Institute (Institut fur Lehrerbildung) for an eight-semester (four-year) course, thus straddling the upper secondary and higher stages of the system. (See Fig. 3). Thus, East Germany has not gone as far as several other countries in the bloc in developing a totally graduate teaching profession.[2]

Yugoslavia, outside the bloc in any case, has always been a law unto itself. But there are further complications: one of the poorer East European countries, Yugoslavia has often lagged in the rear of developments, especially when they involve large-scale expenditure. Furthermore, the great variety of nationalities (and the extreme decentralis-ation of the system) makes it difficult to generalise about the country as a whole. Broadly, however, federal policy

Fig. 3: Structure of Teacher Training in East Germany

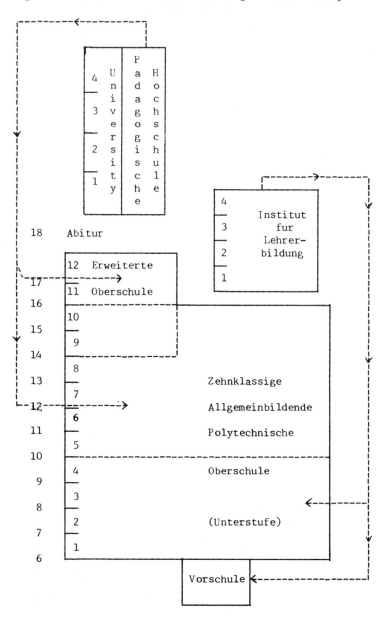

seeks to ensure that educational developments move in the same general direction, but the devolution of authority to the constituent Republics (and, more to the point, their differences in economic state) make for great unevenness in pace. Usually, the more affluent Republics, notably Croatia and Slovenia, are years ahead of Bosnia-Herzegovina, Macedonia, and indeed of Serbia itself. Yugoslavia was one of the countries with a three-tier system: teachers' schools (učiteljske škole) at upper secondary level for teachers of the primary classes, higher pedagogic schools (više pedagoške škole) at post-secondary level for the lower secondary stage, and universities (or equivalent) for the upper secondary school (gimnazija). Since the 1960s, the process of phasing out the teachers' schools has been virtually completed, though something quite like them, in an extended form, remains in Serbia (pedagoška akademija). Generally, the trend is towards post-secondary training, and from there to higher institutes of one kind or another. Apart from the unevenness of implementation (Yugoslavia has also been going through a major school reform since the mid-1970s) the general pattern holds good.[3]

In the USSR, the effects of transition can be seen plainly enough. There are overlaps at every stage. Pedagogical schools (pedagogicheskie uchilishcha) are either upper secondary extended schools, or post-secondary schools, after the pattern of secondary specialised schools generally; that is, they offer four-year courses of combined general education and professional training after class VIII (age 15), or two years of professional training only for graduates of the ten-year school. (See Fig. 4). Either way, their graduates enter their careers at the age of 19 or 20. There are also such schools for pre-school "educators" or "upbringers" (vospitateli), but most of them train primary teachers for classes I-III of the general school. Pedagogic institutes (pedagogicheskie instituty, pedvuzy) are higher educational institutions with four-year courses for one special subject, or five years for two subjects, the latter being usually preferred, since it makes for greater flexibility in employment. These (chiefly) train teachers for classes IV upwards. Universities also train teachers; this is not their main function, but virtually all courses include an element (though a relatively modest one) of pedagogy, psychology, didactics, methods and teaching practice, whether the students intend to teach or not - they are qualified for it if needed. Figures for students in the three types of institution are given in Table 1.[4] Not all of these entered in the universities go into teaching, but a large proportion do - something of the order of 60 per cent, though they still make up a fairly small minority of the total secondary teaching force. Generally, they are said to be about a year

51

Fig. 4: USSR - Structure of Teacher Training

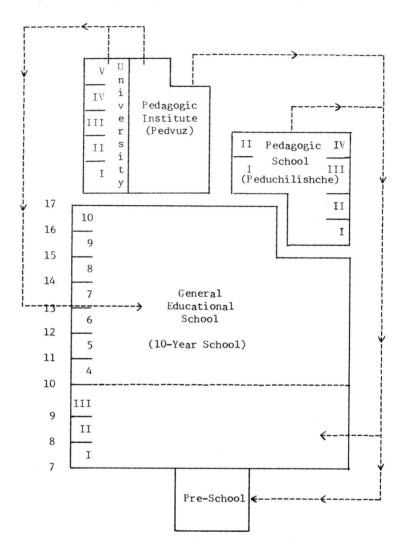

Table 1: USSR: Students in Teacher Training, 1965-1980

	1965-66	1970-71	1975-76	1976-77	1977-78	1978-79	1979-80
Higher Education: Total (000s)	3,860.6	4,580.6	4,864.0	4,952.2	5,037.2	5,109.8	5,185.9
Universities	279.4	344.5	368.1	374.3	378.5	381.8	386.5
Pedagogic Institutes	797.1	880.6	871.1	883.7	896.1	906.6	913.7
Secondary Spec. Schools: Total (000s)	3,659.3	4,388.0	4,524.8	4,622.8	4,662.2	4,671.2	4,646.5
Pedagogical Schools	299.0	340.1	395.0	402.9	410.3	415.0	421.5

ahead of their pedagogic institute colleagues (as one might expect from the length of the course, five years for one subject), but about a year behind in teaching competence. This is difficult to verify, but fits in reasonably well with the balance of subjects in their courses.[5]

But pedagogic institutes also train teachers for the primary classes, with four-year courses in "pedagogical faculties". It has long been declared policy to shift all preparation for primary teaching to this level, but ever since the early 1960s this has been met with difficulties.[6] On the one hand, there is general agreement that the pedagogical school courses were too short (allowing for the general educational component) and produced teachers who were rather immature, and that the tasks of the primary teacher were becoming more complex anyway, requiring a longer and more advanced training. Many of the pedagogical schools were closed down in anticipation of the transfer to what would be called here an "all-graduate profession", but within a fairly short time some were being reopened and enrolments generally being raised. This was not only because there had been miscalculations in the projections of the number of pupils (though there was an element of that); it had also to do with developments in the general school system. In 1966, the Minister of Education of the USSR, M.A. Prokofiev (he is still there) announced plans for the future development of the general educational school.[7] Among other things, it was envisaged that universal secondary schooling (that is, to age 17 at least) would be achieved by 1970 in one form or another. There was some scepticism at the time about the target date - rightly, as it turned out - not least because of the qualifications in the Minister's own pronouncements. (He declared that ten-year schooling would be universal by that date v osnovnom - basically, substantially - which is generally interpreted as meaning "in the towns more or less right away, in the countryside when we can get round to it"). But expansion went ahead, and by the middle 1970s was pretty well complete. But it strained resources, including teacher supply, to the utmost; some teacher shortages remained, and the pedagogic institutes were hard enough put to it to meet the increased demand for teachers at the upper secondary level, without trying to take over the whole of primary training as well. At the same time, the expansion of pre-school education proceeded apace; and these developments between them produced a renewed demand for the services of the pedagogic schools. Even though it is still insisted that "the future lies with the higher institutions"[8], the pedagogic schools are still needed, and their continued existence is envisaged for some time.

There are other factors at work too. There is still a

54

problem of teacher shortage, especially in certain basic
subjects and the rural areas:

> In the basic disciplines, the shortage of teacher
> specialists with higher education in the 1977/78 school
> year ranged between 7 per cent (for elementary teachers)
> and 16 per cent (for biology teachers) ... The Moscow
> schools are faced with a constant shortage of teachers
> in certain subjects (mathematics, Russian language and
> literature), while the number of geography and biology
> teachers exceeds the demand.[9]

Some of these shortages (especially of Russian in Moscow)
are a little surprising, and in any case can hardly be met
by the pedagogical schools. That task rests with the higher
institutes, but once again it inhibits their capacity to
develop courses to take over the role of primary training
as soon as planned. Further:

> Since the shortage is reflected largely in rural
> schools, resolution of one of the most urgent problems
> of our society - the reduction of differences between
> town and country - is being impeded.[10]

Although the rural population of the USSR has dwindled
proportionally - it was down to 38 per cent in the 1979
Census - it is still a substantial figure, and the remaining
gap in educational provision between the urban and rural
sectors is one of the authorities' greatest worries.
Because of the lower standards of living and amenity in the
countryside, most teachers are reluctant to work there,
despite fringe benefits; and although there are (in effect)
powers to direct teachers to posts and to require them to
stay in them for up to three years, this has always proved
difficult to enforce - a salutory reminder of the limitations of political power, even in a country like the Soviet
Union. As long as shortages remain at all, the rural
schools are likely to bear the brunt of them.

But although efforts have been made to plan entry to
the appropriate institutions, this proves far from easy in
practice. It is one thing to plan a specified intake into
the pedagogic institutes, quite another to be sure that this
will produce the numbers required. All higher institutions
have a problem of drop-out (of the order of about 20%),
which makes forward planning difficult; the authorities show
a continual reluctance to allow for drop-out in their
calculations. There is also a marked tendency for trained
teachers to go into other jobs if they can. It is difficult
to quantify, or even, sometimes, to express:

This diversion of cadres from education is an adverse phenomenon for the national economy in general ... A spontaneous exodus of specialists disrupts planned proportions for the national economy in cadre training (and) the diversion of teachers from education increases the cost of specialist training; they do not use the knowledge they have gained in a higher educational institution, and expenditures for the training of teachers in other occupations are inevitable.[11]

In other words (and fewer) forward planning is based partly on guesswork, which again increases the burdens on the institutes.

But some recent policy developments have also produced new demands. There have been plans to increase the number of teachers of Russian as a second language in native-language schools in non-Russian areas.[12] This drive for effective bilingualism two well-marked trends from the last two Census returns: firstly, although the proportions of other nationalities claiming fluency in Russian as a second language increased, sometimes dramatically, between 1970 and 1979, they remained a minority in most cases. Secondly, the balance of the population has been changing: the Russians are now down to 52% of the total, and some other groups, particularly the peoples of Central Asia, have been growing much more rapidly.[13] Geopolitical jitters encourage a drive for the improvement of knowledge of Russian throughout the country, which calls for more teachers, which in turn - again - puts further burdens on the pedvuzy.

Lastly, there are the demands created by the growing emphasis on labour training and polytechnical education.[14] It is not possible to go into details here, but it will be remembered that one of the reasons for the relative failure of similar attempts in 1958-1964 (the "Khrushchov Reforms") was the lack of teachers adequately trained for this task. This time, much more co-ordination and sophistication is needed, and it is realised that simply injecting an element of work training into the schools and putting pupils into practice in factories and on farms does not achieve a great deal, especially if the teachers themselves are not sure what they are about. The 25th Party Congress spelled out its ideas of priorities clearly enough to require "a major effort to secure further improvement in the professional training and political education of future teachers who will be capable of teaching and rearing the younger generations ... and of effectively carrying out the highly important social function of the school: the preparation of youth for labout in material production".[15] This function, as a multitude of complaints makes clear, is still often inadequately fulfilled - hence yet another burden for the pedagogic institutes.

On top of all this, they have other problems - problems of status (except for a relatively small number of distinguished pedvuzy, they are not as a category always recognised as having equal status to the universities, which is bound to affect the quality of enrolment); problems of intake (there are frequent complaints about "unsuitable persons" being taken on)[16]; and problems of quality (there are frequent complaints - again, certain outstanding pedvuzy excepted - about the qualifications of staff, the volume and quality of research, etc.)[17] The institutes, it would seem, have a task of overhaul and development on their hands, quite apart from the other demands already mentioned. It is small wonder, then, that the pedagogical schools are still needed to cope with primary and pre-school training; the pedagogic institutes, expanding in function though they may be, have enough on hand for the moment.

THE CONTENT OF TEACHER TRAINING

In the USSR, as elsewhere in the communist world, official statements on the aims of teacher training (usually couched in the most optimistic terms) are legion. This one, however, almost an incidental remark in the course of a discussion about textbooks, curriculum planning, teaching aids and the like, expresses the usual expectations as clearly as any:

> No matter how much the school curricula and textbooks
> are improved, however, everything is ultimately decided
> by the preparedness of teachers to work creatively,
> their pedagogic mastery, knowledge, love of work and
> of children, and their understanding of child psychol-
> ogy. In all their work, teachers educate inter-
> nationalists and people with an active stance in life,
> who are dedicated to the ideals of V.I. Lenin, love
> their homeland fervently, and are prepared to work
> actively for the good of the Soviet people.[18]

This is a pretty comprehensive range of desiderata, with a clear emphasis on the teacher's ideological role. Obviously (as many other Soviet commentators make clear), it has its limitations as a guide to actual practice, except that we would expect to see a considerable amount of time and attention given to social and political as well as teaching methods and educational theory.

This is essentially what happens. The distribution of curricular time varies considerably from one kind of institution to another; but where comparisons can be made, as between pedagogic institute and university courses in the same subject, we do find differences of emphasis between the

specialist and pedagogic studies. The universities consistently give a greater proportion of time to the special
subject than do the pedvuzy; they, on the other hand, place
a greater emphasis on the "pedagogic disciplines" of educational theory, psychology, didactics and teaching methods.
Nevertheless, there are some common patterns: all courses
give by far the majority of time to the special subject; and
although the time for specifically political courses also
varies (from about 10% to over 15%), it is in every case
greater than that allotted to the pedagogic disciplines.
(See Table 2). The actual breakdown of curricular time tells
us only so much, of course. When one considers that much of
the content of the educational theory courses is also
politically oriented, it does give some idea of the high
priority accorded by the authorities to this aspect of
training.[19]

How effective this is in forming attitudes is another
matter. Unofficial reports of the response of students to
the compulsory courses in political theory (History of the
Communist Party of the Soviet Union, Foundations of Marxist-
Leninist Philosophy, and Principles of Political Economy)
suggest a high level of boredom and a low level of commitment.[20] Even official statements make it clear that all is
not well:

> Many young teachers and graduates of pedagogic instit-
> utes are not fully prepared to educate pupils
> effectively on the basis of the life and activity of
> Lenin and his works. They learn from master teachers,
> acquire necessary knowledge and skills, and improve
> them in practice. But this does not diminish the
> urgency of the task of improving training within the
> walls of the pedagogic institute.[21]

There is a great deal of discussion of this kind in the
Soviet educational press. It is nothing new; attempts to
make the ideological training more effective come and go,
but the commitment to it as a central task of teacher
training is constant.

The same holds good for the East European area generally. Emphases differ, as does the content to some degree -
some countries are more given than others to flavouring
political education with a strong dose of national sentiment,
for example, and the usual differences between rigid and
more flexible interpretations (e.g. Bulgaria and Hungary
respectively) are also to be observed. But this emphasis,
in one form or another, is universal. In East Germany, the
ideological aspects have always been particularly prominent;
so much so, indeed, that immediately after the War the
authorities appointed Neulehrer ("new teachers"), usually

Table 2: Institut für Lehrerbildung

Semester

	1	2	3	4	5	6	7	8
German Lang. & Lit.	7	7	4	4	3	3	–	3
German Methods	–	–	3	3	3	4	–	2
Local Studies & Methods	–	–	2	2	3	3	–	2
Mathematics	6	6	4	4	4	3	–	2
Maths. Method	–	–	3	3	3	3	–	2
Ped.-Psych. Intro.	4	4	–	–	–	–	–	–
Pedagogy	–	–	2	2	2	2	–	2
Psychology	–	–	2	2	2	2	–	2
Marxism-Leninism	3	3	3	3	3	3	–	2
Speech Training	1	1	–	–	–	–	–	–
Health Education	2	2	–	–	–	–	–	–
Russian Lang.	3	3	2	2	–	–	–	–
Options:								
Music & Methods	4	3	3	3	3	3	–	3
Sports & Methods	5	5	5	4	4	4	–	3
Art Ed. & Methods	3	3	3	3	3	3	–	3
Manual Trg & Meth.	3	3	3	3	3	3	–	3
Gardening & Meth.	3	3	3	3	2	2	–	2
Physical Education								
(non-specialist)	2	2	2	2	2	2	–	2

quite unqualified but politically reliable (which the
teaching force of the Third Reich was not). Subject knowledge and professional expertise could be acquired later,
but ideological soundness was held to be too important to
leave to chance. This view of priorities has remained;
Table 3 may give some idea of it, especially when it is
remembered that the education subjects (and much of the
specialist disciplines too, especially in the humanities)
are even more ideologically flavoured than they are in the
Soviet Union.[22]

At best, the pedagogical and methods training can be
thorough and carefully planned. The programmes for teaching
practice in the USSR, for example, go far beyond putting the
students into schools for three weeks and seeing them take
the odd lesson. There are pre-practice seminars; students
are expected to sit in on lessons being taken by their class
in other subjects, to take part in extra-curricular activities, plan a series of lessons and teach one or two of them,
conduct psychological case-studies on individual children
(which also involves home-visiting), and the whole period is
rounded off with a post-practice seminar. The students are
assigned to a "methods teacher" (uchitel'-metodist), and
constant liaison is maintained between the school and the

Table 3:   USSR: Secondary Teachers by Qualification.   1980

	Total Tchrs. Class IV - X (000s)	% With Qualifications:		
		Higher	T.Inst	Sec
Russian Lang. & Lit.				
Russian-Lang. Schools	201	90.6	6.3	3.1
Non-Russian Schools	116	84.0	8.7	7.3
Native Lang. & Lit.	141	88.1	7.9	4.0
History, Govt. & Law	163	91.4	5.7	2.9
Physics	123	94.7	3.5	1.8
Mathematics	303	90.0	7.2	2.8
Chemistry	83	95.3	2.7	2.0
Geography	98	89.3	6.6	4.1
Biology	105	89.1	6.9	4.0
Foreign Languages	172	93.7	3.2	3.1

training institution, with particular concern for the link
between theory and practice. That, at least, is how it is
supposed to work, though it often happens that students in
areas or subjects of shortage are given a timetable and
expected to get on with it.

Even when the official programmes are put into effect,
however, there is a further long-term problem, which was
hardly recognised as such until about the middle of the last
decade. The programmes can be specific, detailed, serious,
and very thorough, and can turn out teachers who know
exactly what is expected of them and how to go about it. By
the same token, of course, it can be highly inflexible, and
can produce rather rigid, stereotyped teaching in the classrooms. To be sure, this is often alleviated by a caring
attitude on the part of the teachers, sometimes to the point
of sentimentality; but it is not the best preparation for a
continually changing situation, for the flexibility and
variety of approach that the authorities have been calling
for over the past few years. When it was possible to believe
that there was a "correct" approach to every teaching
problem, highly prescriptive training had its uses: at least
the teachers knew where they were. But as the pace of
change accelerates, and the fact that children differ in
their capacities and learning needs is more readily accepted
than it was, demands are placed on the adaptability of
teachers, demands which their careful training has not
really equipped them for - not their initial training at any

60

rate.[23]

IN-SERVICE TRAINING

It is particularly important, therefore, that teachers
should not be left with the tasks of a whole career to
perform on the basis of what they learn in their twenties
or even their 'teens'. Fortunately, the in-service training
system is well developed, and goes a long way to make up for
some of the shortcomings of much initial training. In most
countries, some kind of in-service training is a normal
expectation in the course of a teaching career; it may be
compulsory, as in the USSR and the GDR, or laden with
inducements for advancement, as in Yugoslavia, but it is
there in one form or another.
   In the USSR, for example, there is an institute
specially designed for this purpose, the Institute for
Teacher Improvement (institut usovershenstvovaniya uchitelei),
which operates from national to local level. Other bodies
can be involved in further courses too, notably the pedagogic
institutes, and the Ministries put on conferences and short
courses to deal with specific issues, such as the recent
increase in the role of labour training in the schools. In-
service training is required every fifth year; roughly, the
courses cover the equivalent of one day per week for the
full school year, and in the cities this is usually what is
done, the teachers being released (on full pay) for this
purpose, and the staffing calculations are made to allow for
this. In the rural areas, as ever, there are practical
problems due to distance and staffing shortages. In the
first case, this is tackled by organising alternative
structures - residential crash-courses, etc., the second is
less tractable. Since the mid-1970s, in-service training
has acquired a further significance, since teachers are
periodically regraded. Soviet schools, like European schools
generally, do not have anything like the elaborate career-
structure based on administrative duties that is so familiar
in the UK. There are grades - teacher, senior teacher and
"methods teacher"; but these are based on teaching competence, not administrative position. For teachers seeking
upgrading (or trying to avoid downgrading, a theoretical
possibility, though it rarely seems to happen), performance
in further training is one criterion that can be applied,
which acts as a spur to the intent.[24]
   The system in the GDR is similar. At national level,
there is a Central Institute for the Further Training of
Teachers (Zentralinstitut für die Weiterbildung der Lehrer),
and local branches (Kabinetten für Weiterbildung) in every
province (Kreis) and county (Bezirk); a five-year cycle is
operated, along lines much like those of the Soviet system,

61

though the problem of remote and rural areas does not arise to the same extent. Elsewhere, the system is less formal. Romania, Bulgaria and Yugoslavia all operate a system of further subject and pedagogical qualifications, carrying financial and other advantages, not unlike the French agrégation, and known variously as "didactic degrees" (Romania) or "cycles" (Yugoslavia).[25] It is a less elaborate structure than the Soviet or East German model, but the intention is much the same - to ensure not only that teachers are encouraged (at least) to keep up to date with developments in subject content and methods, but to get them back into the learning situation from time to time. Less formally, but arguably more effectively, the school itself is a centre of further training; schools have their own "method and cabinets", where the staff pool experience, and helping with professional development of staff is a normal part of the duties of school heads. (In this connection, it is relevant to mention that school directors and their deputies are specifically trained for the job before they take up their posts).

In short, the in-service training network is probably the most effective part of the teacher training system in the long run. As we have seen, initial training in the communist countries has its problems, some of them hauntingly familiar in the West. They have come in for a good deal of criticism, much of it just, but two considerations need to be borne in mind. Firstly, the shortcomings have to be measured against the high expectations for the teaching force - their level of academic training, professional competence and personal commitment. Of course they often fall short, but that is an index of the level of expectation as well as of performance. Secondly, further training is taken very seriously indeed, is planned for, and is regarded as an essential part of the educational system. There are, perhaps, not many lessons for us in the teacher training systems of the Eastern Countries; but, especially in our current climate, the commitment to the lifelong learning of teachers would seem to be one worthy of serious attention.

NOTES

1.   For a more detailed account of the post-war changes, see N. Grant, Society, Schools and Progress in Eastern Europe, Oxford, Pergamon, 1969.
2.   Siegfried Bär and Rudi Slamma, Initial and Further Training of Teachers in the GDR, Berlin, GDR Ministry of Education and UNESCO Commission of the GDR, 1973. Also personal communications, Berlin, Potsdam, Karl-Marx-Stadt and Rochlitz, 1978.
3.   Personal communications, Belgrade, Skopje, Zagreb

and Novi Sad, 1976.

4. Narodnoe khozyaistvo SSR v 1980 godu: Statist-icheskii ezhegodnik, Moskva, Statistika, 1980.
5. The desirability for more university-trained teachers has also been voiced. E.g., V.K. Rozov, "Sotsial' no-ekonomicheskie problemy pedagogicheskogo obrazovaniya i povysheniya effektivnosti ispol'zovaniya pedagogicheskikh kadrov". Sovietskaya pedagogika, 1980, number 2, pp. 97-102.
6. ibid.
7. M.A. Prokofiev, "K novomu pod'emu sovietskoi shkoly", Uchitel'skaya gazeta, 26 November 1966.
8. "The future, however, is with the VUZy". Oral communication in the Ministry of Education of the USSR, Moscow, 1968, at the end of a discussion of the continuing role of the pedagogic schools. Rozov (loc. cit.) makes the same point.
9. "Sotsial'no-ekonomicheskie problemy narodnogo obrazovaniya (Obzor materialov Vsesoyuznoi nauchno-praktich-eskoi konferentsii)". Sovietskaya pedagogika, 1980, number 3, pp. 15-34.
10. ibid.
11. Rozov, loc. cit.
12. ibid.
13. Naselenie SSSR (Summary of 1979 Census figures). (M., 1981). For a fuller treatment, see N. Grant, "The education of linguistic minorities in the USSR", in J. Megarry, S. Nisbet and E. Hoyle (eds), The Education of Minorities: World Yearbook of Education 1981, London, Kogan Page, 1981, pp. 67-84.
14. See Note 9. Also, Yu.Yu. Ivanov, "Pedagogicheskoe obespechenie vseobshchego srednego obrazovaniya", Soviet-skaya pedagogika, 1980, number 8, pp. 3-7.
15. Rozov, loc. cit.
16. See Note 9.
17. I.F. Kharlamov, "Nekotorye voprosy sovershenstvo-vaniya vuzovskogo obucheniya", Sovietskaya pedagogika, 1981, number 5, pp. 86-93.
K.V. Gusev, "Attestatsiya nauchno-pedagogicheskikh kadrov: itogi i perspektivy", ibid., pp. 3-6.
"Kadry pedagogicheskoi nauki", ibid., pp. 7-15.
18. Ivanov, loc. cit.
19. Bär and Slamma, op. cit.
20. Personal communications, Moscow, 1976.
21. V.S. Gribov, "Izuchenie marksistko-leninskoi teorii budushchimi uchitelyami", Sovietskaya pedagogika, 1980, number 4, pp. 53-59. (Emphasis supplied).
22. E.G. Ministerium fur Volksbildung u. Ministerium für Hoch- und Fachschulwesen, Lehrprogramm für die Ausbildung von Diplomlehrern der allgemeinbildenden poly-technischen Oberschule im Fach Pädagogik an Universitäten

und Hochschulen der DDR, Berlin, 1975.

23.   Discussions at the City Institute for Teacher Improvement, Moscow, the Institute of Pedagogy, Kiev, and the City Institute for Teacher Improvement, Erevan, 1976.

24.   Discussions at the Zentralinstitut für Lehrerweiterbildung and the Akademie für pädagogische Wissenschaften der DDR, 1978.

25.   Discussions at the Ministry of Education and Institutul de Ştiinţe Pedagogice, Bucharest, 1966, the Ministry of Education, Sofia, 1969, and Jugoslovenski Zavod za Proučavanje školskih i Prosvetnih pitanja, Belgrade, 1976.

DEVELOPING COUNTRIES

J.S. Farrant

The term 'developing' is applied to countries where, generally
speaking, population increase is rapid (more than 2% per
year), natural resources are few or incompletely exploited,
G.N.P. per capita incomes are less than $3000, service and
administrative infrastructures are weak and technical aid
is vital. In educational terms, such countries spend more
than one quarter of their national budget on education, have
literacy rates of less than 70%, have fewer than half their
teachers professionally trained and fewer than nine years of
compulsory education.

Nevertheless 'developing' is a misleading term for it is
used to group more than two thirds of U.N. member countries,
giving the impression that they have much in common. Nothing
could be further from the truth, for these countries offer a
rich range of geographical, cultural and economic conditions.
No part of the Seychelles is more than two miles from the sea
but the nearest sea to the Republic of Chad is more than a
thousand kilometres distant. The population of Nauru could
be fitted into a third division football stadium, but what
enclosure would be required for India's 600 million people?
To own a pig in some Pacific islands is to be regarded as a
man of substance, but to keep pigs in some other places is
to be despised. Tuvalu has little in common with Trinidad
or Singapore with Senegal, yet to all these countries with
all their variety is applied the label 'developing'.

It is important, therefore, to remember that, for every
generalisation made about developing countries, there are
likely to be a host of exceptions, and no example can be
assumed to be typical since each country is unique.

By examining the reports of national and international
conferences on education in developing countries, it is
possible to identify the changing priorities in education
that these countries have experienced since World War II and,
with them, the implications for teacher education. In
colonial territories, for example, the immediate post war

65

period was often marked by a determination to modernise teaching and improve the quality of education. It was attended by expansion of the system and increased emphasis on teaching in English, French, Portuguese or whatever was the language of the colonial power.

The independence period which followed was an optimistic period. Huge sums of money were invested in education and ambitious projects launched. The early period of independence was above all a time for setting the course for national development and establishing in the education system what was authentic in national culture and tradition. This led to programmes of curriculum development which, in some cases, are still not complete and to the abandoning in some countries of the foreign language, that had been the medium of instruction, in favour of an indigenous language. Countries such as India, Sri Lanka, Malaysia and Tanzania adopted this policy; others restricted mother tongue policy to the early stages of primary education.

Following independence, many developing countries tried to improve both quality and quantity in education. But the two experienced a see-saw relationship as first one then the other received special attention. The limited educational resources at the disposal of governments rarely permitted both to be improved simultaneously. Usually, more meant worse and better meant fewer. Nevertheless, many countries made significant strides to improving both. However, a number of problems have seriously disrupted the optimistic schedules for educational development that were set in the heady days of new-found independence.

PROBLEMS AFFECTING NATIONAL SYSTEMS OF EDUCATION

Four main factors have contributed to the difficulties that developing countries face in building their educational systems. They are worldwide in their effect, though the relative impact they have made on individual countries has depended largely on the stage and nature of each nation's development.

1.   Rapid growth and movement of population

A dramatic contrast between developed and developing countries is to be seen in their population trends. In contrast to the nil or negative growth of most developed countries, developing countries are experiencing growth rates that will more than double their populations before the end of the century and, if left unchecked, will continue to increase until no government can feed or control, far less educate, its people. Improved medical knowledge and health services have so reduced infant mortality that the

66

normal age distribution of these countries has been seriously disturbed and, in many of them, more than half the population is under 15 years of age. This is the opposite of the age distribution to be found in developed countries where longer life expectancy has greatly increased the proportion of the elderly.

Aggravating this problem have been the mass movements of population caused by the attraction of rural people to the towns and the disturbance of communities by war and famine. Depopulation of rural areas, with all its implications, has taken place on a dramatic scale. In contrast, many townships and cities have been overwhelmed by the flood of migrants.

Vast refugee camps have sadly become an increasing feature of demographic change in developing countries. Political unrest or climatic change in one area have led with increasing frequency to mass migrations into neighbouring territories and created acute difficulties for the countries involved. It is almost impossible to provide a satisfactory formal system of education in such circumstances. Meaningful educational planning depends on accurate statistical data and trends that can be anticipated. In the disrupted conditions that exist in some developing countries, this is not possible.

Massive movements of population have also contributed to social changes that have made traditional institutions very insecure. Books such as Things Fall Apart and No Longer at Ease[1] have described these changes and illustrated how family life, traditionally accepted customs, and standards of behaviour have been affected. Such changes have placed teachers in new roles and called for pressing changes to be made in their training.

2. Excessive demands for education

If the natural increase in the population of developing countries presents a frightening prospect to educational planners, it is not nearly so immediately pressing as the educational expectations that independence has brought to their people. Whereas a generation ago in some countries, parents had to be bribed to send their sons to school and cajoled into sending their daughters, today the clamour for places in school for their children is often an acute embarrassment to the authorities. School building and the supply and training of teachers cannot keep pace.

Governments, in their pursuit of national development, have been in a dilemma as to where to place their main investment in education. Priorities have fluctuated. At times, universities and higher education have benefitted from a major share of the educational budget, while primary

67

and secondary education have remained deprived. More
recently, economic beliefs concerning the higher returns to
be obtained from investment in primary education have led
to policies of provision for universal primary education
with tentative plans to extend this into three or more years
of secondary education.

While governments have debated these priorities, the
public have clamoured for education at all levels. They
have provided nursery schools, used community resources to
open primary and secondary schools, and done all in their
power to ensure vocational and training facilities for
their young people when they leave school. Examples of
these enterprises such as the 'harambee schools' and
'village polytechnics' of Kenya have attracted considerable
interest. But the fact remains that only a small proportion
of the children of developing countries can hope to enjoy
more than eight years of schooling. Resources are not
available to provide the schools, teachers and learning
materials in the quantities required for further rapid
educational expansion.

It is easy to understand the insistent public demand
for education in developing countries when it is remembered
that the path that begins in the primary school and leads
on to secondary school and university assures the person
who follows it of wealth and power. It is not so easy to
understand how governments will react to this demand. One
thing is clear, however, and that is that teachers are
needed in the future in far greater numbers and with very
different training than was the case in the past and that
this calls for fundamental changes in teacher training.

3. The need to make curricula and methods relevant

Most developing countries that attained independence in the
years following World War II inherited an educational
system that had different objectives and was geared to a
different pace of development from what was soon to follow.
In consequence, changes of a substantial nature were
inevitable.

National development became the primary aim of the
system and this had far reaching implications on access to
education, curriculum development, and teacher training.
As already mentioned, independence brought about a huge
increase in demand for education and high expectations as
to what it could achieve both at a personal level and a
national level. The school system, as previously organised,
was unable to meet the challenge of these changes and a
quiet revolution began.

The curriculum was the first target to be attacked,
and many countries entered into national debate concerning

68

their primary school curriculum. For example, the Nigerian
National Curriculum Conference held in 1969 brought together
educationists of various levels and representatives of
leading groups within the community, and tried to decide
what the aims of Nigerian primary education should be.
This was followed in 1971 by a National Workshop on primary
education at which objectives for each area of the curriculum were discussed and new syllabuses worked out. Then,
in 1973, there was held the seminar on National Policy in
Education. Each of these meetings was an attempt to get
wider participation in determining the curriculum used in
the schools and to ensure that this curriculum was set in
the context of the cultural traditions of the country,
adapted to its varied local conditions, and geared to its
manpower needs. Action in other countries varied in detail,
but the aim everywhere was the same: education must be
relevant.

At the same time, new ideas about methods in education
were circulating which complicated the curriculum revolution.
For example, new theories of how children learn called for
new methods of teaching in the classroom, new instructional
technologies seemed to offer prospects of solving the
problems of mass demand for education, and proponents of
deschooling were suggesting that more effective education
could be achieved without schools. There was little
response from developing countries to the last of these,
perhaps because, from a government point of view, primary
schools are the most widely distributed national institution,
and teachers are the largest single occupational group in
paid employment; but also, no doubt, because with such
enormous public pressure for schools, their elimination
would be impossible even if it were desirable.

Some developing countries, notably El Salvador, the
Ivory Coast and American Samoa, heeded the siren song of
new technology and adopted a systems approach to education.
It is noteworthy that these did not work out as was hoped
and there has been a return to more traditional methods.
But other countries went part way, investing vast sums of
money in broadcasting and audio-visual equipment in the
hope of good returns on their capital.

Adopting these developments, together with new ideas
on learning, presented teachers who had received training
of only a formal kind with intolerable difficulties and
brought a new urgency for in-service training.

4. Soaring costs in education

If curriculum development is the aspect of education to
which teachers find it most difficult to adapt, that which
frightens educational administrators most is its escalating

69

costs. Any country which still has some way to go before achieving universal primary education, but adopts a UPE policy in response to public demand, must accept daunting capital costs, because the cumulative total of even low cost school buildings can go far beyond the means of such a country. Such is the case with Bangladesh, where a large programme aimed at achieving UPE is being launched by the World Bank. Other countries anxious to make existing buildings more cost-effective are tackling the problem with varying success in other ways such as shift systems or the resource centre concept where the building is used for both formal and non formal education.

In most developing countries, teachers' salaries account for almost 90% of the recurrent expenditure on Education which itself may be over 30% of the total national budget. This leaves little room for any course of action which necessitates increasing the number of teachers or raising their salaries. Consequently, pupil-teacher ratios tend to be high and the use of unqualified teachers is widespread. Whatever balance is left from current expenditure is usually devoted to teaching materials but the sum is meagre and leads to constant complaints from teachers for more to be supplied. Gone are the days when a slate and a pencil served all a pupil's needs and a few sticks of chalk were the teacher's stock in trade. The simple business of learning and teaching has grown in developed countries into a complex industry with sophisticated technology. But for many developing countries, such prospects are still only a dream. Harsh reality requires that their teachers make do with the limited equipment that is available.

NEW PRIORITIES IN TEACHER EDUCATION

From the brief account given above of the problems faced by developing countries in providing education for their people in the post-war years, it does not take special gifts of insight to see that traditional ideas of teacher education no longer apply. The concept of a single period of training being sufficient to equip a teacher for his whole career, even with the aid of personal study, is an anachronism. Passing years have brought such changes and new demands on the training of teachers that even the tidy cycles of training suggested by James have little relevance. In developing countries, for many teachers, induction is the first experience of teaching and is supported by minimal supervision. In such circumstances the term pre-service training ceases to have meaning and all training is in-service in one form or another.

Teacher education has always been a service industry. Its priorities have always been a response to the changing

priorities set by governments for educational development.
In outlook it has tended to be conservative rather than
radical, with the result that changes have come generally
out of necessity rather than from a pioneering spirit. That
is not to deny that teacher education has been innovative.
Indeed it has proved itself capable of considerable
innovative action. What it does mean is that teacher
education has almost always been engaged in a catching up
process, unfortunately sometimes, too little too late.

What follows is a description of the various priorities
in teacher education being pursued by developing countries.
They are identifiable as priorities by the effort and
expenditure spent on them, but they illustrate the enormity
of the task that faces teacher trainers and some of the
imaginative solutions they are offering.

1.   Improving the cost effectiveness of training

(a) By reducing wastage   One of the largest factors
in the high cost of teacher education in developing countries
is the continuous loss of trained teachers from the classroom.
They leave for many reasons: further training, promotion into
other branches of the education system, and personal advancement outside the system. Many countries face this problem
but few have come up with successful solutions.

The basic problem is that, for many young people,
teacher training provides opportunity for furthering general
education. It provides an educational ladder parallel to
that of the secondary school. Understandably, students who
fail to enter the secondary system often enter the training
college with little commitment to the teaching profession.
Further education is all they want because they know where
it can take them. Perhaps it is significant that so many
leaders in developing countries have been teachers at some
stage in their careers.

To overcome this problem, various types of action have
been taken including bonding and a requirement for a teacher
to have taught for a specific number of years before he is
released for further training. A more positive approach has
been taken by some countries such as Hong Kong and Singapore
to improve the status and morale of teachers. But, for the
most part, this kind of solution has been left to teachers'
organisations who, in addition to improving conditions of
service have sometimes provided in-service training for
their members.

(b) By reducing the time spent in training college
Sandwich training has been introduced by many countries,
particularly in Africa, as a means of shortening the
expensive college based element of formal training. In

Lesotho, at the National Teacher Training College, a sandwich course involving a total of ten weeks' residential attendance spread over several vacations interspersed with correspondence assignments sent out by the Lesotho Distance Teaching Centre and backed up by supervised help at the local Centre, offers teachers an opportunity to qualify with a minimum of college based training.

In Tanzania, a similar programme of two years' duration involves face to face teaching three times per week, radio broadcasts, correspondence assignments and supervised teaching of about fifteen hours per week.

In Zimbabwe, where the independence bush war ravaged the country's school and teacher training programme, a new sandwich training scheme for teachers has begun with the Zimbabwe Integrated Teacher Education Course (ZINTEC). The prime task of this programme is to provide training for two thirds of the 15,000 untrained teachers currently employed in the country and to do so as quickly as possible. To achieve this, conventional training has been replaced by a system of sixteen weeks residential training in college at the beginning and end of the course with three and a half years of correspondence assignments and supervised teaching practice in between.

There are numerous other examples which illustrate the varying differences between the length of time devoted to face to face teaching as compared with distance learning and between the alternating frequency of college based and school based training.

Another method used to shorten the length of time spent in college is by accelerated training. In Nigeria, for example, at the universities of Kano, Lagos and Nsukka, an experimental study programme for the B.Ed. degree has enabled students to graduate after two years instead of the usual three. Currently, the performance of teachers trained in this way is being evaluated against that of students who have followed the accelerated course.

Grenada has also introduced an accelerated programme of in-service teacher education, in this case, aimed at producing within three years all the teachers the country needs. In this programme, teachers are categorised as temporary, student, probationer or certificated, and the courses they follow demand of them one day per week in term time and five hours per day for six weeks in the long vacation. There are examinations every six months set by the University of the West Indies as well as continuous assessment and supervised practical teaching. To carry out this training using the facilities and methods that previously existed would have taken more than a generation, and so, if the programme succeeds, very significant improvements in the cost effectiveness of training will have been achieved.

(c) <u>By using mass training methods</u>   During 1975-76
the Satellite Instructional Television Experiment (SITE)
provided an opportunity for India's Centre for Educational
Technology to launch a mass in-service training course for
teachers coming to terms with a new science curriculum.
Four seminars of twelve days' duration were organised for
teachers at the 2,400 villages covered by SITE. At each
village, ten teachers from the village concerned and from
neighbouring villages met under the supervision of a science
teacher who had received training for the project at an
earlier stage. The training materials for the seminars were
in the form of multi-media packages incorporating radio and
television programmes, activity guides, enrichment materials
and tutorials. The television programmes were transmitted
by the ATS-6 satellite and the seminar groups used the
equipment and infrastructure of SITE. As each twelve day
seminar provided training for 24,000 teachers, the total
covered in just two months actual teaching time was 96,000.

The National Teachers Institute in Nigeria is another
example of a developing country's solution to the need to
train teachers in massive numbers. It was conceived in the
days when the country was facing up to the full implications
of universal primary education in terms of the need to expand
teacher training facilities. It was estimated that, by the
time that UPE had worked its way through every primary grade,
enrolments in the college would have to be of the order of
250,000 students if the intention of raising all unqualified
teachers in the country to the Grade II were to be achieved.
A task of such proportions clearly demanded something out
of the ordinary for a solution. The NTI was established,
therefore, to combine effective methods of distance education, self instruction, curriculum development, evaluation,
research and examination. Today, its School of Basic
Studies has responsibility for preparing the self-instructional materials sent out to its students. Its School of
Educational Innovation assists with course development and
evaluation. It also conducts classroom research aimed at
providing data of relevance to course writers about the
process of learning and teaching in this medium. The
Facilities Department accommodates the highly specialised
equipment and systems necessary for operating an effective
large scale distance education programme. These include a
graphics and printing unit, an audio-visual and photographic
unit, and a computer centre for processing student records,
evaluating their progress and analysing the effectiveness of
the instructional materials. The Facilities Department is
also responsible for the physical links between NTI Headquarters and the Field Centres. The Field Network aims at
providing a Field Centre in each State capital with the
assistance of the State Ministry of Education. These Field

Centres feed NTI materials into a number of Study Centres
and it is the Study Centres which serve as the contact point
for students. They are located within commuting distance of
students' homes or schools and provide a resource centre
where they can listen to audio-tapes, view slides, use laboratory kits, study from reference books and obtain a limited
amount of tutorial assistance. Completed assignments are
handed in to the Study Centres for marking at NTI Headquarters.
Although, currently, the enrolment is approximately only
some 10,000 students, the NTI intends to build up steadily
to its full potential as its staff gain experience.

2.   Improving the quality of training

(a) By upgrading qualifications   A number of developing countries, mainly in Africa, employ a high proportion
of untrained and unqualified teachers. In several countries
at least half the teachers are untrained while in one the
figure rises to 68 per cent. Causes for this state of
affairs vary. In poor countries, the reason is largely one
of cost; the budget resources available are insufficient to
train and pay full teaching rates for all the teachers
required. In other cases, especially where educational
expansion has been rapid, the output of the training colleges
has been unable to keep pace with the rate of increase of
the pupil population in the schools, with the result that
untrained teachers have had to fill many vacant teaching
posts.

Under-qualified teachers, on the other hand, comprise
those teachers who have undergone training and have been
employed even though they have failed the examinations,
together with those teachers who were trained many years
ago, but whose qualifications have since been superseded by
higher national requirements.

For such untrained and under-qualified teachers, most
countries provide training facilities. For example, Malawi
organises courses of this kind; responsibility for the
written assignments is in the hands of the Malawi Correspondence College, the teaching and inspection being carried
out by the Institute of Education at Domasi. Uganda has two
entire colleges devoted to similar two-year upgrading
courses. The Zambian National In-Service Teachers' College
runs a one year residential course leading to the award of
the Advanced Primary Certificate.

(b) By introducing new curricula   Curriculum
development and the need to train teachers to implement the
new curricula has been a priority in most developing
countries. The pattern has followed well tried methods of
curriculum planning involving panels of specialists,
including teachers, and the production of materials using

74

trained editors, graphic designers and printers in the process. Dissemination has generally followed the centre--periphery model.

In Sri Lanka, for example, while the Curriculum Development Centre devised new syllabuses in every subject in the schools, in-service courses were organised to help teachers teach them. The underlying principle of the approach was that of curriculum dissemination through the training of master teachers. In this, serving secondary school teachers were selected and trained at the Curriculum Development Centre to act as a permanent cadre of in-service trainers providing local monthly and fortnightly courses in various subject areas for their fellow teachers. At primary level, a similar group of pilot teachers were specially trained by the Primary Education Curriculum Committee to introduce new programmes into their schools and supervise the work of other teachers testing the new curricula.

In Malaysia the same strategy of training key personnel at national level to organise and conduct courses at state and district levels is used. The method was pioneered by the Curriculum Development Centre in Projek Khas between 1969 and 1975 in respect of primary science and mathematics, and a network of thirty-two local centres of excellence, each with two key personnel, was set up to serve as resource centres for local teachers in these subjects. The current 'back to basic skills' thrust in primary education will be promoted by means of a similar strategy.

While curriculum development in developing countries has, on the whole been successfully implemented, there have been some spectacular failures as evidenced by the number of countries that have made U-turns on 'new mathematics'. The lesson, however, is clear: new curricula can be developed and successfully introduced to the schools if the necessary commitment is there and all the preparatory stages are carried out in full.

(c) By introducing new methods   The vocabulary of education is international but the practice of it is open to local interpretation. This is the case with some of the developments in educational theory which have so revolutionised teaching in western countries. Child-centred education is alien to traditional custom in some countries and has found acceptance difficult. Likewise, in countries where literacy is recent and memorisation is still highly prized, it is difficult to persuade teachers to abandon rote learning. Nevertheless new methods have come to developing countries and been given strong support in the quest for quality in education.

Individualised learning, group learning, resource-based learning, programmed learning and a number of other

types of learning are taught in teacher training courses.
So also are team teaching, open plan teaching and educational
technology. But in some developing countries the local
conditions, lack of facilities in the school and inadequate
training of teachers makes nonsense of the assumptions that
underpin these techniques and so they frequently fail.
Consequently, in countries where development is most difficult to achieve, a facade of modern methods may cover the
practice of well established traditional methods. Elsewhere,
significant strides have been made and children learn with
an enthusiasm and genuine pleasure that teachers in western
countries might well envy.

(d) <u>By increasing teacher support services</u>   It is
widely recognised that pre-service teacher education is an
inadequate preparation for a teacher's whole career and
that in-service training experiences are essential. In
addition, the fact that the normal resources of the classroom and even the whole school are, by themselves,
insufficient for the teacher to do an efficient and
effective job, is not so readily recognised. Increasingly,
however, developing countries are becoming aware of the
important role that advisory and technical support services
play, and are giving new-found priority to them.
Schools' broadcasting was one of the first support
services to be adopted on a large scale. In the late 1960s,
its adoption accelerated on a wave of cheap transistor radios
and the comforting belief that the teaching weaknesses of
untrained and under-qualified teachers could be compensated
for by radio teachers who provide a model of excellence.
The disillusionment that followed the discovery that the
link between the presentation of the radio teacher and the
learning of the pupils was not as direct as was imagined
caused a cooling off in attitudes towards schools' broadcasting and a substantial reduction in funding for it. Only
as the need for expatriate producers and technicians has
declined and local personnel have taken over these roles,
have developing countries begun to show renewed interest.
Many countries have added television to their broadcasting
and produce programmes not only for schools but as an
important element in their provision of non-formal education.
Teachers are also receiving increasing training in how to
use the medium to the greatest advantage.
The provision of much audio-visual equipment in the
post-independence years, without complementary training for
teachers in its proper use and maintenance, led to a sorry
situation in many developing countries with school cupboards
gradually accumulating stocks of unused and broken-down AV
equipment. India was one of the first countries to plan a
network of repair services for this problem. It did so in

connection with the SITE programme in order to ensure that
television sets were always in working order. Each cluster
of villages had a team of engineers to staff one main repair
workshop and three subsidiary workshops all strategically
located to give speedy access to every village in the
cluster. The operators in charge of the television sets in
the villages were supplied with postcards which were
illustrated with pictures of the different parts of the set.
If a failure occurred, they put a mark on the card against
the part that appeared to be faulty and posted the prepaid
card to the maintenance depot. A team would respond by
taking a replacement set to the village or by trying to
repair the set on the spot. The latter was simplified by
the design of the sets which incorporated several circuits
on printed cards which could be slipped out and replaced in
moments with a new one. The system worked very well and
ensured a very high percentage of sets in working order
throughout the experiment. Since then, a number of countries
have established workshops, some of them mobile, to service
and repair scientific and audio-visual equipment.

Correspondence courses and other forms of distance
education to help teachers further their general education
or receive in-service training have multiplied in recent
years. Some idea of the rate at which this expansion has
taken place is to be seen in the surveys of noncommercial
correspondence institutions undertaken by the Commonwealth
Secretariat. In 1974 when the first survey was carried out,
there were only 59 such institutions in the Commonwealth.
When the survey was revised two years later the number had
risen to 75, but the most recent revision carried out in
1980 indicated no fewer than 170.

Teachers' Centres and Resource Centres are another
support service for teachers that developing countries are
beginning to provide in increasing numbers. The separate
identities of these two kinds of centre, as developed in
the United Kingdom, have tended to merge when they have
been transplanted into developing countries. What has
resulted has been Regional Teacher Resource Centres which
lack the intimacy and responsiveness to local needs of the
original concepts but offer an allocation of resources more
in keeping with the economies of developing countries.
Malaysia is moving ahead with four large regional multi-
purpose centres to promote decentralised curriculum
development and in-service education. Nigeria is moving
in the same direction with its Educational Resource Centre
in Kano, offering on one site the services of the State
Inspectorate, Curriculum Development Unit, Multi-Media
Library and In-Service Training Centre.

Media Production Units, usually in attachment with
Curriculum Development Centres, are another important

service for teachers. They are the most suitable agencies for the production of locally developed teaching materials and, in developing countries, are helping to break the monopoly of multinational publishing houses. In some countries it is possible for individual teachers to get materials printed at these Units which they have themselves created, but more common is the arrangement by which the Units publish the materials devised by the Curriculum Development Centre.

Other support services for teachers are provided by the supervisory staff, including inspectors, college tutors and other appointed trainers who concern themselves with the in-service training of teachers. How they organise this training varies. In some cases they simply arrange and lead in-service courses at vacation times; in others, they act as mobile teachers, moving from school to school to assist teachers with particular problems in the classroom. Another approach is to help teachers at field centres with any difficulties they experience while working their way through self-instructional modules. As a reassurance for teachers experiencing the sense of isolation in a small village school or struggling with the problems of a school in an urban slum, such support is invaluable.

Another support service for teachers is to be found in teachers' professional associations. While it must be admitted that most of these in developing countries still act as pressure groups only to improve conditions of service for their members, an increasing number are taking on responsibility for improving the professional competence of members by in-service training.

3. Widening the scope of training

(a) By increasing the training options   In developing countries in the immediate post-war years, it was common for primary school teachers in training to undertake a course that offered no options. On completion of the course, they were expected to be competent in teaching all subjects in the primary curriculum. Now, most developing countries offer a range of options within the course, enabling teachers, even at non-graduate levels, to specialise to a considerable degree.

Specialisation has always featured in the training of secondary school teachers, but some countries are incorporating, even in primary training, a number of new specialisations such as teaching the handicapped, remedial teaching and politics. The need for the former has been highlighted by programmes of universal primary education which have drawn into schools children with defective hearing and eyesight and those who are educationally sub-normal. The

78

need for training in remedial methods has been brought about by policies of automatic promotion and also by the very high pupil-teacher ratios found in developing countries. Politics have been introduced as a special study by countries which favour a strong ideological path to development. Sri Lanka is an example of a country which has responded to the problem of special training needs by assigning to particular colleges responsibility for training in specific subjects. Giragama Teachers' College, for example, specialises in training teachers in both traditional and western art, craft, music and drama, and Hingurakgoda College specialises in the training needs of teachers in small schools in rural communities.

Broadening the training base may have other implications. In Bangladesh, for example, which is a country where the enrolment of girls in school is traditionally very low, special efforts have been made to recruit female teachers in greater numbers in order to correct the imbalance.

(b) <u>By training for new roles</u>   In recent years, changes in the schools of developing countries have been so great that teachers trained in traditional ways can no longer cope. The UNESCO Conference in Geneva in 1975 identified a number of trends in education which placed teachers in new roles. These included a shift in emphasis from transmission of knowledge to organisation of the pupil's learning, greater individualisation of learning with a changed structure in teacher-pupil relationships, wider use of educational technology and the new skills this requires, more co-operation between teachers in planning teaching strategies, closer involvement with parents and other people in the community, greater participation in extra-curricular activities and a decrease in authoritarian attitudes between the teacher and his pupils.

The training for teachers whose new roles are school-based differ naturally from that given to teachers about to undertake out-of-school responsibilities. An example of a course for teachers destined to leave classroom teaching is a five month course to train school supervisors held in Zimbabwe in 1980. The course offered a wide range of skills in administration, classroom organisation and subject methodology. Other countries offer training for curriculum developers, evaluators, teachers' centre leaders and personnel about to take up posts in the other kinds of support service that provide the infrastructure of educational systems.

A variety of courses also exists for teachers who will remain school-based. In Plateau State, Nigeria, for example, the Primary School Supervision Course trains Grade I teachers, most of whom are already headmasters, to be responsible for the in-service training of unqualified teachers in selected primary schools near their own school. The nine month course, operating on a two-week-per-month sandwich basis also equips this new category of supervisory headteacher to disseminate new curriculum units and to administer attainment tests. Lagos University has a similar plan to assist headteachers and inspectors with Grade II qualifications and at least ten years' experience in the training of unqualified teachers in their care.

Another area of training receiving increasing priority is that for teacher trainers. Traditionally, training college tutors have been recruited on a haphazard basis, either by promoting competent primary teachers and head-teachers or by drafting graduates, some of whom have never themselves taught. Zambia now offers a two year Diploma in Teacher Education for tutors in teachers' colleges, and Makerere in Uganda has a similar three year course for Grade III teachers in which the middle year is spent on 'supervised lecturing practice' at a college. The curric- ulum of these and other courses like them lays emphasis on the skills of diagnostic testing, classroom observation and coaching teachers.

In developing countries, the problem of rural depopu- lation and communities in decline has caused considerable attention to be given to the training of teachers for rural areas. Hingurakgoda Teachers' College in Sri Lanka concentrates on preparing teachers for village schools and is an example of the approach taken by a number of countries. Two key assumptions underlie the planning of the course. The first is that the village constitutes the smallest unit of administration in national terms; and the second, that progress in rural areas is basic to national development. In consequence, the aims and content of the course are designed to make the teacher an acceptable and effective change agent for improving the quality of life by way of the villages to the country's total rural population.

The objectives of the course relating specifically to community education are:

(i) To deepen the teacher's understanding of
- development problems in terms of rural populations.
- the relevance of education to rural development.
- the need for interdisciplinary thinking and cross sectional co-operation for overcoming rural problems.

(ii) To develop in the teacher specific skills which will enable him to participate in an effective and practical manner in village development programmes.

(iii) To enable the teacher to make the village school the

80

operational centre of community development by:
- encouraging self-reliance in the community.
- fostering traditional skills and culture.
- promoting activities that offer economic and employment benefits.
- developing an awareness in the community of local resources that can be utilised for development.

In order to increase the effectiveness of the course, a project was launched which involved the adoption of three villages by the college. Students from the college went to live in the villages and carried out full socio-economic surveys using questionnaires, interviews, observation and discussion in order to identify the demographic characteristics, local resources and pressing needs. Surveys of educational provision were also conducted. On the basis of these studies, and in consultation with relevant authorities, plans for action were drawn up.

The immediate outcome was a greatly improved relationship between the school and community in each village with a number of important developments taking place such as the introduction of bee and poultry keeping, brickmaking, lime production and a number of handicraft projects. A bus service and mobile dispensary were also introduced together with schemes for the collection of medicinal herbs on a commercial basis and the preparation of medicinal oils from seeds. On the educational side, a curriculum more relevant to the educational and health needs of village children was introduced. New techniques of teaching were adopted in which the children were taken to resources of the villages to learn in a practical manner about daily life. More and better teaching materials were provided as a result of the link between the college and the villages, and educational programmes for adults were introduced.

At a local level, there have been grounds for considerable encouragement from this programme. Unfortunately, because the government has recently downgraded priority for community education, the programme has not been replicated elsewhere in the country. Nevertheless, it offers a useful model for study.

CONCLUSION

The changing priorities of teacher education have all involved innovation, and successful innovation is extraordinarily difficult to achieve. If an analogy may be used, innovation is akin to surgical grafting where, unless the metabolism of the donor matches very closely that of the recipient, the graft is likely to be rejected. That is why innovations that are 'homegrown' have a higher success rate than those that are 'imported'.

But there is more to it than this. For an innovation to succeed, there must be an urgent need for it and strong official backing. There must be on the part of those people planning it a thorough understanding, not only of the educational system with which it will interact, but also of the cultural milieu into which it must fit. Those who implement it should have a meaningful role in its planning as well as adequate preparation for their role in it. Any technology adopted should be of a kind that can be utilised and maintained by indigenous personnel and with materials and equipment that are readily available. But most important of all, it must be given sufficient time to allow for effective planning, piloting and final implementation. Without this, it is almost certainly doomed to failure.

An example of such an approach is to be seen in an innovation introduced in one developing country that could be of significance to many. This is project Impact, an acronym for Instructional Management by Parents, Community and Teachers. It was proposed as an experiment in mass primary education and was intended to be effective, economical and efficient.

It arose as a result of the Southeast Asia Ministers of Education Organisation (SEAMEO) authorising INNOTECH the regional centre for educational innovation and technology to undertake a research project. The project was to solve an urgent educational problem in Southeast Asia caused by the rapid growth of population, the pressing demand for educational expansion and the realisation that most of the countries in the region could not cope financially with universal primary education. Two pilot schemes were proposed, one in the Philippines, the other in Indonesia.

Project Impact in the Philippines has now developed beyond an experiment. It is a viable delivery system for mass primary education, innovating on the basic technology of programmed instruction. The Impact system takes advantage of the close family ties among Filipinos by organising the school population into mixed age 'families' of 40 to 50 children. This enables older pupils from primary grades 4 to 6 to teach younger ones by programmed teaching techniques. Using the same method, more senior pupils learn through peer-group sessions or by individual self-instruction using self-instructional modules.

At the heart of the Impact system are the programmed instructional booklets called 'learning modules' which together cover the bulk of the nationally determined curriculum content of all six levels of primary education. A module is divided into lessons calculated to give an average child what he can digest in one session without becoming bored. Pupils using the modules both in peer-

groups and individual self-instruction are able to move at
their own pace. For fast learners and those who propose to
go on to secondary school, advanced modules are available.
A system of pre-test and post-testing determines whether a
pupil has mastered a module.

The teacher in the Impact system is called an 'Instructional Supervisor' because her role is the management of
the pupils' learning. She takes responsibility for two to
three 'families' of about 48 in each, thus making a pupil-
teacher ratio of nearly 150:1.

Assisting the Instructional Supervisor are a number of
non-professionals who include 'Programmed Teachers' who are
pupils selected from classes 4-6 in the school and who, after
basic training from the Instructional Supervisor, each give
one hour per day to teaching groups of four to eight
children in the lower classes. They follow a prearranged
programme in a set sequence that presents what is to be
taught and how it is to be taught. They receive this
instruction from the Instructional Supervisor each afternoon
in preparation for the next day's lessons. Half of the
teaching hour each day is spent teaching. The other half
is devoted to giving special help to slow learners. Pupils
in classes 4-6 study in peer groups of six to eight children
using learning modules. Each group makes a 'contract' in
consultation with the 'Instructional Supervisor' promising
in writing to complete a number of modules each week.
Completion of a contract is recorded on a progress chart.
In addition, group members have scheduled individual learning
activities.

'Itinerant Teachers' are professionally trained teachers
who take charge of specialised (non-modularised) subjects
such as physical education, practical arts and music. They
also take extra-curricular activities such as farming and
scouting. In small schools, such itinerant teachers move
from school to school, but in larger ones they may be
permanently based.

Routine tasks in the school are undertaken by aides in
return for a minimal wage. These aides are all non-
professional community members. Instruction in practical
skills such as sewing or carpentry may be provided by other
non-professional community members but usually on a
voluntary basis. Additional voluntary help comes from
secondary school pupils who give one day per month to
various kinds of community service, and from brothers or
sisters, and from parents.

Overall supervision of a group of Instructional Supervisors is provided by an 'Instructional Co-ordinator' who
will meet with her staff from time to time. Her role is
similar to the headteacher in the formal system. Liaison
between the school and the community is undertaken by the

'Field Co-ordinator' whose role is similar to that of the district education officer in other systems.

An interesting feature of cost saving in the Impact system is that the only permanent building required is the 'Community Learning Centre' housing the instructional modules. The children learn in 'kiosks' built by parents from local materials and these provide adequate shelter from sun and rain.

The success of learning in Impact greatly depends on the Instructional Supervisor who has to orchestrate all the elements of the Impact learning management system. Evaluation, however, has shown that Impact pupils have achieved higher averages than pupils in the normal system. And these better results go across all subjects. Impact costs have proved to be significantly less than the traditional system in relation to teachers' salaries. And, even allowing for the greater expense of providing the large number of learning modules required, total costs for Impact amount to only half that of the traditional system.

The striking thing about this innovation is the way in which it was developed. It started in response to an urgent need. It incorporated the cultural tradition of the Filipino family system as a basic element in the design. It encouraged wide participation by teachers both in developing the learning modules and discussing the new roles of those who would share in its implementation. It adopted technology well within the handling capability of local personnel and used only equipment and materials that were readily available. And it allowed an adequate timescale for implementation and possible replication. But perhaps the most significant feature was that, although expatriates had a share in the discussions and planning that led to its development, at no stage were they in any sense leaders. The real action was undertaken by Filipinos.

This innovation and the way in which it was implemented provides an interesting lesson for developing countries, for what these countries need are not more and more imported solutions but help with developing their own innovations by being involved at all levels in the planning and implementation process. The ultimate priority in teacher education, as with national development, is self-reliance.

NOTES

1.   Chinua Achebe, Things Fall Apart, London, Heinemann, 1958, and No Longer at Ease, London, Heinemann, 1960.

THE NEED TO PROBLEMATISE EDUCATIONAL KNOWLEDGE

Robin Burns

Crisis is a word which is applied so widely and frequently these days it has almost become trivialised. From culture to individual lives, the term is used to express a state of malaise. What appears to be general in many of the usages is a breakdown in problem-posing and problem-solving. This breakdown seems to approximate Kuhn's depiction of the need for a paradigm shift.[1] The central argument in this paper is that the dominant paradigm for the process of generating, transmitting and applying knowledge is itself in crisis, insofar as it is no longer allowing problems to be posed or solved in a fruitful fashion. Further, since this paradigm has affected not only the conceptualisation of knowledge, but of the socio-cultural processes including the definition of the individual and her/his role in those, the various crises are inter-related. And while these crises are perhaps most acutely felt in the capitalist, industrialised world in which the dominant paradigm originated, they are, like the paradigm, not confined there since a basic feature of that paradigm has been its assumed universality.

Thus, in education, the central crisis stems from the epistemological one. That it has been seen in predominantly instrumental terms - problems with the structure of institutions and the delivery processes and content within them - is in itself an aspect of the dominant paradigm and the power structure which has been developed to legitimate and maintain it. This has led to a failure to problematise knowledge itself. In this paper, a brief outline of the nature of the knowledge crisis will be given, and some implications for three aspects of teacher education will be considered: its role in knowledge generation, the changing social world in which education is sited and knowledge of which it transmits, and the ways that knowledge is selected, organised and evaluated in the curriculum.

1. Changing Knowledge Paradigms

It is now becoming evident in most traditional disciplines that the old paradigms no longer provide adequate guidance for either theorising or theory testing. This is perhaps most dramatically evident in physics, where the work of David Bohm[2] on the hologram challenges the very concept of the nature of matter. Similarly, Karl Pribram[3] has applied holographic imagery to the functioning of the brain, challenging the dominant mechanistic and topographical model of brain activity.

The changes are less clear in the social sciences, although two trends are evident. The first is the dissatisfaction with theories, evident in most disciplines except perhaps economics, regardless of the particular type of theory. For example, there is almost as much criticism of Marxist theory, at least insofar as it is able to handle late capitalism/post-industrialism within its framework of class analysis, as there is of other, more traditional or conservative theories in such fields as sociology, social anthropology and political science. Such criticism is often directed more specifically to, or is at least linked with, methodological criticism. This has several thrusts, including both a weariness with the pursuit of ever more refined empirical tools when the validity and meaning of their application can be questioned, and the critique of positivistic research itself. In particular, the concept of the value neutrality of such research has been questioned in the light of its use - and misuse - in various aspects of social steering, as well as its implications for a view of human nature as object of, and amenable to, such inquiry.[4]

The second trend partly grows out of the first. It is directed more at a critique of the nature of theorising itself. There are now evident three major paradigms for social science - the logical-empirical, the hermeneutic and the critical.[5] The dominance of the logical-empirical is waning, yet neither of the others looks like replacing it. Further, there is little possibility for inter-paradigmatic dialogue, for there is no way in which the basic postulates of the one can be admitted to the other in such a manner that their competing claims can be tested. The nature and desirability of objectivity, what constitutes a "test", and indeed what the very aim of theorising should be, is questioned. And a new perspective on the debates is arising which questions the possibility that any of the presently conceived tools - theoretical, metatheoretical or methodological - can deal with the crisis in both "science" and "life".[6]

What is the impact of such trends on education and teacher education, especially from a comparative viewpoint?

I contend that, with the possible exception of the new
sociology of education, there has been little impact. At
the level of theory, this may short-circuit some blind
alleys found in the approach towards a scientific paradigm
by occurring after the ground has been broken in other
fields. But such a view implies that education, including
teacher education, is reactive, rather than playing an
active role in knowledge generation and transmission even
within its own sphere.

Comparative studies in particular have been useful in
showing the extent of, and variations in, concerns in
education with demography, course structure, lifelong
education, ideology, education and working life and so on.
Thus, given socio-cultural and system-specific characteristics, a certain range of structural and institutional
problems and solutions occurs. If, however, it is asserted
that the educational crisis lies at least partly in the very
nature of our approach to knowledge, its selection and
organisation for transmission in education, which is
essentially a cross-cultural and transnational dilemma, then
a new context for the discussion of crisis is presented.
And one approach to penetrating the crisis is to problematise
the way in which knowledge is presented in teacher education,
in order to see if teacher education is contributing to both
the debate about and quest for knowledge, and the trying out
of new frameworks and practical solutions.

2.   Teacher Education and the Generation of Knowledge

One aspect of the dominant knowledge paradigm which has
received extensive criticism is the control of the generation
of knowledge by narrowly-defined experts, who are in turn
partly controlled by the funders of research. Knowledge
generation is a question of search and research, and while
there has not been a lack of educational research, it has
been largely empiricist and often unrelated to the notion
that knowledge is problematic. In this way, research is
conceived in teacher education in narrow terms, which include
both a division between researchers and others within teacher
education, and between researchers and teachers in the school
system.

Such a division is partly due to the uncertain "status"
of education as a field of inquiry, its often uneasy
relationships with "parent" disciplines and over-emphasis on
quantitative methodology. Two effects have followed from
this. The first is a paucity of theory, despite a plethora
of theories in sub-fields such as educational sociology or
psychology, which tend to fall somewhere between education
and the parent discipline in a way that fragments knowledge
of both education and the parent discipline. This tends to

further lower the status of education, and to decrease the possibility for general theories of education. The second is a division of labour or further fragmentation in both the knowledge generation and transmission areas, in part legitimated by a mythology which sees teaching either as an "art" which is minimally amenable to scientific processes, or as a competence which can be enhanced through the application of research findings in which teachers-as-objects have little active role. Thus, there is often an hierarchical arrangement in education. In the institutional divisions (universities, colleges, governmental departments and schools), each participates differentially in research, and research itself is of different kinds. Further, staff are allocated to either a predominantly generating or transmitting role, and students are divided according to level, the lower ones gaining very little notion of educational research as either product or process.

Teacher education and educational research have often become so separated that the former is little more than the transmission of selected research findings and skills and not part of an ongoing knowledge-generation process. On the other hand, educational research is divided into the "pure" and the "applied" with neither theories nor actors overlapping in most instances. We turn in a little more detail to the two main divisions:

(i) <u>Teacher education and research</u>   It is broadly true to state that the division of labour between research and teaching is greater in the education of educators than in most other professional fields. In Australia, for example, even the move in the 1970s to upgrade and diversify the institutions into more multipurpose ones has not led to significant changes in their research capacities. Staff still teach approximately twice as many hours per week as their university colleagues in Faculties of Education, find it harder to attend conferences, have little access to research funds and have fewer, and shorter, opportunities for study leave for research or professional development.

A second division is found, even within universities, between the different levels of teacher education, from skill-oriented pre-service education and some in-service work, to higher degree studies. Those teacher educators who are actively engaged in research often prefer to work at the post-graduate levels and justify this in terms of the "disinterest in" or "irrelevance for" lower levels of teacher education. Certainly the task of teaching is ever more complex, and initially at least survival and instrumental skills are of uppermost concern to new teachers. The staff who work with these students often adapt their courses accordingly, work with the students during their practical teaching rounds, and have better relationships with school staff. Beginning teachers are thus reinforced in their opinions that teaching is a practical matter, and "theory", a loose term applied to research and theorising alike, is seen as largely irrelevant. When other staff find such students disinterested in broader issues and perspectives, so that they either try not to be involved in their education or are reluctantly recruited for it, and when on the other hand experienced teachers who also play a role in socialising the new teachers feel that research and researchers have little to offer them, a vicious, self-reinforcing circle is established.

Another contributing factor to this division of labour and attitudes stems from the way in which education itself is conceived. It tends to be a social institution that is easily used as a scapegoat for a variety of social ills, and is relatively easy to control through the threat of withdrawal for its products and processes and through the use of financial sanctions. It is considered at least in its formal schooling aspects as a socio-cultural tool, and little more: even at the "best" of times the individual-societal dialectic is a contradictory and unacknowledged one.[7] There is a further contradiction between research and theory on the one hand, and practice on the other. As Levin depicts it, "To a very large degree it appears that educational research is expected to solve educational dilemmas because such problems are considered to be technical in nature ... Given this presumption, educational research represents the investigatory approach that can provide appropriate technically valid answers. Many of these problems are not technical at all, but political".[8] And the research paradigm mostly used does not admit values or implementation strategies within its premises. It is practice, and not theory, which enables particular sorts of political and administrative-technical decisions to be made about the implementation of research studies and findings.

An interesting example of these dilemmas is found in a country like Sweden which has prided itself on its progressive educational reform policies and strategies, including the use of research for these. It has, however, been predominantly structural, organisational and psycho-metric research, with little attention to either broader philosophical or general curricular issues.[9] In Australia, a recent national inquiry concluded that "teacher education research and development ... is deficient in most areas".[10] This is also true of the policy aspects of broader educational research, and few guidelines were provided for future development. Questions of resources and forms of decision-making have been given most attention, while issues like aims and objectives were only beginning to emerge

in the late 1970s.[11] Now, a year after that report was
released, the Educational Research and Development Committee
was abolished, so that the prime responsibility for research
initiative and funding is to be in the hands of the state
governments, most of whose record in this field is weak, and
concentrated on short-term, classroom-oriented and
administrative issues.

Thus, the whole relationship between teacher education
and research is an uneasy and vulnerable one. Further, it
is open to the very criticisms which have led to the
reduction in funds and in perceived usefulness: increasing
isolation or conformity to the policymakers' directives,
leading to decreasing legitimacy amongst the practitioners
and the public at large.

The technical approach to educational change and to
teacher education flows from the dominant research paradigm.
This is not to deny that valuable research takes place, but
the situation is largely one of stalemate. If this is seen
to be at least partly due to the need for a new paradigm,
and if a new definition of knowledge, admitting value
statements, provides a basis for problematising which seeks
to affirm the dialectical inter-relationships between theory
and practice, and which attempts to find new methodologies,
then new knowledge can again be generated which is based on
the very notions of humanity, society, culture and change
which education should imply.[12]

(ii) _Teachers and research_   It is argued that the
division between "educational research" and "practical
teaching" is perpetuated through students' experiences in
initial teacher education. Those attitudes are not entirely
negative, however. In an evaluation of the diploma programme at La Trobe University, it was found that the students
considered that the aims of their courses had not been
achieved very well in areas of general issues in education,
including educational theories.[13] It is not clear how
students ranked these areas in importance in their
expectations from the courses, but clearly what they "got"
in the way of theory, which could be considered to include
research, they considered to be badly conceived and
communicated. On the other hand, practical skills,
understanding children, development of self-awareness and
becoming an informed critic of school practice was seen to
be well achieved.

If such perceptions form the basis for later negative
attitudes to research, then the actual practice of
educational research tends to further the exclusion of
teachers from active involvement in it. They are either
expected to use the results of research, without having
participated in more than experimental groups on which some

90

findings have been based, or are the objects of research. They are becoming more and more resistant to both approaches, and since promises to communicate research results are rarely kept, the situation is a stalemate.

There seem to be two routes at least out of this dilemma. The first is suggested, perhaps surprisingly, in the recommendations of the Australian National Inquiry: "that the study of methods of inquiry and research should be included in pre-service courses for teachers at all levels. This should assist in producing teachers able to use research and research findings to develop their teaching".[14] Admittedly this limits the role of teachers to the practical and passive field. It does, however, suggest that some orientation to and acquisition of skill in research should be an integral part of teacher education. There is a need to integrate the general education of teachers, in which they have either studied other subjects to a level well beyond the approaches and demands made in their teacher training, or have undertaken the two in tandem in a way that has limited their general education. Surely in any tertiary studies an orientation to the process of and controversies in research should be an integral part?

Another aspect of breaking down the division of labour is found in the concept of the teacher as researcher. This has been best worked out in the context of new approaches to evaluation. As Stake points out, "Resisting the presumption that they are truth-tellers, evaluators may enable educators and other people to be better truth-seekers".[15] Proppe takes this further and suggests that "evaluation needs to become dialectical (two-way communication) ... It is of no less importance to help the audiences to see the relationship of the program with the 'outside world' than to see what is happening inside the program".[16] Taken together with a case study approach to the general process of social inquiry, such evaluation implies self-reflection, and a different concept of the nature of generalisations. Dialectical, illuminative evaluation can become a powerful tool for the involvement of the teacher in evaluation, for the development of the teacher's capacity to evaluate (which implies a research orientation to the process of education), and for a new relationship between school and world to be perceived and implemented. Such changes, and the development of relevant skills need to become a part of teacher education - and in what more practical way than through the task of evaluation in teacher education?

3. Social Knowledge and the Changing Social World

If the foregoing argument is valid, that classroom teachers

and even some teacher educators have little to do with the
active generation of knowledge, what is the role of both in
the selection and organisation of knowledge for transmission,
and its evaluation? I shall limit myself here to consideration of "social knowledge", for two reasons. Firstly, it
is a more over-arching concept which can be used as a
shorthand expression of the way in which other specialised
forms of knowledge are brought together, given meaning and
used in and for social participation. Secondly, one of the
main dimensions of the educational crisis is the confused
conceptualisation and often-contradictory practice of
education as a social institution. This latter is in turn
related to the nature and pace of socio-cultural change
today, and to the inability of old paradigms to continue to
provide satisfactory explanations and guides for conceptualising and living in the world of today and tomorrow.
There are plenty of diagnoses of socio-cultural change.
Some elements are the pace and direction of change itself,
the role of technology, the future of work, and underlying
and persistent problems of poverty, inequality and
oppression which signify a violent structure in relationships
within and between nations. These in turn lead to the
possibility of destruction and annihilation, from the
impoverishment of human relationships to each other and the
environment, to the threat of nuclear holocaust.

To what extent do such diagnoses and debates about
their significance and solution play a role in teacher
education? To some extent the new sociology of education
has been a channel for them. What it has done for teachers,
Richard Bates concludes, is to "offer a challenge and an
opportunity to reassert the purpose of education, not in
furthering the processes of social control by social,
cultural and economic elites, but by furthering the cause
of human betterment and increasing the ability of
individuals to control their own destiny through processes
of educational, political and social change".[17]

Some research has been undertaken on the ways in which
teachers perceive the relevance of social issues in education
and their ways of conceptualising these issues. In a series
of investigations in Sweden, it was found that teachers
considered that the teaching of international problems was
as important or more so than teaching about anything else.
70% claimed that they were at least "rather interested" in
doing so themselves, interest amongst pupils was judged to
be great, but half considered that such problems were rarely
treated in their own teaching or that of the comprehensive
school in general.[18] Both teachers and pupils had
significantly different opinions of the main issues than the
population at large, and teachers differed from pupils in
their emphasis on the world of work. There was also a

difference between teachers' own concerns, their perceptions of their pupils' concerns, and the actual concerns of pupils.19

There is thus a range of perceptions of the world, and a gap between ideals and practice in raising these issues in schools. The teachers in the Swedish surveys thought that greater coherence would be gained if they had an opportunity to acquaint themselves further with both contents concerning the issues, and methods for their incorporation into teaching.

In an attempt to find out what some Australian teachers thought about the teaching of social issues, I questioned one pre-service group (mostly adult, part-time students) and three in-service (post-graduate Bachelor of Education) ones. They were simply asked to nominate the three most important concepts about the world that they thought children should consider in the course of their formal schooling. No differences between teachers occurred according to sex, age or amount of teaching experience, nor birthplace, experience in foreign countries and disciplines of specialisation. There were differences between primary and secondary teachers, the former nominating broader, more general concepts whereas the latter gave a greater variety of more specific ones. The other difference was found between courses at the B.Ed. level. Those studying the anthropology of education were interested in culture, inter-cultural understanding and skills, individual development and the appreciation of other cultures. Those studying educational administration tended to focus on cultural diversity, the need for understanding and tolerance, the importance of social change and the interdependent nature of the world.

There are clear differences between teachers in their worldview and their preferences for conveying this in the classroom. The small Australian survey indicates that the content of teacher education at least interacts with the worldview that a particular teacher has developed. This is shown in the characteristics of the two main groups. The "administrators" were older, twice as many were men, and fewer had any overseas experiences than those in the "anthropology" group. There were slightly more women in the latter, the average teaching experience was less, and twice as many women as men had overseas experience. Given free choice in in-service teacher education, it seems that individual characteristics play an important role in the types of educational experiences which teachers seek; whether or not those experiences merely confirm, or extend and modify their worldview, is another question.

Such findings indicate a number of questions about what teachers know about the changing social world, what they would like to know more about in order to incorporate it into their programmes, what they think their pupils should

93

or would like to know, and how they can gain this knowledge, evaluate their own positions, and select and organise into meaningful frameworks and strategies those aspects they can convey in the classroom. Rather than asking specifically how teacher education can meet these needs, and raising thorny issues about whether or not "contemporary world studies" should be a core subject in teacher education, and what alternative means and sources exist (such as journals and subject teachers' associations), the following areas are suggested as significant for considering the role of teacher education in the ongoing process of relating education to the changing socio-cultural world:

(i) The basic education of teachers   Teachers are still mostly trained initially at an early age and have little experience outside the classroom. While some may have undertaken undergraduate studies in particular disciplines and courses which give a broad spectrum of ideas about content and research, others will have experienced a more narrow, hierarchical and non-exploratory learning situation. Either way, they are often told to "forget all that" when it comes to what they will be teaching in the classroom, and further dissonance is produced when the knowledge and skills acquired in their general tertiary education have little coherence with their teacher education (at least subjectively, my experience of a concurrent degree and diploma programme versus a sequenced degree followed by end-on diploma is that students are more ready and able to inter-relate their degree and educational work in the former). The selection and organisation of social knowledge in teacher education needs to take much greater cognisance of the backgrounds - both strengths and weaknesses therein - of trainee teachers, in order to start a process of reflective conceptualisation of the relationships between education and the socio-cultural world, and its translation into classroom practice.

(ii) The ongoing education of teachers   While more and more attention has been paid to in-service education of teachers, this has often focussed too narrowly on methodology and skills areas. Teachers are required either to take more responsibility for the generation of the content of their teaching, or to encompass new areas and approaches. In the anxiety which either situation has created, both the presentation of new approaches to knowledge generation and of new ways for its selection and organisation, have been underplayed, perhaps not least because teacher educators may be out of touch outside their own specialised and narrow fields. The selection and organisation of means for teachers to update - and perhaps participate in the ongoing generation

94

of - socio-cultural knowledge is problematic, but that is no
excuse for ignoring it. In my own institution, staff have
been divided over the validity of allowing up to three units
of the B.Ed. to be taken, for the purpose of updating, in
another faculty and it is not entirely due to the delicate
book-keeping (who gets teaching hour credits?) that there is
no course designed for their needs by teacher educators and
"subject specialists" together. The fact that a new socio-
cultural area, World Studies, which is achieving legitimacy
in schools in the U.K., has largely been promoted, and
organised through combined content and methodology workshops,
by a non-governmental and non-educational group, the One
World Trust, throws interesting light on the whole process
of the legitimation of new educational knowledge and the way
it is conceived and transmitted.

(iii) Teachers as representatives of socio-cultural
change   Issues of culture and social class have increasingly come under scrutiny in the educational literature.
From supposed bearers of enlightenment and "better" culture,
teachers have been criticised for imposing their middle
class values and concepts, and in multicultural societies
their "culture" and role as cultural carriers has also
become controversial. This has had the effect of calling
into question the role of education in cultural production
and reproduction, and opinions have tended to become
polarised. What has largely been overlooked in the debate
is the changing socio-cultural base of many teachers who are
now being trained. For those, for example from cultural
minorities, who "receive" knowledge about the supposed
culture of the groups they represent and its place in
society and education, their teacher education must surely
create cognitive and affective dissonance! In forging new
approaches to socio-cultural education, and to knowledge
about social and cultural change, new ways are needed to
incorporate the experiences of these new recruits to
teaching, as a point of entry into educational theorising
and practice, an active agent in social and cultural
dynamics.
These are just some aspects of the problems of and
prospects for new paradigms for incorporating all the
participants in education in the knowledge selection and
organisation processes. One should ask to what extent has
changing socio-cultural reality - from the facts of demography to vital issues such as changing sex roles and
perspectives, time perspectives and frameworks for
understanding society and culture - a critical place in
teacher education? The fragmentation and partial presentation of such issues leads to the possibility for ideological
manipulation of education, and to its continued reproductive,

95

dependent status.[20]

4.   The Curriculum

Some reasons why the curriculum has become so problematic today include the so-called knowledge explosion, the effects of reproduction theories, the impact of child-centred theories of education and relativistic theories of knowledge, as well as the loss of general legitimacy for formal education. The aspect which I wish to underline is the confusion about the nature of knowledge which can be seen to underlie many of the problems about curriculum.

Knowledge today is increasingly fragmented. There are different knowledge systems, of which our western one is an example. Within it, there are the "two cultures" of science and the humanities, classical and romantic traditions of thought, divisions into functional types,[21] ever-refined disciplines and branches, and new inter- or multi-disciplinary, theme or problem oriented re-combinations. Over against the increasing specialisation is the notion of the knowledge of "everyday reality",[22] which in itself must become more complex if it is to contain adequate guides for the lay person to find the right specialist, assuming that s/he has the "right" to do this. Cognitive, rational knowledge; emotional and aesthetic; intuitive and spiritual; male and female; social and individual; theoretical and applied - logically, anthropologically, politically or on the basis of the organisation within and/or between classifications of knowledge, we are aware of the many different ways of knowing and of selecting from these for transmission in particular situations.

Given this state of diversity and confusion in the knowledge generation, organisation and selection processes, it is little wonder that the choice of curriculum guidelines and content has become so problematic. Some questions which arise in teacher education which bear on its role in the curriculum debate include:
- what, if any, paradigms for knowledge generation are applied in the education of teachers?
- what relationships are there between research and teacher education, and teacher education and the models for knowledge generation both advocated for and practised in schools?
- how is the curriculum conceived in relationship to the solution of a particular problem, the selection and organis-ation of educational knowledge?
- what contradictions are apparent and acknowledged in the current ways in which the curriculum is selected and transmitted (including contents, processes and evaluation)?
- what is the role of teacher educators and teachers, separately and together, in curriculum debate and development?

96

- how is this debate and development conceived in terms of the broader process of knowledge generation, transmission and application?

On the whole, the content of teacher education seems to fall behind such debates, and to treat curriculum as a technical problem. Thus, in the field of social knowledge, Hicks' investigation of global perspectives in the initial education of teachers in the U.K. showed that 63% of the college respondents and 30% of the university ones said that they were teaching courses or units on contemporary global problems. This was largely limited to aspects of discipline-based courses, the aims and frameworks varied enormously, and a world perspective was least likely to be found in general education courses. Here, the roles of women and ethnic minorities received more attention - quite unattached to a global framework! And both were largely unrelated to the study of the curriculum.[23] A similar situation was found in Australia.[24]

It is clearly simplistic to think that a compulsory course on new views of knowledge, world problems and the curriculum could solve some of the problems of the contemporary curriculum. But if our approaches are limited to tinkering, adding, subtracting, amalgamating in diverse and often unrelated parts of teacher education, we and our students will continue to be passive agents of transmission.

5. Conclusion

Perhaps it is because the delineation of what constitutes a better society and the role of education in it is so diverse and controversial, and because we have perhaps become too conscious of the ideological and perspectivist nature of knowledge, that we hesitate to stand up for a particular view of education and society on which a renewal of teacher education could be based. We thereby fall into a relativist dilemma and become the object of radical and conservative critics alike.[25] A fruitful current approach broadens the debate into the sphere of culture, from different viewpoints but recognising that education is part of cultural generation as well as reproduction.[26]

If we as teacher educators remain content with a passive role, with accepting a commitment to lifelong education and continuous teacher education which can so easily be merely a job-saving adaptation to the latest political directive, we drift ever further out on the periphery of socio-cultural and educational renewal. As one critic of the Australian National Inquiry into Teacher Education stated:

More than ever before, we need a thorough and sober

97

assessment of teacher education concepts and practices...
More than ever before, we need an increasing variety of
patterns of teacher education ... More than ever before,
we need the support of educational research, curriculum
development and community involvement. But the current
climate sees the emasculation of substantial enterprises
in these fields, and the result is that teacher
educators are adopting a fortress-like response, as
they overstate their case for contribution to excellence
in teaching.[27]

And even more than ever before, we need to explore the
concepts of knowledge, society and culture on which our
approaches to and role in education are based. In the words
of an old Maori proverb:

The old net is full of holes, its meshes have rotted and
it has been laid aside. WHAT NEW NET GOES A-FISHING?[28]

NOTES

1.   T.S. Kuhn, The Structure of Scientific Revolutions.
Chicago, The International Encyclopedia of the Social
Sciences 2 (2), 1970.
2.   D. Bohm, "The Unfolding-Enfolding Universe: a
conversation with Renée Weber", Re-Vision, Summer/Fall, 1978.
3.   K.H. Pribram, "Problems concerning the Structure of
Consciousness", in G.G. Globus, G. Maxwell and I. Savodnik,
(eds), Consciousness and the Brain. New York, Plenum Press,
1976.
4.   J. Habermas, Legitimation Crisis. Boston, Beacon
Press, 1975 (transl. T. McCarthy).
5.   See, e.g. S. Lindholm, Paradigms, Science and
Reality. Stockholm Institute of Education, Stockholm
University, 1981; G. Radnitzky, Contemporary Schools of
Metascience, 2nd edn. Göteborg, Akademiforlaget, 1970, and
H. Strasser, The Normative Structure of Sociology, London,
Routledge and Kegan Paul, 1976.
6.   P. Schwartz and J. Ogilvy, The Emergent Paradigm:
Changing Patterns of Thought and Belief, Menlo Park,
Analytical Reports, VALS Program, 1979.
7.   R.D. Herman, "A Theoretical Look at Knowledge,
Schools and Social Change", Comparative Education Review,
Volume 18, number 3, 1974, pp. 411-418, and J. Hinkson,
"Pierre Bourdieu and Reproduction Theory", Working Paper,
La Trobe University Centre for the Study of Innovation in
Education, 1981 (mimeo).
8.   H.M. Levin, "Why isn't Educational Research more
Useful?", Prospects, Volume 8, number 2, 1978, p. 166.
9.   R. Burns, "Process and Problems in Educational

Reform in Sweden", Compare, Volume 11, number 1, 1981, pp. 33-44.

10. J.J. Auchmuty, Report of the National Inquiry into Teacher Education, Canberra, AGPS, 1980, p. 216.

11. J.V. D'Cruz and P. Sheehan (eds), The Renewal of Australian Schools, 2nd edn., Melbourne, ACER, 1978.

12. e.g. M.L. Simmons, "Toward a Critical Theory of Education", Paper presented to a conference of the American Educational Research Association, 1975 (mimeo).

13. G. Rowley, "DipEd Evaluation, 1980", La Trobe University School of Education, 1981 (mimeo).

14. J.J. Auchmuty, op. cit., p. 211.

15. R.E. Stake, Evaluating Educational Programmes, Paris, OECD, 1976.

16. Ó.J. Proppé, "Dialectical Evaluation", Interim Report, CIRCE, University of Illinois, 1979, p. 31.

17. R.J. Bates, "What can the New Sociology of Education do for Teachers?", Paper presented to the annual conference of the Sociology Association of Australia and New Zealand, 1979, p. 19 (mimeo).

18. E. Almgren, The Swedish Report of the European Study on Education for Development at the Post-primary level, Malmö, 1973 (mimeo).

19. S. Marklund, The Internationalization of Education: Some Concepts and Questions, Institute for International Education, Stockholm University, 1980.

20. See, e.g. M.F.D. Young and G. Whitty, Society, State and Schooling, Brighton, Falmer Press, 1977; R. Burns, "Knowledge for Peace and Education", Bulletin of Peace Proposals, Volume 12, number 2, 1981, and M. Haavelsrud, "On Inclusion and Exclusion", Bulletin of Peace Proposals, Volume 12, number 2, 1981.

21. G. Gurvitch, The Social Frameworks of Knowledge, Oxford, Basil Blackwell, 1971 (transl. M.A. and K.A. Thompson).

22. P.L. Berger and T. Luckmann, The Social Construction of Reality, New York, Doubleday, 1967.

23. D.W. Hicks, Global Perspectives in the Initial Education of Teachers, World Studies Teacher Education Network, 1979.

24. C.G. Coffey (ed), Proceedings of the Australian UNESCO Seminar on Teacher Education for International Understanding, Canberra, Curriculum Development Centre, 1977.

25. Compare, e.g. R. Saraudy, The Alternative Future, Harmondsworth, Penguin Books, 1972; R.M. Pirsig, Zen and the Art of Motorcycle Maintenance, London, Corgi Books, 1974 and Young and Whitty, op. cit., with T.S. Eliot, "The Aims of Education", in T.S. Eliot, To Criticize the Critic and other Writings, London, Faber and Faber, 1950.

26. See e.g. J. Berque, "Towards a better transfer of

Knowledge and Values", Prospects, Volume 6, number 3, 1976;
Hinkson, op. cit.; R. Pring, Knowledge and Schooling, London,
Open Books, 1976, and M. Skilbeck, "Core Curriculum: An
Essay in Cultural Reconstruction", Canberra, Curriculum
Development Centre, 1980 (mimeo).

27.   P. Jones, "Problematics in Teacher Education:
Lessons from Auchmuty", SPATE Newsletter, May, 1981.

28.   P. Buck, Vikings of the Sunrise, New York, J.B.
Lippincott Co., 1938.

THE IMPLICATIONS FOR TEACHER TRAINING OF CONFLICTING MODELS OF COMMUNITY SCHOOLING

Linda A. Dove

The central argument of this paper is that government-sponsored community schooling schemes in less developed countries are geared to reformist rather than transformational goals. Yet if teachers are genuinely to serve the needs of disadvantaged communities they must be prepared to conceive of and perform their tasks in radically different ways. Teacher training, therefore, must be revolutionised. But no government can encourage the development of a teaching force dedicated to fundamental changes in the status quo. Therefore teacher education and training for community schooling remains conservative and ineffective. It fails to help teachers resolve the conflicts which arise between their responsibilities as agents of national governments and their responsibilities to local communities.

In the twenty years after World War 2 many less developed countries invested heavily in their education systems as ways of encouraging economic growth, fulfilling needs for high level manpower and stimulating national unity.[1] In the 1970s governments grew uneasy over the disappointing returns from their investments. Schools were criticised for over-producing school-leavers whose skills and values were inappropriate to national economic needs. They were blamed for exacerbating social inequalities, between urban and rural areas, between rich and poor, between majority and minority ethnic populations and for perpetuating social injustices by serving the needs of economic and political elites while neglecting and alienating the poor and the oppressed.[2]

COMMUNITY SCHOOLING

One response to these problems was the shift of policy away from the development of imported "colonialist" models of education towards more indigenously authentic community-oriented ones. The community school concept was adopted as

101

a remedy for some of the economic and social ills of the time. Community schools were to perform a number of functions.[3] They would very closely serve the needs of the communities in which they were located and encourage community development. They would provide a curriculum for young people which would prepare them for productive work locally and thus slow down the drift of alienated youths to the towns in search of jobs. They would encourage positive attitudes between community and school, and integrate child and adult education. They would economise on costs through the shared use of teachers for school and community activities.

Community schooling policies have been more and less comprehensive, radical and determined.[4] In some countries community schooling is run by non-governmental organisations, sometimes with their own distinctive ideologies or counter-culture. In others it is adopted by governments but only for disadvantaged ethnic minorities or areas, such as urban slums and remote rural areas. Only a very few countries have adopted community schooling as a radical and wholesale strategy for the transformation of the national educational system. Even then it tends to be most thoroughly developed at the level of basic education for children and adults. At secondary and tertiary levels community-oriented experiments in community service or work experience tend to be tacked on to conventional programmes rather than being an integral part of them.

Objective and dispassionate evidence on the success of community schools in achieving their purposes is scanty.[5] A few isolated experiments which appear to be successful become over-exposed, the success of others proves ephemeral. Many fail through lack of clarity or consensus on their purposes or through problems of implementation. Nevertheless, the community school idea retains its attractiveness into the 1980s for governments in search of new educational strategies.

The idea of community schooling is by no means new. It runs throughout the entire history of modern school systems.[6] Nor does the adoption of community schooling as official policy indicate that there is necessarily anything more in it than rhetoric and the mere re-naming of existing institutions. But for those countries which are seriously trying to implement it teacher training has become the new priority.

COMMUNITY-ORIENTED TEACHER TRAINING

In many educational innovations the need to prepare the teachers for their new tasks is often recognised belatedly if at all. Teacher training and re-training is often poorly

102

financed and the teachers are badly prepared. But in appraisals of the weaknesses and failures in community schools, the inappropriate skills and attitudes of teachers are frequently identified as crucial. Common sense suggests that a community school with everything else in its favour cannot succeed if the teachers who give life to the institution are inadequate to the task. Many teacher training programmes, therefore, particularly at the initial training level, include some components intended to prepare teachers to work in community schools.

Despite efforts to gear teacher training to the changing tasks of teachers, there has been little success in producing large numbers of teachers who willingly and effectively stay for any length of time in community schooling. This is often for very practical reasons. Community schools are often low status or disadvantaged in terms of their location or their pupil intake. Teachers find it very taxing to pay adequate attention to classroom tasks and to community development, adult learning and all the other activities which community schooling demands of them and prefer to concentrate on their traditional, uncontroversial tasks as teachers of children in the classroom.[7]

But the fundamental reason for lack of success in revamping teacher training to produce committed community school teachers stems from a confusion of ideological perspectives.[8] It is this issue to which we now turn.

REFORMIST STRATEGIES OF CHANGE

Policy makers and planners tend to work with a view of social processes which derives from the evolutionary tradition of Durkheim. This was refined by the structural-functionalists such as Parsons and Merton in the 1950s and more recently adopted by systems analysts. Society is like a machine with many interlocking parts. If the machine breaks down, all the human beings whose lives depend on it suffer so its maintenance in working order is the over-riding goal of the managers. All the members of the society who work on the machine have their allotted roles and tasks which they must perform efficiently to maintain the social machinery. Within the machine are sub-systems of working parts such as the economic, political and educational systems. The educational system performs two tasks essential to the smooth functioning of the social machine. It socialises the young into values, attitudes and behaviour conducive to maintenance of the machine and it allocates them future economic, social and political roles. If members of the society are imperfectly socialised or do not fit into their assigned roles the social machine may falter or even break down. From the assumptions of this model, changes in society are welcomed only if they enable the machinery to function more efficiently. Radical changes which threaten to alter the whole structure of the machinery or change its nature are opposed.

In the post-war years policymakers and planners worked within this perspective. They envisaged the development of their societies in terms of enabling the machinery to work more efficiently, to create more wealth, more education, more centres of modernity. They did not question the ultimate goals for society only the means. When, for instance, school systems began to over-produce school leavers who had no jobs the remedy was to raise the level of qualification for entry to the more desirable jobs. Thus demand was artificially dampened for existing jobs but the occupational and social structure remained the same.

TRANSFORMATIONAL CHANGE

When such ameliorative measures no longer sufficed because political unrest and the economic cost of rising numbers of educated unemployed threatened the efficient working of the social machine, policy makers began to accept an alternative view of how society remains stable or falls apart. The conflict perspective owes its origins to Marx, and later Max Weber, and in educational thinking has recently been developed by Carnoy, Bowles and Gintis and theorists of the dependency school. According to this model society is not a self-balancing machine which occasionally needs to be tinkered with to correct malfunctions. Rather it is like a rope taut between teams in a tug of war. The struggle is between the wealthy and ruling groups who pull hard on the rope to maintain their own power and privilege and the exploited groups. The latter may pull on the rope for a while but if they make no headway they may let go. The rope goes limp as they refuse to play the game. They may even organise to overthrow the existing rules. The conflict model implies that only changes which meet the demands of the underprivileged can improve society. But such changes necessitate radical structuring such as a massive redistribution of educational opportunity, and therefore of economic resources, to the excluded groups.

Policy makers came to accept this diagnosis of their society's problems but could not fully effect the radical remedies required. New policies, for instance, emphasising increased educational opportunities for disadvantaged children were promoted but were not totally effective in practice. Dominant groups who favoured the status quo diluted any educational changes which threatened their own privileges and thereby perpetuated mere reformist change

104

strategies.

TEACHERS AS COMMUNITY CHANGE AGENTS

The idea that local communities should participate in educational change is attractive to policy makers. It appears to give scope for change from below which may satisfy the demands of disadvantaged groups without major disturbance to the existing social order. But community schooling reforms promoted by national governments pose fundamental dilemmas for the roles and tasks of teachers. These dilemmas go a long way to clarifying why such reforms rarely become large-scale or last very long.

Teachers are government servants. They are expected to inculcate in pupils the dominant values of society and to prepare them to fit into roles in the existing social structure. At the same time they are expected to be mobilisers in the community encouraging change which will be consistent with governmental development policies. They are therefore expected to act as change agents of a reformist type. But the history of community schooling indicates that such schools need teachers who can act as much more radical agents of change; change which threatens to attack the established social order and its values and which thus serves the long-term interests of disadvantaged communities.[10] Community schools spring up spontaneously in response to discontent of various sorts with the existing society.[11] The discontent may be of an economic-political nature, ethno-cultural or religious. The anti-establishment aims of community schools may range from pursuing changes which are limited to improving the community's opportunities within the existing social order (reformist), to radically re-structuring society in its own favour (transformative) or to seceding altogether from the society in order to set up a new one (separatist).

When governments set up community schools they cannot tolerate teachers becoming the agents of radical types of change. Rather they seek to use the teachers to harness the enthusiastic participation of the community in the schooling of their children and in other "safe" developmental activities. They try to meet community needs in ways consistent with the development goals of government. But if teachers are genuinely to serve the community they must ignore governmental policies when these contradict the interests of the local community as it sees them.[9] Governments are only too well aware of the potentially subversive part which teachers may play in community education. This is why they rarely allow communities a great deal of control over teachers, even though local control is a natural extension of the idea that teachers should serve local

communities. All this means, then, that teachers in
community schools are caught in a dilemma. They cannot
perform their responsibilities both as government servants
and as community servants at the same time (except in the
rare cases where a community's interests coincide exactly
with governmental policies).

The implications of these conflicting demands on
teachers with respect to their participation in community
schooling are far-reaching. They imply different aims and
approaches to their tasks in the education of children in
school and in community development. Teachers operate in
four areas of responsibility: acculturation, preparation
for economic production or work, political education and
the integration of school and community. Each of these
activities may be carried out in school and among youth and
adults in non-formal education and community activities.
Table 1 charts out the implications for teachers' work with
respect to community schooling when they are servants of the
national government.

Table 2 delineates the implications for teachers' work
when they are servants of the local community. In the aims,
content and style these two models conflict. Teachers
cannot serve two masters simultaneously and if they try,
they suffer from role conflict. The natural reaction to
such a situation is to flee from it altogether into more
conventional teaching or to opt for one or the other. Very
few teachers can afford to opt out of a salaried government
job for the sake of community ideals and so independent
community schools lose support and national community
schools are no more than conventional schools under another
name.

TEACHER TRAINING FOR NATIONAL SERVICE

Many teacher training programmes, it was suggested above,
already incorporate components designed to enable teachers
to work in community-oriented schooling. These programmes,
which aim to promote community development consistent with
national development policies, may be dubbed the national
service model. They are merely modifications in the
existing pattern, structure and content of teacher education
programmes. Teacher trainees are selected on national
achievement tests which normally require proficiency in the
national language. Trainees are then given a course which
is mainly college-based, and often residential in rural
areas. The academic programme is the traditional one but
includes topics on community development, sociology, anthro-
pological investigation and the like. Sometimes field
experience may partly replace the traditional practice
teaching, so that trainees may get used to finding out about

106

Table 1: The Teacher as a Servant of National Government in Community Schooling

Teacher's Responsibilities	In School	In Community
Acculturation	**Aim** – To inculcate knowledge and respect for national (mainstream) values and ways of life	
	Approach – Emphasise national culture in the curriculum – Use national language as medium of instruction – Teach national language and literature – Involve pupils in cultural events symbolising national identity	**Approach** – Encourage national cultural events in community – Use national language – Show respect for national symbolic activity – Uphold national moral and spiritual values
Preparation for work	**Aim** – To encourage knowledge, skills and attitudes appropriate to work and jobs available for children and adults in the local community	
	Approach – Teach functional literacy and numeracy – Develop problem solving scientific approach – Instil positive attitudes towards local work opportunities – Select pupils who succeed	**Approach** – Teach functional literacy and numeracy – Develop scientific approach – Encourage work producing a surplus for use in national economy – Liaise with state agencies

107

in national examinations
for jobs in wider world

for developmental
activity (agricultural
extension, population
control, non-formal
adult education)

Aim — To encourage loyal attitudes and behaviour towards national political authorities

Approach — Emphasise socialization into national political culture and system in civics, social studies, etc.
— Emphasise attitudes of respect and deference to national political authority in class and school activities
— Emphasise benefits of stable and benign government for individual well-being

Approach — Exemplify benevolent paternalistic model of government servant
— Participate in national political events (e.g. election officer; voting) and encourage community to do so
— Carry out duties as government servant strictly

Political education

School-Community Integration

Encourage (a) adults to support national aims for education and consequences for own children
(b) children to accept existing political, social and economic structure and processes in the community as part of a national system

Table 2: The Teacher as a Servant of the Local Community in Community Schooling

Teacher's Responsibilities		In School		In Community
Acculturation	Aim	- To inculcate knowledge and respect for local cultural (counter-cultural) values and ways of life		
	Approach	- Emphasise local culture in the curriculum - Use local language(s) as medium of instruction - Teach local language(s) and literature - Involve pupils in cultural events symbolising local identity and self image	Approach	- Encourage local cultural events - Use local language(s) - Show respect and sympathy for local symbolic activity - Uphold local moral and spiritual values
Preparation for work	Aim	- To encourage knowledge, skills and attitudes conducive to development of self-help, life-enhancing and income-generating productive activity		
	Approach	- Teach Freireian approach to literacy - Emphasise problem-posing science - Create critical awareness of existing economic opportunities through	Approach	- Teach Freireian approach to literacy - Emphasise problem-posing approaches to productive activity - Encourage local init-iative in economic

109

formal curriculum and work-experience in locality
- Use tests for diagnosis and encouragement of pupils' potential

activity which benefits community
- Encourage local organ-ization for self-help (co-operatives, literacy circles)

Political education

Aim — To encourage loyalty to community ideals and political activity conducive to the improvement of the community's welfare

Approach —
- Emphasise knowledge of community politics in civics, etc.
- Emphasise "conscientization" through a critical approach to study of national political system
- Encourage political efficacy through participatory approach to school government

Approach —
- Exemplify "animateur" approach to political activity on behalf of community interests
- Encourage community self-confidence in political activity (conscientization)
- Act as political champion of community school

School-Community Integration

Encourage adults to participate in formulating aims of community school with reference to the interests of their children, to contribute to development of the school. Encourage children to respect community activities by encouraging adult participation in school learning and pupil participation in adult learning

local communities and even participating in them. Once
training is over, teachers may or may not be posted to
community schools, but they are equally qualified to teach
in conventional government schools.

TEACHER TRAINING FOR COMMUNITY SERVICE

At this point the discussion must become somewhat unrealistic
for no government would be willing to finance the training
of teachers to act as liberators of community consciousness
and animateurs of community development which runs counter
to national values. Even if voluntary sponsors ran such
training it would have to ride a very fine line between
being moderate in its approach and therefore tolerated by
the authorities and being so radical that it was suppressed.
      Nevertheless, as a finale to this discussion we may
speculate on the form and content of teacher training for
community service. It would be on a very small scale at
local level. Candidates for training would presumably be
selected by the community in terms not just of academic
achievement but positive attitudes to the community, knowledge of the local language and willingness to commit
themselves to participate over a lengthy period of time in
community life.[11] Successful candidates might very well be
local people but others might not be as long as they passed
a period of probation in the community before being judged
acceptable and welcome.
      Initial training proper, then, would only begin after
some time spent in the community. Initial training would
be controlled, conceptualised and organised by the community.
The community would decide on the balance between theoretical
study and practical experience and between school and
community-based study. There would be a very close integration of theory with practice. Specific training
activities would be in the hands of experienced teacher
trainers, teachers and community personnel who would teach
specialised skills in the context of intimate knowledge and
sympathy for the community.
      Formal study would be closely related to on-going
practice in the classroom and the community. Early on
trainees would study the social, political and economic
processes of the community and its cultural and spiritual
ideals. They would compare and contrast these with national
policies and values. They would investigate how various
community educational activities, including the school,
contributed to community development. They would be
encouraged to develop a critical and sympathetic understanding of the educational needs of children and adults.
      Early on also, trainees would be encouraged to study
themselves in relation to the local community; they would be

111

trained to assess their own strengths and weaknesses and to
develop a positive self-image and self-confidence. They
would begin to work out for themselves a personal style and
approach to their work in serving the community. Such
studies would involve experiments in practical situations
and reflective study of them with the support of experienced
people.

The point at which trainees became fully accepted as
community teachers might vary according to how long it took
for them to convince the community of their acceptability.
But by the time they were introduced to the technical
aspects of teaching they would be "on the job". Then they
would continue to learn through part-time study and work for
a number of years. In the early stages they would need to
develop a sound knowledge of the curriculum of the community
school and to become effective communicators in the classroom and out. They would need a working knowledge of the
principles of learning and teaching. Later, an understanding
of human development, language development, ways of planning
and designing and evaluating curricula materials would be
needed much as they would for conventionally trained
teachers. Many more components could be added here but the
important point is that all the various components of teacher
training would be closely geared to community needs and
would be learned flexibly as needs arose and only after the
trainees had gained a very thorough knowledge, critical
understanding and sympathy for the community. Only then
could the teachers serve the community in genuine community
development.

A WAY FORWARD?

Many countries, and not just the less developed ones, are
attempting to cope with the problems raised by the presence
within their boundaries of minority communities, distinctive
in their world views, cultures and educational needs. As
outlined so starkly above, the dilemma for teacher preparation and therefore for the whole future of education in such
countries appears almost insoluble. But if education is the
key to development a way must somehow be found to provide
the sort of teachers who can deliver it.

The argument here is that community-oriented teachers
are potentially subversive and disruptive influences in the
context of nation-state building. But perhaps the message
is less threatening if it is put another way. Surely, all
that is being said is that the genuine education of
communities involves acceptance of new roles for teachers.
If they are to perform these roles well, young teachers need
to develop adaptability, flexibility, creative and independent thinking as well as enthusiastic commitment to helping

112

communities learn those things which will enable them to
help themselves. These are words with which no education-
alist, politician, administrator or aid agency would quarrel.

Finally, then, on a note of optimism, we spell out some
of the important conditions which need to be fulfilled if
teacher education and training is to evolve.

Political Conditions

1.   Maturity of the nation-state. Policy makers and ruling
groups must encourage a climate in which minority communities
are accepted by others, whether or not they themselves desire
to integrate.
2.   Decentralisation. Central authorities must be willing
to allow a degree of local autonomy, both financial and
administrative, particularly with respect to the setting of
teacher requirements, the regulation of teacher training and
certification.

Professional Conditions

1.   Flexibility. Teacher trainers and teacher unions must
accept greater participation by lay people and other profes-
sionals in (a) the selection of candidates for teacher
training; (b) the standards set for the certification of
teachers; (c) the conceptualisation, planning, implementation and evaluation of programmes for teacher preparation.
2.   Adaptability. Specialists in teacher training must be
willing to work over long periods in the schools and
communities in which teachers are being prepared.
3.   Creative Enthusiasm. A paradigm shift among specialist
teacher educators is required, so that community-generated
knowledge, skills and values are legitimated and honoured.
This involves the difficult task of integrating theory and
practice in novel ways.

Special Conditions

1.   Teacher Supply. The society must be capable of generating a sufficient flow of new candidates for training who
are willing to serve in local communities. Much depends
here on the social status of teachers, the respect accorded
them and their pay and conditions of service.[12]
2.   Role Expectations. There must be social acceptance of
teachers trained unconventially. The profession itself can
do much to educate the public into understanding the need
for changing teacher roles and tasks and therefore for new
forms of preparation.

Taken one by one most of these barriers to change should not prove daunting to policy makers. But they do involve a partnership between professional educators, politicians and administrators if they are all to be tackled successfully. Above all they require political will. But this is where we came in ...

NOTES

1. The UNESCO conferences at Karachi, Santiago and Addis Abbaba in 1961 echoed these national needs in an international forum.

2. The World Bank Education Sector Policy Paper, Washington, IBRD 1974, voiced these changing priorities internationally.

3. L.A. Dove, (a) "The Role of the Community School in Rural Transformation in Developing Countries", Comparative Education, Volume 16, number 1, March 1980, pp. 67-79.

4. Special number: School and Communities, International Review of Education, Volume 26, number 3, 1980.

5. M.E. Sinclair and K. Lillis, School and Community in the Third World, London, Croom Helm/Institute of Development Studies, 1980.

6. ibid.

7. L.A. Dove, (b) "The Teacher and the Rural Community in Developing Countries", Compare, Volume 10, number 1, 1980, pp. 17-30.

8. T.J. La Belle and J. Da S. Goncalves, "Control and Service of Schools: the community and the state", Compare, Volume 10, number 1, 1980, pp. 3-16.

9. In this discussion the local community is taken as a homogeneous entity which it may not be. See L.A. Dove (a) op. cit., pp. 76-7.

10. R.G. Paulston, "Education as Anti-structure: non-formal education in social and ethnic movements", Compare, Volume 16, number 1, March 1980, pp. 45-54.

11. Tanzania recruits primary teachers thus.

12. L.A. Dove, "The Deployment and Training of Teachers for Remote Rural Areas in Less Developed Countries", International Review of Education, Volume 28, number 1, 1982.

TEACHER EDUCATION IN BELGIUM: TOWARDS PRACTOPIA?[1]

John Owen

Any modern society in a changing world is continuously faced
with a number of educational questions which need to be
answered and re-answered if that society is to have any
control over its destiny and the future of its citizens.
Among these questions some of the more important are:
What should education try to do?
What sort of educational system would achieve these ends?
What sort of teachers are needed to operate the system?
How can these teachers be produced?
    This suggests that meaningful answers to questions about
changing priorities in teacher education can only be given by
examining, first, changes in the aims of education. Similarly, the way a society perceives itself and the context
within which it operates, and thus the answers it gives to
these questions, will be influenced by its cultural
characteristics, by its history, its political, economic,
religious and linguistic situation, and, in particular, by
its perceptions of the future.

BELGIUM

The case of Belgium, sitting as it does astride the frontier
which separates the mainly-Protestant, beer-drinking,
Teutonic-language-speaking North from the mainly-Catholic,
wine-drinking, Romance-language-speaking South, is a
particularly interesting one. As a small, vulnerable
country, frequently overrun in the past, and now the seat
of many international concerns, it appreciates more than
most the value of supranational organisations and is one of
the most dedicatedly European of all the members of the
Common Market. It is a predominantly Catholic country with
a Protestant work ethic[2] and a community problem which is
probably at least as intransigent as that of Northern
Ireland.
    Grappling with this problem has brought many Belgians

to a realisation that the nation-state is not the ultimate in political development. Recent events throughout Europe suggest that assimilationist or integrative nation-building policies, despite having been often quite brutal and coercive, have in the long-run frequently failed,[3] and other solutions, of a pluralistic or federal nature, must therefore be sought.[4]

As a result, Belgium sees its future in a true "unity in diversity", where localities and regions retain their individuality within a united (though not necessarily unitary) Belgium, which is itself part of a united Europe. It seems to the outside observer more future-orientated than most European countries and seems to see itself fairly clearly entering what Alvin Toffler has called the "Third Wave" of civilisation.[5]

Certain "Third Wave" characteristics, such as that of "demassifying" society,[6] are particularly noticeable in the educational system because, although centrally controlled, it is already divided and duplicated along a number of lines:
3 types of controlling body: State, province/commune, private;
3 language divisions: French, Dutch, German;
4 religious divisions: confessional, non-confessional, neutral, pluralist;
2 pedagogical divisions: "traditional", "Rénové".
Even if we leave out the further complication of Brussels, this means that there are theoretically 72 different possible types of school, and thus 72 different ways of meeting a local need - a good start in the process of "demassifying" mass education.

WHAT SHOULD EDUCATION TRY TO DO?

Since the Second World War increasing demands for mass education have everywhere widened the gap between those who want and value education and those who wish to leave school as soon as possible. But it has also made scholastic failure intolerable, since the inability to express oneself or to write or think effectively creates serious obstacles for the citizen. The teacher, therefore, "is being asked to succeed where society, with its social inequality, fails".[7]

The demands of religious, racial, ethnic, linguistic and economic minorities have made it clear that a single scale of commonly held values no longer exists. In recent years the values of the mass media, recognised by the Belgians as a "parallel curriculum", have become salient. With the emergence of the pluralistic society has come the recognition that education is too important to be left to the schools alone. Parents, local communities, social service organisations and employers must all become involved.

In Belgium educational thinking has inevitably been strongly influenced by educational thinking elsewhere,

116

especially in France, Britain, and, through strong links at
the university level, in the U.S.A. But the biggest
influences have undoubtedly been those associated with
supranational and international organisations: Bertrand
Schwartz's L'éducation demain, the European Cultural Foundation's Plan Europe 2000, UNESCO's Learning To Be[8], the ideas
expressed in many Council of Europe publications on the
importance of "authenticity" and the full development of the
individual, and the work of the OECD.[9]

For the Belgian educator, then, education should provide
all children with the intellectual, physical and social means
to develop into happy, autonomous individuals who will take
the future into their own hands, and not only welcome, but
guide and change it. It will do this, without interfering,
whenever required throughout the person's life.

"Henceforward", we are told in a publication issued by
the Belgian Government for the information of parents of
primary school children, "we are no longer concerned with
the teacher revealing to the child a world regarded as given,
with which he should establish stable relationships; but with
acting in such a way that he explores it, conquers it, makes
it, and, in the end, in making it, makes himself".[10]

The basic concepts believed to contribute towards the
"flowering" of the individual at this stage are creativity,
freedom with responsibility, commitment, flexibility of mind,
and the ability to see things from another's point of view.[11]

With these concepts in mind, "Primary education takes
place when each pupil, under the benevolent and attentive
eye of the teacher, takes his own situation in hand and
progressively masters the set of relationships in and around
himself. Primary education is at once a first introduction
to cultural goods and the first conscious production of
cultural goods; this double step serves the development in
all its forms of a balanced being open to social and human
growth.[12]

The avowed aims of secondary education, expressed in
another official document, Aux Parents[13], are as follows:
To make school a welcoming environment, where the child feels
happy;
To allow each child to go as far as he wants and as far as he
can;
To relate school to life and life to school;
To encourage the achievement of autonomy and the development
of a sense of responsibility and a social sense.

These aims clearly build on those of the primary school
with the additional awareness that the adult world, the
world of work and civic responsibility, is coming closer.

WHAT SORT OF EDUCATIONAL SYSTEM WOULD ACHIEVE THESE ENDS?

Considerations of space and the complexity of the system obviously do not permit a very detailed examination of the reforms undertaken or envisaged by the Belgian education authorities, but some general observations must be made.

BASIC SCHOOL

Pre-school and primary education since the 1930s has been organised on lines suggested by Froebel and Decroly, and the pre-compulsory stage is the most extensive in the world. It has generally been thought of as a series of age-groups corresponding to developmental stages. From $2\frac{1}{2}$ to 5 the aim was to awaken the child's senses through games, songs and dances. The second stage, from 5 to 8, aimed to act as a weaning period between the "école des petits" and the "grande école ou l'on fait des choses sérieuses"[14], which formed the third stage from 8 to 12.

About 1971 considerable concern began to be expressed about what was actually happening. Some 40% to 45% of primary pupils had to repeat a year at some point, and one in five failed first year primary. A Ministerial Circular issued on 21 June, 1971 outlined the underlying philosophy described in the previous section and gave directives for the reform of basic education.

Fundamentally, the aim was to make school from $2\frac{1}{2}$ to 12 a continuous and progressive learning experience. Classes in which a single teacher lavished the same education uniformly on all the pupils were to disappear. Indeed, separate nursery and primary schools were to give way to "complete" basic schools covering the whole age range, and a government project of 1978 prohibited the setting-up or maintenance of any new separate nursery or primary schools from 1 September, 1981.[15]

Teachers were to form a team, led by the head teacher, which would work in co-operation with parents and Psycho-medical-social Centres.[16] The approach to the children would be in two directions:

1. Individualisation, aimed at encouraging and supporting progress, and concerned with identifying and helping with problems and shortcomings;

2. Socialisation, aimed at producing a growing awareness of the society in which he lives. "The extension of social contacts reveals to the child images of the adult different from those he knows in his restricted school circle. And progressively, by confrontation with these varied groups, the child builds for himself a personal frame of reference

118

which helps him to direct his behaviour".[17]

The structure of the basic school is flexible. For some purposes vertical groupings (i.e. "family groupings") are used; for others, "synthesis groups", based on level of maturity rather than age. There are also workshop groups, which carry out projects jointly decided.

Teachers are expected to develop in their pupils the skills of curiosity and imagination, logical, divergent and lateral thinking, evaluation, and work organisation.

SECONDARY SCHOOL

Reform and change in the secondary school has taken place over a long period. The first barrier in the vertically-divided tripartite system to be removed disappeared in 1947. Up to then a pupil had been required to spend the entire six years of secondary school in the same section in order to receive his final certificate at 18. The new legislation reduced this requirement to the last three years (i.e. upper secondary) which immediately introduced the possibility of a change of direction into the lower secondary stage. This possibility was enhanced in some general schools, known as multilateral schools, when technical sections were added to those already existing.

At about the same time research by the Psycho-social Centres, which had been set up in 1945, indicated that vocational interest tests given at 12 years old were 80% invalid by the time the pupils were 18; those given at 15 remained 80% valid at 18. The introduction of some means of delaying choice was strongly indicated.[18]

As further barriers were removed by the laws of 10 April, 1958 and 8 June, 1964,the medical service was combined with the Psycho-social Centres to form the Psycho-medical-social, or PMS, Centres, among whose functions was the advising of parents and pupils on all matters of educational and vocational choice. At the same time various experiments were conducted, inspired by the French "classes nouvelles", with the object of improving relationships between pupils and school.

Studies continued to show that many pupils were mis-placed; even after parents were allowed to choose the type of secondary school: general, technical, or vocational. It appeared that most middle-class parents chose general and most working-class parents chose technical or vocational, regardless of the aptitudes of the children. Expansion of the PMS Centre network improved this situation so that by the late 1960s almost all parents to whom advice was available were following it.

Another response to the misplacement of pupils was the Guidance Course. This was introduced into some schools as

an experiment in 1957 and became obligatory in all new
general schools opened after 1 September, 1963 and all new
technical schools from 1 September, 1964. The main objects
were to avoid premature choice and to ensure that when choice
was made, it was made from an informed position. The
Guidance Course had a "tronc commun" of 30 'hours'[19] for the
first two years and 25 'hours' for the third. Six 'hours'
were devoted to an option chosen from courses corresponding
to the choices available in general, technical, or vocational schools.

A recent development is the "école rénovée", known
officially as Type 1 secondary, which owes its general shape
to the Langevin proposals of the 1940s, and whose aims have
been outlined in the previous section.[20]

Introduced experimentally in 1969 into 24 schools, by
1971 the number which opted to change to Type 1 had increased
to 247. In January 1976 it was decided to make all State
secondary schools Type 1 by 1978-1979 at the latest, but by
1977-78 the French sector had changed only 56% of them.
Figures for Dutch-sector schools are not at present available
but by 1977-78 83% of pupils in State secondary schools were
in Type 1.[21]

Type 1 schools are organised in three stages of two
years each, devoted respectively to observation, orientation,
and determination. The observation stage is identical in
all Type 1 secondary schools. While giving a wide basic
training the aim is continuously to observe and evaluate the
aptitudes and behaviour of each child so as to help him
discover his potentialities and tastes in order to allow him
to choose the most fruitful direction in the orientation
stage. As well as 26 'hours' of common-core curriculum he
is expected to 'have a go' at music, art, Latin, technical
activities, and so on. Gradually, choice has to be made
between options. The choices are joint decisions of parents
and pupils, advised by the class council which consists
effectively of all those who teach or direct the group,
together with the local PMS group.

At the orientation stage secondary education in effect
divides into general, technical, artistic, or vocational
sections, which become progressively specialised in the
third, or determination, stage. At the end of each stage
a pupil either qualifies for the next stage or receives a
qualifying certificate for vocational purposes.

The whole operation of Type 1 secondary education is
conceived as a process in which schools, parents and PMS
Centres co-operate in bringing about the fullest possible
individual development of the pupil. More and more the
running of schools, within the framework laid down by the
State, is being carried out by those partners in a process
known as "gestion associative", or associative management.[22]

At its twelfth annual congress, in November 1980, FAPEO (Féd-
ération des Associations de Parents d'Elèves de l'Enseignement
Officiel) asked for gestion associative to be made obligatory
in all official schools.[23] It has existed in all State
primary and secondary schools in the Dutch-speaking sector
since 1 September, 1972.[24]

The latest development, from 1 September, 1981, is for
secondary schools to group into "Centres d'enseignement
secondaire" (C.E.S.), either to make better use of resources
or in order to create new options.[25] Any new Type 1 State
school must form part of a C.E.S., and no more Type 2 (traditional) schools will be set up, recognised, or subsidised.[26]

WHAT SORT OF TEACHERS ARE NEEDED TO OPERATE THE SYSTEM?

"The school is worth precisely what the teacher is worth and
for this reason an improvement in teacher education is a
first step in any educational reform".[27] Adolf Diesterweg
used these words in 1865, but King William had realised the
fact nearly fifty years earlier when he set up the first
teacher training college in Western Europe at Haarlem in
1816 and a second one at Lier the following year.[28] From
time to time in Belgium, as in most other countries, the
idea has been forgotten, but it was rediscovered in the
recent wave of reform.

The type of teacher produced by traditional methods, who
saw him- or her-self solely as a transmitter of culture, had
only a limited contribution to make to the 'new' education.
Indeed, in some cases, his presence was positively harmful.
In some basic schools the whole process of reform has been
negated by leaving out the parents, or by using the flexible
grouping opportunities to stream children.[29] In secondary
schools teachers who dislike or disapprove of mixed-ability
classes have observed the letter of the law rather than its
spirit regarding marks, examinations, class promotion, and
so on, and "clouaient au sol les élèves défavorisés".[30]

Certainly, to some extent, teachers in the new schools
need to know about new subjects, such as computer science,
modern mathematics, or linguistics. They need to know about
modern educational technology, the use of AVA and CCTV, and
some need to know about technological advance in the world
of work. This is not in itself an insurmountable problem,
or even, except in its scale, a new problem. There has
always been the necessity, or at least the desirability, of
keeping up-to-date with one's subject.

What is new, and difficult, is that the 'new' education
demands, in some cases and for some purposes at least, a
different kind of person. A Ministerial Circular of 11
April, 1973 tells us that the future primary school teacher
must be "a leader, a mind-awakener, a team leader, and a

121

model of emancipation".[31] If he is to lead others towards autonomy, he must himself be autonomous. If he is not to suppress or denigrate the creative or imaginative impulses of his pupils, he must be open-minded and not himself have fixed ideas about how the world is, or ought to be. He must be able to work in a team with other teachers and co-operate, when occasion demands, with psychologists, social workers and parents.

The secondary teacher must have similar characteristics and perhaps in addition should have a wider perception of the world at large, and especially the world of work, than is common among the traditionally trained teachers.

At higher education levels it is believed that in view of the growth of permanent education[32] teachers will be required in firms, social organisations, unions, and so on, as well as in the school system. More than 50% of graduate economics students at Antwerp University undergo teacher training, and a 1977 survey showed that 20% of those who became teachers did so outside the educational system.

Teachers at this level are expected to show "curriculum-proof" behaviour (i.e. adaptability to change), to be able to choose teaching strategies which correspond to the learning preferences of their pupils, and to know that teaching is not to be equated with explaining.[33]

HOW CAN THESE TEACHERS BE PRODUCED?

The proposals of the various international bodies regarding teacher education have progressively veered towards models of recurrent training within a context of widespread continuous education.[34] Belgium has naturally favoured this approach.

Traditionally, Belgian teachers have been produced by normal schools, recruiting at 15+ for teachers of levels up to the end of lower secondary, and by universities, recruiting at 18+, for upper secondary. Normal schools were, in fact, part of upper-secondary education. Since 1962 the tendency has been to separate teacher education from general education.[35] In 1967 primary training was increased to five years (two post-secondary) and secondary training became entirely post-secondary. From 1 September, 1974 all teacher training became post-secondary and part of higher education. All non-university teacher training is now the same length (two years post-secondary) and has much in common, whether it is for nursery, primary, or lower secondary school teachers. Unions are now demanding equal pay for equal training.

Contrary to expectations, the demand for an extension of the period of training has receded. This is explained by the proposition that since the educational situation is changing so rapidly it is more profitable to spend money on in-service training than on initial training.[36] A recent order (1979) doubling university fees stipulated that one third of those fees should be spent on research and organisation of in-service training for teachers.[37]

The changes which may be required of teachers fall into three categories: (a) changes in knowledge; (b) changes in skills; (c) changes in attitudes.

The problems of introducing innovations into educational systems have been widely researched, and research in Belgium itself, as well as elsewhere, has shown that, whatever teacher training does that is new, conservative forces in the school tend to negate it.[38] Some of the difficulties which have been encountered in practice have already been mentioned.

One Belgian researcher, Professor de Landsheere of the University of Liège, takes an extremely pessimistic view of the possibility of innovation. Throughout history, he claims, man has striven for stability and immobility. "The transition to a dynamic civilisation has been accompanied by a cultural crisis so acute that it is not even certain that our civilisation will be able to survive the shock. In any event it seems pointless to attempt, over a very short period, to change mentalities, attitudes and Weltanschauungen which have been developed over thousands of years".[39]

Probably de Landsheere both overrates the stable nature of the past and underrates man's capacity for change. As Buxton Forman has commented, history was largely written by the immobile but made by the mobile. Moreover, systems theory suggests that where a positive feedback loop exists, very extensive changes may be brought about in a very short time[40] and the work of Ilya Prigogine and others at the University of Brussels suggests that causation in non-mechanical systems, including human societies, is much more complex than previously thought.[41]

Belgian teachers have, in fact, shown themselves more willing to change than one might have supposed. A 1975 survey[42] indicated that most of them accepted the principle of continuous retraining; 8 out of 10 expressed a willingness to retrain and 2 out of 3 had already undergone retraining courses of some sort.[43] Further questions, however, revealed that, if given a sabbatical year, 41% would use it to improve their knowledge of the subject they taught, 25% to improve their general culture, 18% to learn more about the social sciences, and only 12% to improve their pedagogical knowledge.[44]

It seems that changing knowledge and skills is no great problem, in that one is likely to have the co-operation of those who are to be changed. Initial training courses have been modified accordingly, and extensive in-service courses have been provided in such areas as modern mathematics,

computer science, linguistics, AVA, and so on. All courses
are voluntary, since it was found that retraining had the
least effect on those who undertook it with feelings of
compulsion or restraint[45], but inducements are offered in
the form of a reduced teaching load for those attending
such courses.

It will be clear, however, that the Belgian view of the
future, in the creation of which education will play a key
part, demands new attitudes.[46] Much effort has therefore
been concentrated on this aspect of both initial and in-
service training by State and Catholic education authorities
alike.

The approach has been largely through various aspects
of group dynamics and social psychology. T-groups are
extensively used with the object of bringing about new and
changed perceptions and attitudes in teaching-learning
relationships through authentic communication. Discussions
on power and authority are held; authority being understood
in its etymological sense as arising from auctor, one who
creates, who causes to progress; and power understood as
"frequently nothing more than constraint and the preservation
of older unchangeable and reassuring ways".[47]

Great emphasis is placed on the affective life of
groups and group-work methods "such as Philipps 6/6, round-
table, beehive, working group - resonance group, discussion
group, panel, think tank, as well as creative problem-
solving techniques" are all brought into play.[48]

It is important to note that these courses are directed
not only at classroom teachers but also at principals,
inspectors, administrators and training college lecturers.
The one great gap in all this reform is with respect to the
licenciés-agrégés, the products of university teacher-
training, whom Breuse describes as "notoriously ill-
trained".[49] The existing legislation on teacher-training
in universities, as Rigaux has pointed out, dates from 1929
and is in urgent need of revision; but the reforms so far
proposed are concerned almost entirely with improving teacher
effectiveness rather than with changing the sort of teacher
produced.[50]

Three features of the reform programme are of particular
interest in that they are designed to avoid some of the
pitfalls encountered by innovations elsewhere. The first is
that the design of the retraining courses has been carried
out, not simply by specialists, but by teams of teachers,
including teachers from levels other than those for whom
the courses are intended, teachers from practice schools,
lecturers from teacher training colleges, and, in the case
of secondary courses, representatives of the Office Belge
pour l'Accroissement de la Productivité.[51] It is hoped
thus to avoid the problems of schools negating the work of

124

colleges, secondary schools negating the work of primary schools, industry negating the work of secondary schools, and so on.

The second feature is that teacher trainers and inspectors are included in those who need retraining. This, again, should reduce conflicts within the system.

The third, and perhaps in the long term most important feature is the encouragement of those who have been retrained to become, not only their own educators, but animateurs who will encourage, and even organise, retraining for their colleagues. This might well prove to be the positive feed-back loop which will turn the potential failure inherent in all educational innovation into potential success.

Whether this will in fact be the case, it is yet too early to say. But a study published in 1978[52] indicated that there were already detectable differences, in what might be regarded as desirable directions, between those children who were educated in the 'new' schools and those educated traditionally.

SUMMARY

Shifts in European educational thinking have had the effect of changing the emphasis from teaching to learning and from effectiveness (how to convey facts, skills, and so on more efficiently) to emancipation (how to produce citizens who can discover, analyse and synthesise for themselves).[53]

Compared with her Common Market neighbours Belgium has enjoyed certain advantages which have helped her to adapt to these shifts. Throughout its history, Belgian education has had to accommodate many conflicting demands within a State-controlled system, and the result is thus extremely flexible, especially from the pupil's point of view. The gradual development of an independent guidance system through the PMS Centres has resulted in an informed parental involve-ment for which it is hard to find parallels. Thirdly, for various complex reasons, Belgium had no shortage of teachers even during the boom years of the late 1960s. "La classe surpeuplée n'existe donc pas," wrote Mertens in 1969.[54] This, added to the policy of using the surplus of teachers in recent years to reduce class sizes even further, has made in-service training on a large scale possible.

In teacher training itself the most important shift in priorities has been that which has altered the emphasis from what a teacher knows towards what sort of a person he is. In future his base must be authority rather than power, he must be a facilitator of learning situations rather than a manipulator, be relativist rather than absolutist, work within networks rather than hierarchies, and think in terms of co-operation rather than competition.

The pious hopes are familiar. There is plenty of
criticism of the new schools, not least from the pupils
themselves. But, as Pirson-de Clercq has pointed out, the
criticism is "very frequently both highly relevant and
extremely sound", and may thus be regarded as a sign that
the schools are succeeding in at least one essential aim,
that of producing an environment where critical and
analytical attitudes can flourish freely.[55] And if, as the
Violon and Skinkel study[56] has suggested, the new schools
are also indeed producing citizens who are more passionately
devoted to freedom, more concerned about the inequalities of
the world, more tolerant, more flexible, and less concerned
with material possessions than those produced by the old
schools, then perhaps at least some of the hopes may be
realised.

NOTES

1.   Alvin Toffler, The Third Wave, London, Pan Books,
1981, p. 367. Although not referred to in detail in this
essay, Toffler's contention that industrial, or Second Wave,
society is rapidly becoming unworkable, and that we are
heading towards a new civilisation, as different from the
present one as that was from the agricultural society which
preceded it, is assumed to be substantially correct.
Practopia, not a perfect but a workable society, is seen as
a possible goal which we might achieve if we point our
efforts, including our educational efforts, in the right
direction.
2.   Renee C. Fox, "Why Belgium?", Archives Européennes
de Sociologie, Volume XIX, number 2, 1978, p. 227.
3.   The literature on this subject is vast, but see,
for instance, Cynthia H. Enloe, Ethnic Conflict and Political
Development, Boston, Little, Brown, 1973.
4.   Martin O. Heisler, "Managing Ethnic Conflict in
Belgium", Annals of the American Academy of Political and
Social Science, Volume 443, September 1977, pp. 32-46,
provides an excellent summary.
5.   Alvin Toffler, op. cit., passim.
6.   ibid., especially Chapter 13.
7.   Mario Reguzzoni, "European Innovations in Teachers'
In-Service Training", in Donald E. Lomax (ed); European
Perspectives in Teacher Education, London, John Wiley, 1976,
p. 162.
8.   Bertrand Schwartz, L'éducation demain, Une étude
de la Fondation Européenne de la Culture, Paris, Aubier
Montaigne, 1973; European Cultural Foundation, Plan Europe
2000, The Hague, Martinus Nijhoff, 1974; Edgar Faure et al.,
Learning to Be: The world of education today and tomorrow,
Paris, UNESCO, 1972.

9. Mario Reguzzoni, op. cit., gives a useful summary of OECD and Council of Europe views on teacher education.

10. Ministère de l'Education Nationale et de la Culture Française, Eduquer pour le monde de demain: la renovation de l'enseignement primaire, Bruxelles, M.E.N.C.F., 1973, p. 5. N.B. Translations of this and other texts are by the present writer.

11. ibid., p. 10.

12. ibid., p. 16.

13. Ministère de l'Education Nationale et de la Culture Française, Aux Parents, Bruxelles, M.E.N.C.F., 3rd edn., 1978, pp. 7-10.

14. Council of Europe, "Belgique: Réforme de l'enseignement primaire", Newsletter Faits Nouveaux, 3/78, Strasbourg, Documentation Centre for Education in Europe, 1978, p. 7.

15. Council of Europe, "Belgique: Projet de rationalisation et de programmation de l'enseignement fondamental", Newsletter Faits Nouveaux 2/78, Strasbourg, Documentation Centre for Education in Europe, 1978, p. 8.

16. The Psycho-medical-social, or PMS, Centres are a unique feature of the Belgian educational scene. They combine many of the services offered in other countries into an integrated whole, independent of the schools.

17. Joseph Michel, Education Minister, in a document dated 15 June 1978, reported in Council of Europe 3/78, op. cit., p. 8.

18. Yves Roger, "L'enseignement «rénové»", Les Amis de Sèvres, No. 81/1, March 1976, p. 76.

19. The period referred to as "une heure" in Belgian timetables, is of fifty minutes' duration.

20. For full details see Organisation des Etudes, L'enseignement secondaire rénové: organisation générale, Series 'Faire le point sur ...', Bruxelles, M.E.N.C.F., 2nd edn., 1978.

21. Calculated from statistics published by the Ministère de l'éducation nationale et de la culture française and the Ministerie van nationale opvoeding en nederlandse cultuur.

22. For details see Organisation des Etudes, La Gestion Associative, Series 'Faire le point sur ...', Bruxelles, M.E.N.C.F., 1974.

23. Council of Europe, "Belgique: Politique de l'éducation et parents d'élèves", Newsletter Faits Nouveaux 5/80, Strasbourg, Documentation Centre for Education in Europe, 1980, p. 9.

24. Edouard Breuse, "Belgium: Experiments in Continuing Teacher Training", New Patterns of Teacher Education and Tasks. Country Experience: Belgium, France, United Kingdom, Paris, OECD, 1974, p. 13.

25. Council of Europe, "Belgique: Création de Centres

d'Enseignement Secondaire", Newsletter Faits Nouveaux 1/81, Strasbourg, Documentation Centre for Education in Europe, 1981, pp. 7-8.

26. Council of Europe, "Belgique: Plan de rationalisation de l'enseignement secondaire", Newsletter Faits Nouveaux 3/80, Strasbourg, Documentation Centre for Education in Europe, 1980, pp. 8-9.

27. Quoted in: Wolfgang Mitter, Educational Research and Teacher Education in the Perspective of Comparative Education, Frankfurt am Main, German Institute for International Educational Research, 1979, p. 38.

28. Vernon Mallinson, Power and Politics in Belgian Education, 1815-1961, London, Heinemann, 1963, p. 20.

29. Council of Europe 3/78, op. cit., p. 8.

30. Yves Roger, op. cit., p. 78.

31. Edouard Breuse, op. cit., p. 11.

32. Belgium has one of the most extensive permanent education systems in Europe and the law of 10th April 1973 allows workers, within certain limits, to take educational leave without any loss of wages. For details, see Commission of the European Communities, Educational Leave in Member States, Social Policy Series No. 26, Brussels, 1975.

33. See J. van Daele's report in Gordon H. Bell, Developing Teacher Education in the European Community: A Case Study, Department of Educational Studies, Teesside Polytechnic, 2nd edn., 1980, and J. van Daele, "Teacher Training in Economics: A Flemish Belgian View", in Raymond Ryba and Brian Robinson (eds), Aspects of Upper Secondary Economics Education in E.E.C. Countries, London, Economics Association of Great Britain, 1977, pp. 143-150.

34. Mario Reguzzoni, op. cit., p. 161.

35. Sylvain de Coster, "The Historical Development of Teacher Training in Belgium", G.Z.F. Bereday and J.A. Lauwerys (eds), The Education and Training of Teachers, The Year Book of Education 1963, London, Evans Bros., 1963, p. 233.

36. Edouard Breuse, op. cit., p. 7.

37. Gordon H. Bell, op. cit., p. 16.

38. Gilbert de Landsheere and E. Bayer, Comment les maîtres enseignent. Analyse des interactions verbales en classe, Series 'Documentation', Bruxelles, M.E.N.C.F., 3rd edn., 1974.

39. Gilbert de Landsheere, "The Causes of the Resistance of Teachers to Innovation" in OECD, The Teacher and Educational Change: A New Role, Paris, OECD, 1974, Volume 1, p. 357.

40. See, for instance, Ervin Laszlo, The Systems View of the World: The Natural Philosophy of the New Developments in the Sciences, Oxford, Blackwell, 1972.

41. See G. Nicolis and Ilya Prigogine, Self-Organisation

in Non-equilibrium Systems: From Dissipative Structures to Order Through Fluctuations, New York, John Wiley, 1977.

42. M.L. Digneffe, G. Leroy, A. Roosen and J. Therer, Enquête sur la Formation Professionelle Continue des Enseignants du Secondaire, Series 'Recherche en Education', Bruxelles, M.E.N.C.F., 1975.

43. ibid., p. 156.

44. ibid., p. 159.

45. Edouard Breuse, op. cit., p. 17.

46. OECD, The Teacher and Educational Change: A New Role, Paris, OECD, 1974, Volume 1, p. 16, lists many of these new attitudes, and Douglas A. Pidgeon's chapter, "The Implications of Teachers' Attitudes for the Reform of Teacher Training", pp. 361-394, makes a detailed examination of the research in this field.

47. Edouard Breuse, op. cit., passim.

48. ibid., p. 14.

49. ibid., p. 7.

50. H. Rigaux, "The Future Education of Teachers at the Belgian Universities", in Donald E. Lomax (ed), European Perspectives in Teacher Education, London, John Wiley, 1976, pp. 91-110.

51. OBAP, the Belgian Productivity Office, is a private establishment managed jointly by the State, The Federation of Belgian Industries, and the trade unions.

52. Jacques Violon and Raymond Skinkel, Opinions et attitudes des jeunes sortis de l'enseignement secondaire rénové en 1975 et en 1976, Bruxelles, M.E.N.C.F., 1978.

53. See Mario Reguzzoni, op. cit., especially pp. 167-169 on the Bristol Symposium of April 1973.

54. J. Mertens (ed), L'Emploi de la radio et de la télévision dans la formation des maitres, (Etudes Pedagogiques Internationales 25), Hamburg, Institut de l'Unesco pour l'Education, 1969, p. 17.

55. Jacqueline Pirson-de Clercq, "The Qualification Stage of the New Secondary Education in Belgium: a sociologically based evaluation", European Journal of Education, Volume 15, number 2, 1980, p. 159.

56. J. Violon and R. Skinkel, op. cit., p. 13 and passim.

PREPARING FOR NEW FUTURES: PERSONALIZED TEACHER EDUCATION IN BRITISH COLUMBIA

Anne MacLaughlin and Peter Murphy

INTRODUCTION

Over a century ago, the British North American Act delegated to provincial governments the responsibility for financing, co-ordinating, and regulating public education systems. Due to the physical geography and cultural diversity of the nation, this legislation was considered essential for protecting the educational rights of minority groups and ensuring that an appropriate standard of education was maintained throughout the nation.

The governance of education was further decentralized by provincial governments establishing local school districts. Initially, there was a multitude of these educational systems. However, economic factors, as well as educational issues, have significantly reduced the number of districts over the past three decades.

Recently, legislation, in many provinces, has further decentralized the governance of public education by allowing school boards to recruit their own superintendents. Previously, these executive officers were civil servants who reported to the Minister of Education. These administrators are now employees of the local school board. The full impact of this change, on the public education system, has yet to be assessed.

Similarly, the development of curricula was significantly decentralized in the early 1960s. As a result of more children remaining in school for a longer period of time, curricula had to be modified. School districts were permitted to develop local courses; a policy which the Ministry of Education believed would enable schools to better satisfy the educational needs of the communities they served.

Concurrently, teachers were lobbying the Minister of Education, through the British Columbia Teachers Federation, for more control over the learning environment. In response to this political pressure, procedures were established so

130

teachers could be involved in curriculum development at both the local and provincial levels. With one policy, the Ministry of Education was able to satisfy teachers' demands for greater autonomy and to offer children a greater diversity of learning experiences.

Within a decade, parents were expressing concerns that a uniform standard of education was no longer available throughout the province. A series of investigations, which examined the scholastic achievements of students, appeared to substantiate that significant differences in performance existed from one school to another.

A 'core' curriculum was introduced into the public school system to improve the quality of education and to ensure 'basic' subjects were the focus of instruction. The establishment of a Learning Assessment Branch, for monitoring students' achievements, provided the provincial government with an agency for exercising its regulatory power over the learning process.

During the 1980s the local appoint of superintendents and more prescriptive curricula are going to have a substantial impact on classroom teachers. However, these are only two of numerous dynamic forces influencing how they perform their professional duties.

In the 1950s, when public school systems were relatively simple social service agencies, school teachers performed well-prescribed roles, rarely had their authority challenged and viewed teaching as a lifetime career. The systems teachers now serve are complex, political organizations endeavouring to effectively respond to the needs of an ever-changing environment. These conditions place tremendous demands on teachers. Therefore, it is not surprising that many of them are experiencing serious health problems.

Three decades ago, teacher training programmes were limited in scope, of short-term duration and primarily concerned with preparing students for appointments in elementary schools. Furthermore, all students, irrespective of their abilities, interests, and aspirations, were required to complete a similar programme of studies. This type of professional training is unsuitable for preparing teachers for the schools of the future.

Young adults, who are interested in joining the teaching profession, must be provided with a number of career preparation programmes which offer unique learning experiences. With appropriate guidance and counselling, a student can be assisted to select the programme which 'best fits' his/her career aspirations, special abilities, and general interests. By employing this personalized approach to teacher training, students are better prepared to cope with the challenges they will encounter in their first appointments.

131

This paper provides a brief description of several teacher training programmes, which are in operation or are being developed, at the University of Victoria, British Columbia, Canada. Due to limitations of time and space, the authors are unable to comment on the following teacher preparation programmes also offered by the University:

(1) The Native Indian Programme;
(2) The Bachelor of Education Programme;
(3) The Post-Degree Professional Programmes; and
(4) The Arbutus Project.

All these teacher preparation programmes are based on a philosophy of personalized professional growth. These programmes, due to the small number of students involved, are more expensive to operate than traditional teacher preparation programmes. However, students, faculty members, and practising teachers are very supportive of both ventures. A brief description of each programme is provided for the reader.

The Saanich Project

The most distinguished feature of the Saanich Project is that students are assigned to the staff of a specific school, in the Saanich School District, for a year. Under the direction of a practising teacher and faculty members, a student teaches one class in his/her teaching area full-time and assists in the teaching of one class in his/her second teaching area. At the end of each semester, a student's workload is changed so he/she can teach full-time the second subject area. As a member of staff, a student is expected to participate in extracurricular activities and assist senior colleagues to perform routine school duties.

During the school year, students are required to complete a number of professional courses. Several of these courses are taught, by faculty members, in one of the sponsoring schools. Students complete remaining course requirements during Summer Studies. Once course requirements are satisfied, students are eligible for certification by the British Columbia Ministry of Education. All students, who participate in this internship programme, receive $200.00 per month for any services they provide the Saanich School District.

The Secondary Internship Programme

The Secondary Internship Programme is designed for prospective secondary school teachers. All applicants must possess a degree (a B.Ed. degree) from a recognized university in

teaching areas appropriate to British Columbia secondary
schools. Admission is usually very competitive.

After being accepted for the programme, students are
required to attend a one-week orientation in the school
district. This provides the students with an opportunity
to meet sponsor teachers and principals, to visit schools,
to be informed of teaching assignments, and to become
familiar with the community in which they are going to work.
After this orientation, students complete four professional
courses during Summer Studies.

Early in September, students join the staff of the
schools where they are going to complete their internships.
Students cannot be involved in teaching for more than 50
per cent of the school day. The remaining time is devoted
to preparation, marking, discussions with sponsoring teachers
and observing senior teachers. Academic studies are tempor-
arily suspended in the internship phase. In most cases,
students spend five months of the internship at a junior
secondary school and three months at a senior secondary
school.

The course requirements for certification are completed,
after the internship, during Summer Studies. All students
receive $300.00 per month for the services they provide a
school district. Presented on Figure 1 is the total programme.

Comment

By exposing teachers in training to the realities of their
future careers, in a controlled situation, enables them to
eliminate a variety of weaknesses which characterize
beginning teachers. Upon joining the staff of a school,
graduates from these internship programmes can quickly
adjust to the demands of a regular teaching position. Not
only are they better prepared to teach, but possess a high
level of confidence in their own abilities.

There are now indications that an extended practicum
will become an integral component of many teacher preparation programmes in western Canada. Presently, the Ministry
of Education, Province of Alberta, the Alberta's Teachers'
Association, University of Calgary, and University of
Alberta are discussing the feasibility of all teachers in
training being required to complete an extended practicum.
The group formulating this policy are in general agreement
that students should spend a greater proportion of their
preparation period in the classroom.

At the Master's level, a six-month internship is now
available, on an experimental basis, to practising administrators who are interested in studying educational
administration. This intense, 14-month programme provides

133

graduate students with an opportunity to work with senior educational administrators. In the near future, the internship option will probably be available to practising teachers who are interested in studying other aspects of education at the graduate level.

RURAL TEACHERS PROGRAMME

Introduction

Rural school districts in British Columbia are continuously faced with the problem of a high rate of staff turnover. Every year senior administrators endeavour to recruit new teachers for their schools, a task which is expensive in terms of time, energy, and financial resources. Often the teachers hired are beginning their careers or are new Canadians from overseas. Both groups possess limited experience and knowledge of the British Columbia public education system. This situation, naturally, has an adverse impact on school climate, community-school relations, quality of education, and continuity of programmes. A similar phenomenon exists in metropolitan areas where teacher turnover is high in "down town" schools.

An unstable school staff has many long-term effects for regional growth and development. Parents are reluctant to remain in a community, if they are mobile, once they become aware that their children are being provided with an inferior quality of education. This intensifies the present trend of people to migrate to large urban centres.

Industrial development in northern regions is often hindered by shortages of skilled manpower. If local secondary schools are unable to offer a selection of career programmes, students move to communities where they can secure the education they desire. Few return to their 'home' towns to seek employment after graduation.

Existing teacher training programmes, at the University of Victoria, were obviously not adequately preparing students for teaching positions in rural communities. A team of researchers under the direction of Cross endeavoured to identify skills and characteristics needed by country school teachers.[1] Based on the findings of this investigation, a new preparation programme is being developed for students who are interested in teaching in rural areas and small school districts. The principal features of this programme are noted below.

The Elementary Rural Teacher Preparation Programme

The major objectives of this new programme are:
(1) To provide adequate rural experience and course

134

preparation for pre-service elementary teachers so that when accepting rural placement, they will do so with a realistic understanding of the rural community situation; and
(2) To provide small school districts and rural schools with more realistically trained beginning teachers who will seek rural placement and tend to remain longer in such placement.

Satisfying these objectives the high teacher turnover in rural educational systems should be substantially reduced.

All students, who are admitted into the programme, will complete the third and fourth years of their studies at the David Thompson University Centre. This institution, a satellite campus of the University of Victoria, is located nearly 500 miles from Victoria in the foothills of the Rocky Mountains. In the immediate proximity of the Centre are a number of small school districts with a variety of rural schools. Therefore, students will have access to excellent teaching practice positions.

As part of their programme of studies, these students must: (1) have instructional experience in a multigrade class; (2) be involved in extra-curricula activities; (3) teach both at the primary and intermediate levels; (4) receive career counselling from staff of participating districts; and (5) participate in community activities.

Comment

The majority of vacancies for teachers are presently, and will continue in the future, to be in rural school districts. Staff turnover is high, due to teachers being inadequately prepared for professional responsibilities in a rural setting. The future development of northern and interior regions of British Columbia is going to be dependent upon the adequacy of manpower resources available to local industries. Therefore, it is imperative that rural schools are staffed by competent teachers who are willing to remain in these schools for several years. This will enable senior administrators to organize school programmes so they better satisfy local educational and manpower needs.

EXCHANGE PROGRAMMES

The modulations in the governance of education, reported for British Columbia, have occurred, at different rates and magnitudes, in other provinces of Canada. Consequently, differences among public education systems have increased over the past decade.

The public schools of Canada are becoming characterized by a degree of uniqueness, in terms of educational philosophy, learning experiences, and curricula, which is frequently a surprise to a visiting foreign educator.

National Exchange Programme

Recently, the Faculty of Education, University of Victoria, received a grant, from the Canadian International Bureau of Education, to establish a teacher-in-training exchange programme. Students from the University of Western Ontario will fly to British Columbia for a two-week teaching practice. Professional, social, and cultural activities are planned to acquaint these students with the public education system of the province. Visiting students will reside with their exchange partners. This arrangement enables students to establish bonds of friendship as well as becoming familiar with the socio-economic culture of each other's region.

Early in April, students from the University of Victoria will visit London, Ontario, as part of the exchange agreement. The primary focus of this visit will be professional enrichment. The students will teach in local schools, participate in professional seminars, and visit cultural centres. All participants in this exchange programme are preparing for teaching positions in elementary schools.

Presently, the University of Victoria is negotiating with the Canadian International Bureau of Education to form a similar exchange programme with the University of Manitoba for secondary students. If both these pilot projects are successful, a proposal will be submitted to the Ministry of Education for funds to establish this exchange option as an integral part of the University of Victoria's teacher preparation programme.

International Exchange Programmes

Advances in telecommunication systems are bringing into existence the concept of the world being a global village. Reports on important issues are transmitted, at a very rapid rate by television, radio, and satellite, from one socio-cultural setting to another. This information often has a significant impact on a local populace. Furthermore, political conflicts, in the international arena, directly impinge on the economic climate of many nations.

If school systems are to effectively respond to the dynamic forces of a complex, industrialized world, practising teachers must widen their horizons. This can be partially achieved by modifying existing teacher preparation programmes.

The Faculty of Education, University of Victoria, is seriously examining the feasibility of establishing, as an experimental project, an international exchange programme for teachers-in-training. Students preparing for teaching

136

positions, at both the elementary and secondary levels, will be provided with opportunities to visit either a developed industrial state or a developing nation. The national exchange programmes would serve as the base for these international ventures.

A two-year exchange programme is similarly being developed for practising educational administrators. This programme is designed to enhance the professional growth and to enrich the personal lives of the educators who participate in the exchange programme. Educational administrators must be offered new professional development programmes if they are to continue providing educational systems with effective, dynamic leadership.

Comment

The world in which we live is becoming more complex as nations increasingly depend upon each other for survival. The global village is quickly emerging as a reality which many people have yet to accept. In the next two decades, teachers are going to play a greater role in assisting people to adjust to an ever-changing environment. The exchange programmes, under discussion, will sensitize a small group of future teachers to the social, political, economic, and cultural diversity existing in our world.

CONCLUSION

As our society becomes more complex and technologically oriented, school systems are accepting a greater degree of responsibility for shaping the future of the nation. The expansion and diversification of programmes reflects this trend. At the 1980 Annual Conference of the Canadian Education Association a debate was held on the purpose of education: the topic - "Resolved that schools of the 1980s must broaden their mandate to address the problems of the community, the country and the World". Over two-thirds of the 400 delegates who voted on the issue supported the affirmative speaker.

If the delegates, who attended the C.E.A. Conference, were representative of educators across Canada then schools, over the next two decades, can be expected to widen their sphere of influence. There appears to be a general consensus that school systems must provide learning exper- iences which will assist children, upon reaching adulthood, to cope with the demands of an ever-changing environment, to effectively utilize increased leisure time, to fund productive employment and to function as responsible citizens. New missions will emerge and existing priorities altered to accommodate the changing focus of education.

137

Schools of tomorrow will undoubtedly differ from those of today. The consequences of changing societal forces will have a significant impact on the services, programmes, and learning experiences they provide. Similarly, the role of the teacher will undergo substantive change. According to Anderson, teachers in the future

> ... will expect their job to be of relative short duration, they will anticipate changes in both substantive content and method of presentation, and they will anticipate changes in the composition of the "teaching profession".[2]

Also, he maintained that teachers will become more responsible for the total development of a child. Perhaps, the situation can best be summarized by the fact that the term 'educator' is beginning to gradually replace that of 'teacher' as a more appropriate description of the primary role performed by members of the profession.[3]

Preliminary deliberations on the future suggest that teachers of tomorrow must be flexible, mature, knowledgeable, and skilful, if they are to effectively cope with the contingencies of a complex, industrial state. Also, Harrison[4] proposes that teachers must be more aware of the socio-political consequences of specific actions than their colleagues of today. Teacher preparation programmes must regularly be modified and revised to accommodate the changing needs of teachers. At the University of Victoria, students are presently offered a number of career paths which provide alternative learning experiences. The students who graduate from these programmes, enter the teaching profession with enthusiasm, a high level of confidence, and a desire to teach children. What better attributes can young teachers possess at the beginning of their careers?

NOTES

1. William Cross, Helen Bandy and Norman Gleadow, The Identification of Skills and Characteristics Needed by Country School Teachers, Victoria, Faculty of Education, University of Victoria, British Columbia, 1980.

2. Barry D. Anderson, "Diversity in Teacher Education: a Rationale", in Ontario Teachers' Federation, Concepts in Teacher Education, Toronto, Ontario Teachers' Federation, 1971, p. 6.

3. Ronald J. Goldman, "A Concept for Teacher Education", in Ontario Teachers' Federation, Concepts in Teacher Education, Toronto, Ontario Teachers' Federation, 1971.

4. John L. Harrison, "A Concept for Teacher Education", in Ontario Teachers' Federation, Concepts in Teacher

Education, Toronto, Ontario Teachers' Federation, 1971.

IDEOLOGICAL TRENDS AND THE EDUCATION OF TEACHERS IN LATIN
AMERICA

Pilar Aguilar and Gonzalo Retamal

This paper focuses attention on the problem of the education
of teachers in Latin America, with particular reference to
the primary sector. It also deals with the problem of priorities which must be considered when relating the education
of teachers to challenges promoted by an underdeveloped and
dependent socio-economic context such as that evident in
Latin America. In recent years these priorities have been
determined from the outside and fused with ongoing traditions
of teacher education of Latin America. In order to underline
this point of view, the ideological evolution and political
trends attached to the Latin American tradition of Normal
Schools and the education of prospective primary teachers is
analysed in detail. This is partly to demonstrate the
existence of a tradition, and partly to demonstrate the
assertion that even such a long standing tradition has been
overruled by a decision-making structure which does not share
its values or its historical contribution. This recent and
widespread policy orientation has been effected on the basis
of combatting a supposedly alien and invading ideology of
"modernisation". This shift of priorities in the education
of teachers in Latin America cannot be considered as a
purely technical decision, regardless of the existent
historical and ideological traditions. Such a technical
view would conform to an ideological pattern which in the
name of "modernisation" plays the role of cultural invasion.[1]
     The theme of changing priorities in teacher education,
when applied to the Latin American context, does not necessarily carry the same positive connotation as may be
generally applied in a developed industrial society. In most
of Latin America teacher education is either still frozen in
the grip of inertia or is subject to external pressures
which, though involving "modernisation" do not necessarily
assist a process of structural development. Such a process
is absolutely necessary for most Latin American countries to
effect their detachment from dependency: a vital first step

towards genuine development.

However, the persistence of anomie is not a constant feature of the Latin American educational sphere. It has been partially overcome at different moments, under particular historical circumstances, within the framework of populist or revolutionary change. Illustrative of such processes of re-awakening are the developments in Chile between 1970 and 1973, the case of the Peruvian Educational Reform between 1964 and 1975, and the more contemporary cases of the Cuban and the Nicaraguan revolution. Within the tide of such events the education of teachers has played an important role in leadership formation and political engagement.

Nonetheless, it should be said that the present political situation of most Latin American societies, under the severe control of conservative military governments, constitutes a dominant framework in the light of which the actual developments of teacher education should be understood and evaluated. Perhaps, the most important consequence emerging from this situation is that official priorities for programmes of teacher education and training are dictated from above, and thus, very little participation is permitted to teachers at any significant decision-curbing level. Consequently, in order to assess the real needs and priorities of Latin American teacher education it is necessary to examine the deep-rooted and persistent characteristics of the ideologies behind the different programmes and trends. This will necessarily involve an historical survey in order to identify the basic elements of a radical tradition which at present is in danger of extinction.

During the colonial period of Latin American history elementary education was limited to some Catholic sponsored schools whose importance was minimal. The teaching profession was in the hands of friars, and mostly orientated to the education of a minority sector of society, namely the upper criollo[2] class.

Most Latin American countries attained their independence by 1825 under conditions of fierce struggle against the Spanish Crown, and under the influence in most cases of the ideas of the French Revolution and other European liberal trends. However, as has been pointed out by Davies[3], the ideas of popular sovereignty, equality, fraternity and liberty were, to a certain extent perceived by criollo landowners and merchants as a threat to their inherited colonial privileges. It is in this context that the political swing towards conservatism, observed around the third decade of the century, should be considered. The radical ideas of the Libertadores, such as Bolivar, San Martin, Morazan and O'Higgins, were misappropriated and redeveloped in a less forceful manner when merchants and

141

landowners regained the domination of the State. Nevertheless, one element which was built up during the revolutionary
period was deeply rooted in the ideology of the dominant
Liberal elite of Latin America: "that the changes had to be
effected through the minds of the individuals and that the
natural means to achieve this was education".[4]

It was precisely during the first decades of the nineteenth century that this belief flourished. The Libertadores
inherited a distressing situation of intellectual poverty
and began looking forward to the betterment of conditions of
schooling able to provide the children with at least the
rudiments of education. The educational thought and experiences of Joseph Lancaster made a deep impression on the
Latin American leadership of the day. Lancaster was invited
to Colombia by Simon Bolivar and created the first network
of Republican elementary schools. The training of local
monitors, a very important feature in the mutual education
system of Lancaster, could be considered as the original
step towards teacher training in Latin America.

Similar educational schemes were laid down by the
missionary work of James Thomson who, under the sponsorship
of The British and Foreign School Society, took upon himself
the responsibility of spreading the reading of the Bible,
throughout Latin America, as well as popularising the
Lancaster system of education in the new Republics. Between
1818 and 1837 he travelled widely throughout the Americas,
enjoyed the enthusiastic reception of all the governments
visited, and energetically built up the basis of modern
schooling in each country. Over 5,000 children attended the
Lancasterian schools of Buenos Aires within a year of his
arrival in 1818. His success was enormous in Chile where
Bernardo O'Higgins declared him an 'Illustrious Citizen'.
O'Higgins's faith in education as a prime fundamental tool
for the development of his country is typical of the
general feeling of that period in Latin America. The
Lancasterian system was expected to "extend throughout Chile
the benefits of education, to promote the instruction of all
classes but specially the poor".[5] However, it was in Peru
where Thomson improved the aspects concerning the training
of teachers for the Lancasterian schools.

As it was stated by Jose de San Martin in a special
decree concerning the development of the system:

> All the masters of the public schools shall attend the
> central school with two of their most advanced pupils
> in order to be instructed in the new system, and, in
> studying, they shall attend to the method prescribed
> by the director of the establishment.[6]

It was perhaps upon this experience that Thomson

developed his training scheme in Uruguay, Ecuador, Colombia, and finally perfected it in Mexico in 1822. A special central school for the training of Lancasterian Teachers was organised. La Escuela del Sol (The School of the Sun), of Mexico should be considered as the first serious attempt to lay down the blueprint of a Latin American teacher training scheme.

As was reported by Sr Rocafuerte, Mexican Chargé d'Affaires in London and later an active member of the Lancasterian society of Mexico, this school was not only orientated towards the instruction of children, but it also had two departments dedicated to the training of teachers:

> It is a model or central school for forming teachers and good professors who are afterward to be sent into the different provinces in order to fulfil the desire of the government which is to place in every village throughout Mexico a Lancasterian school, a printing press and a chapel.[7]

However, a certain decline of the activity of the Lancasterian schools by mid-century must be explained not merely by the pedagogical disadvantages of the system, but rather along the lines of a reaction towards some of the popular and liberal undertones which underlied the Lancasterian scheme. The political shift towards authoritarianism and conservatism by 1830-1850 must be considered to be at the root of the problem. Perhaps the revival of elementary education could therefore be traced from the 1850s in Chile and later in Argentina and Uruguay.

This Liberal rewakening was able to undertake, under the leadership of Sarmiento of Argentina and Varela of Uruguay, the development of state-sponsored education. Their educational thought was heavily influenced by the ideas of Horace Mann, but the social commitment was pervaded by the myth of 'Civilization or Barbarism' as the only possible choices for Latin American development. 'Civilization' was everything which came from Europe, while 'Barbarism' was rooted in the mixed Hispanic/Amerindian heritage and had to be eradicated from the country in order to bring in 'Civilization'. For Sarmiento two tools were fundamental to the achievement of progress: immigration of Europeans, and the propagation of European 'civilized' values through schooling. However, his first experiments were carried out while in exile in Chile where he was commissioned by the government to create the first Escuela Normal (Normal School) in Latin America in 1842.

As described by Ebaugh:

The original course of studies contained only one

professional subject - methods of mutual and simult-
aneous instruction, according to Lancaster's monitorial
plan. Other subjects offered were reading and writing,
religion, commercial arithmetic, Spanish grammar and
spelling, descriptive geography, linear drawing and
elements of general and Chilean history. As can be
seen this Normal School offered little more than a
modern elementary curriculum, Director Sarmiento was
a great teacher and student of education ... (it) was
he who taught most of the classes, so that those who
finished the three year course were far better trained
than elementary teachers in Chile had ever been
before.[8]

Nonetheless, this development was not a generalised feature
in the educational scene of Latin America. Moreover, it was
a selective process of educational development which followed
the rapid integration of some countries into the international economy as exporters, which gave its characteristic
to the period. Sarmiento in Chile and Argentina, Varela in
Uruguay, Rebsamen in Mexico, Ruy Barbosa in Brazil became
key interpreters of an educational situation challenged by a
context of striking economic transformation.

For Sarmiento, it was clear that in the mining enterprise ...

for using the drill it is necessary to learn how to
read. In Copiapo, (a silver mining centre of the 1850s)
the local driller received 14 pesos ... and 50 pesos the
English driller, given the fact that he knows how to
read he is able to perform strippings and tunnels and
all that work which requires the use of intelligence.[9]

The possibility of progress was then linked to the development of elementary schooling. As has been pointed out by
Luis Reissig, in respect of Argentina:

After the sudden transition from cattle-breeding to an
agricultural economy, and from the illiterate cowboy
to the farmer spurred on by progress, teaching ceases
to be an inferior or degrading occupation; nobody is
lowered by being forced to take up teaching. Schools
and teachers multiply in answer to the felt needs of
the environment.[10]

At this level it could be said that at the turn of the
century liberal and positivist educators were successful in
the development of schemes for teachers in those countries
where the dominant elite was able to meet adequately the
integration of their interests to an external market which

144

required better standards of production. Profits from
mining in Mexico and Chile, intensive agriculture and cattle-
breeding in Uruguay and Argentina were important economic
motives helping to explain the relatively superior development of primary education, and related teacher training
projects in those countries.

However, in other countries the situation was rather
stagnant. As described by the Peruvian educational
historian Valcarcel, the situation in his country showed a
relative continuity:

> The colonial educational system displaced de jure, kept
> its empire de facto, in spite of the new regime. The
> external symbols were modified but not the spirit, for
> a sharp class difference was still dominant at school.
> The state lacked the power and worry to develop a real
> reform. Also there were no suitable teachers and
> buildings, so the children had to grow up in a primitive
> environment not having the benefits of education to
> perceive.[11]

Burrough's opinion in respect of Venezuela helps us to
picture the exact realm of public education and its consequences in the majority of the Latin American countries by the
beginning of the twentieth century.

> If during this period achievements as measured by pupils
> in schools and educational attainment were slight, the
> period was not barren either in the necessary slow
> growth of institutional structures or in men's thinking.
> The concepts of education as a means of eliminating
> social inequality, as concerned with matters of
> practical as well as academic, as responsible for the
> personal development of children as well as the accum-
> ulation of knowledge, found growing appreciation.[12]

If we take into account the above descriptions, it is then
reasonable to state that during the nineteenth century an
educational system prevailed whose effective range of
schooling action was very poor. It was directed mainly
towards the needs of a small but strong power elite and
accidentally played a role for the legitimization of the
State as a formal democratic entity. This process of
formalization was to a considerable degree expressed in the
law, but seldom in an actual programme for universal primary
education. However, this ideological element had the effect
of generating a process of sensitization to the value of
education among wider sectors of society.

In this aspect we agree with Illich, that:

The constitutional history of Latin America since its independence has made the masses of this continent particularly susceptible to the conviction that all citizens have a right to enter and, therefore, have some possibility of entering their society through the door of a school.[13]

It was under this situation that the teaching profession became one of the new possibilities for social mobility in a society which was beginning to open its tight dual social structure under the pressure exerted by a growing middle sector and the increasingly organized urban working class. As was described by Monroe[14] in 1928, a rather common pattern of teacher training schemes had developed in Latin America. The typical normal school was of a secondary grade, students were directly admitted from the elementary school usually to a five year course study. These courses were normally made up of the secondary school "scientific-humanistic" subjects, with the professional element added in the last two or three years. Side by side with the normal school, the Escuela de Aplicacion (Practice Training School) was founded. By the end of the 1920s at least one national normal school existed in each country. In Argentina, Brazil, Chile, Uruguay and Mexico, provincial normal schools were widely distributed over the country. In most cases normal schools were free of charge and generally developed as boarding institutions where students were subsidized by the state. In return they were bonded to serve as teachers for a period of three to five years after their graduation within the public system.

For obvious reasons this subsidized education attracted the lower middle-class and working-class children into a profession which was regarded by the dominant sectors of society, as one with little social prestige. Normal education became also an open professional ground for women. According to Freyre this was also the case in Brazil:

> Until the end of the nineteenth century women were rare in this as well as in other branches of the teaching profession. Now it is rare to find a man as a regular teacher in a primary school in the most advanced or progressive regions of Brazil. Men school teachers are to be found in a considerable number only in ordinary schools of backward areas.[15]

By 1947 in Chile from a total enrolment of 6,162 normal school students 5,549 were women[16]; around the same time in Haiti 47.7% were women.[17] In brief, by the mid-century the teaching profession at the primary school level had become in Latin America a "women's profession".

Moreover, men and women who had become maestros[18],

usually survived on a very low income and normally were sent to isolated one-teacher rural schools, where they exerted some sort of intellectual leadership among the poor peasants and at the same time became integrated to a humble way of life.

As was pointed out by the Colombian educator, Nieto-Caballero:

> And in view of the remuneration he perceived, the teacher has no choice but to be humble. The case of the primary school teacher is the most dramatic of all. In general, he earns less than a foreman, a chauffeur, or a policeman. In the top rank his monthly salary is only $130 to $200. It is a miracle that he manages to keep alive.[19]

Well into this century, the bureaucratic measures devised by the state to control teachers remained largely as a heritage of nineteenth century conservative authoritarianism. Ross, an American sociologist who visited Mexico in 1920, was appalled by the social situation of primary school teachers. He denounced "the political tyranny which now weighs upon them and makes them easy victims of their superiors when these wish to use them for their personal ends".[20] In addition to this situation in many countries teachers had to suffer extra hardships in the form of partial default on their salaries because of inadequate state funds.

Mariategui, a precursory figure of Latin American marxism and one of the more influential Peruvian intellectuals of the century, was able to make by 1928 a precise description of the social condition of the maestro.

> The Latin American maestro emerges from the people, especially from the middle sectors. The normal school trains him for an unselfish function relinquished of economic ambitions. He is destined for promoting the gratuitous and compulsory state elementary education to the children of the poor. Beforehand, while a normal school student, he becomes aware that the state will scantly remunerate his efforts. Primary education - education for the proletarians - proletarianizes its servants. The state compels its maestros to endure a tense financial situation, denies them nearly every means for cultural and economic betterment and keeps them away from the perspective of mobility towards a higher rank ... In one aspect the maestros are deprived of economic welfare. On the other hand, they lack the possibility of scientific progress. Normal school studies are not recognised by the University. Their fate can be an oblivious confinement to a primitive

147

village, dependent on a political boss, without books and journals, segregated from the cultural movement, deprived of basic elements of study.[21]

It is within this context that early attempts to overcome this backward social and economic situation were undertaken by Latin American teachers. Such efforts were accompanied by the declaration of common principles and aims, which by 1930 were expressed in highly radical terms. There were two basic political guidelines which most of them followed; the need for national self reliance and the achievement of basic goals for social justice.

The first Union of Teachers was created in Chile[22] during the early 1920s and by 1930 a militant association of 6,000 maestros existed throughout the country. Integrated to populist orientated governments between 1920 and 1930, the Union was responsible for one of the most impressive educational achievements of the period. The illiteracy rate of 49.7% by 1920 was reduced to 25.6% by 1930 under the effort and guidance of the teachers union. This social commitment of maestros has not been always recognised by the State and a situation of persecution and harassment has prevailed as a common feature in the history of Latin American education. The case of El Salvador as described in the late 1940s by a former Professor of San Salvador's Normal School, helps to illustrate the point:

> For the past thirty years teachers have not been able to organize their own associations independent of official control. They have not made a single demand nor have they been able to express their views as a group on professional or administrative questions in the field. Here is to be found the tragic impotence of the teaching body and the definite clue to their isolation, poverty and backwardness.[23]

However, the educational thought of Latin American maestros emerged from this conflicting situation, from the concrete economic and social problems which constituted a central issue in the confrontation between the teachers and the State. The problem of teacher unionization was not alien to the ideological bias prevailing in the normal school.

Other factors were also important in the determination of the orientating values of Latin American teacher education. The curriculum of the normal school incorporated the discussion and practice of the latest pedagogical ideas. The work of Herbart, Pestalozzi, Decroly and especially the 'progressivism' of Dewey, were of prime importance as conceptual vehicles for explaining the pedagogical practice of most normalistas of Latin America.

148

Such was the view of an important leader of the Chilean Union of Teachers by 1950:

> Whatever remains valuable and longlasting of the teachers' actions of 1915 and after, whatever was substantial in the reform of 1928 and even during the generals' counter-reform after that year; whatever has become practical achievement in the last years of democratic evolution, is rooted in that doctrinary compendium called Education and Democracy.[24]

However, in areas subject more directly to the interventions of the United States of America, such as much of Central America and the Caribbean, 'progressivism' had different effects. The case of Haiti, as reported by Schmidt, helps to illustrate the point:

> Haiti thus became a test-case of isolated technocratic progressivism, devoid of its liberal democratic trappings, with all the stops pulled ... Educational policy, focusing on normal-technical training similar to contemporary functional education for blacks in the U.S. was variously blighted by cultural and racial difficulties ... These efforts were largely unsuccessful because of racial and cultural prejudices which tended to undermine the development of effective master-disciple relationships. Instead of modeling after the Americans, many Haitians came to despise them.[25]

Notwithstanding such reactions, during the first 50 years of this century most of the educational leaders and policy makers of the Latin American countries were trained at Columbia Teachers College, New York, and many under the direct influence of Dewey. Two prominent examples were Moises Saenz, the Minister responsible for the organization of profound educational reforms during the first decade of the Mexican Revolution, and Amanda Labarca, the Chilean educationist who played an important role in the educational policy-making during the reformist years of the Popular Front, between 1938-1947. There were many others of similar stature, profoundly influenced by Dewey's idea that education in itself was a tool for social change; a scientific and technical tool capable of developing the values of democracy and social harmony.

Such concepts were not lacking in incorporation in various educational initiatives of the mid-twentieth century. For example, the striking achievements of the Mexican revolution on rural education, as well as the model set up by socialist indigenistas in Bolivia with the experience of Warisata, were perhaps the basic blueprints on

149

which the maestros of Latin America trained and operated.

The Mexican idea of making out of the rural school a centre not only for basic instruction but also for the mobilization of the rural community in terms of the general political and economic goals of the populist revolution, was encouraged and discussed in the Latin American normal school of the day. The dual idea of education as a national mission of social redemption, and that of the maestro as a social apostle set down by Vasconcelos was welcomed and internalized by many young normalistas of the 1930s and 1940s. For Gamio, a leading educational figure of Mexico, it was clear that education was not necessarily a good thing per se. He recognised that educational attainment was intimately linked to social and political reform, and that in order to "attempt this, it would be necessary to reform completely not only machinery but specially the existing criterion".[26]

As a concrete expression of this aim, the first ambulant system for in-service rural training was set up in Mexico as early as 1924. The Misiones Culturales were mobile teams composed of a social worker, a doctor, a teacher of education, midwife, visiting nurse, an agronomist and an expert on light industries and mechanics. They were to promote in-service training of teachers in rural areas in the field, promoting at the same time projects of community development where practical skills and leadership training was immediately tested and evaluated.[27]

The Bolivian experience emerged, not as a pattern promoted from above under the orientation of a state project, but rather as a contesting grass root experience in the heart of the Indian community of Warisata. In 1931, Elizardo Perez, a socialist teacher imbued by the indigenista ideas of Mariategui and other progressive Latin American intellectuals, came to Warisata when the community was threatened by the expansive aggression of the big landowners of that particular region of the Bolivian highlands. In order to strengthen the bonds of community action and self-defence the idea of nucleo escolar campesino (rural nuclei school) was organised. A community constructed central school radiated the 3R programme to the children and adults of the small peasant settlements around the nuclear village. The Consejo de Amautas – community elected board – was to assume all the administrative decisions in a democratic fashion as well as the different social and economic problems which affected the community. The teaching function served as a propagator element for the problems and ideas discussed by the Consejo de Amautas.

In the later stages of the project a normal school was established in Warisata so as to recruit the student teachers from the same community. This situation was considered crucial, not only to give the whole project a

150

more autonomous character, but also to communicate in fluent Aymara the social expectations of the community, as well as to train children in reading and writing in their own native languages as well as in the Spanish "lingua franca".

The project followed the upheavals of political confrontation within Bolivia, and when a conservative military government took over, the school was closed. In 1946 under the sponsorship of a U.S. international aid mission the school was reopened. By 1950 Warisata was considered an international experiment under the sponsorship of the Pan American Union and UNESCO. The final result was a dry scheme of technical demonstration of pedagogical instructional methods, stripped of the spiritual central core which gave life to the overall experience.[28]

Positive actions were developed at the normal schools of various countries between 1940 and 1960, along the lines of more participatory schemes, and normally within the framework of "populist" governments.

At this level it is interesting to analyze the case of Guatemala[29], which between 1944 and 1953 underwent a series of important political and social transformations under the first democratically appointed governments of Aravolo and Arbentz.

Central to the ethos and political commitment of the Guatemalan Government was the idea of education as proposed by 'progressivism'. Indeed, President Arevalo, a teacher himself, defined this national commitment to education as the first priority of his government. As a consequence of such proposals, important changes were produced in the education of teachers, which was urgently redirected towards diverse projects of rural and community education. Teachers and their education became important components of schemes promoting radical changes within the economic structure of the country, such as agrarian reform involving national-ization of the best land of the country which was in the hands of American fruit companies.

However, the changing attitude of the American govern-ment in favour of a 'Cold War' policy had a profound effect on Guatemalan development. In 1950 the Government was labelled as "communist" by the State Department and a military intervention financed by the U.S.A. brought down the 'progressive' educational achievements of the Guatemalan "Decade of Dignity".

Nonetheless, at the regional level the idea of "redemption through education" was still a central feature of the ideology reproduced by individual normal schools and disseminated somewhat ironically by the OAS and American aid agencies. Official mobilization efforts towards "eradication of illiteracy" and "fundamental education" were pervaded with this ethos. For, though the basic and explicit

151

motivation was for education per se, the fact that such
action was directed to the working class and the peasantry
gave to the literacy task a specially militant relevance.

Even in the 1960s some Pan American bureaucrats would
still define such efforts in critical progressivist terms:

> The people and the governments are not satisfied with
> the educational situation as it is. There is a
> pervading attitude of reform, which is one of the
> significant features - perhaps even one of the most
> important - of Latin America today. There is an
> acknowledgement that education should lead to social
> and economic development.[30]

In most normal schools such sentiments formed the
rationalisation provided for a task which, because it used
the borrowed knowledge of 'progressivism' to explain reality,
was surpassed by the actual social practice of the normalistas. Educational theory was in fact trailing some way
behind social and educational practice. This in turn created
a situation often leading to a sort of purely pedagogical
activism.

However, it should also be recognized that the rein-
forcement of the militant, political and 'leftist' choices
orientating the teachers' educational institutions of Latin
America mostly emanated from a different and more basic
source. This was simply direct contact with the illiterate
peasantry and the phenomenon of their mute acceptance of
dependency and exploitation. Likewise the problems of
poverty as mirrored in the urban working classes.

The example of certain countries, such as Guatemala,
helped to reinforce the idea of a national self-reliance
which could only be achieved by challenging U.S. imperialism.
The triumph of the Cuban revolution beginning in 1959, and
the subsequent striking achievements of that country in the
educational field, were central issues and powerful
components in the formation of an ideology of teacher
education which gained some acceptability in Latin America.

As a counter-action to "Castroism", the problems of
teacher education in Latin America were by the mid-1960s
being discussed within a new scenario. Massive amounts of
aid from the U.S.A. were poured into the various education
systems of Latin America so as to produce certain desired
reforms. Many of the contributions of the previous decades
of teacher and community education were taken into account,
but most of the generative themes which gave force and
energy to Misiones Culturales or to the scheme of Nucleo
Escolar were understated: they were polluted by ideology,
they were value orientated. Pedagogical neutrality,
scientific education as proposed by Bloom and Tyler,

152

educational technology and behaviourism became the passwords
of an increasingly remote set of international experts. The
domination of Latin America by the new American educational
outlook was orientated towards a theory and policy of
"modernisation". This was proffered under the guise of the
'Alliance for Progress', and shaded the state educational
ideology of the 1960s and 1970s.

The Alliance for Progress included 'packages' of aid
for 'modernisation' which have been introduced into most
Latin American programmes of teacher education. They follow
a common pattern which emphasises administrative and
methodological change. Critical appraisal by American
specialists is notably aimed at these particular areas, thus
avoiding the central and crucial problems of inequality,
disparity and social justice.

Schiefelbein and Russell evaluated the situation in
Chile between 1965 and 1970 and give a wider significance
to the positive aspects of a teacher education programme
under threat of extinction when confronted by technical
models of reform:

> In this case the model taught Chilean educators nothing
> new about education reality. All of them were aware at
> varying levels of explicitness that the normal schools
> were not serving only their primary function - training
> teachers. The educators also knew that the normal
> schools were serving an important social function,
> nonetheless, in offering inexpensive and available
> secondary level education to lower class children who
> would not have access to the preparatory schools ...
> The model does not insure that the new normal schools
> will be better. The result of the new program may be
> that poor quality and irrelevant secondary level
> institutions have been changed into poor quality
> irrelevant post-secondary level institutions.[31]

It should also be remembered that educational intervention in
the system of Latin America on the part of the U.S.A., while
stressing the priority for technical and administrative
modernisation[32], has always linked this with a wider
rationale. This indicates that the central aim of modernisation is to improve the efficiency of the production of
the human resources required by external capital investment
in the industry and other sectors of the Latin American
economy. In effect this is a further sophistication of
dependency mechanisms.

One may agree with Carnoy that:

> The United States uses assistance for education now, as
> the British and French used assistance in the nineteenth

153

century, to expand that education which is complementary
to keeping order in the 'empire' and which subsidizes
the expansion of capitalist enterprise, particularly
(for U.S. assistance) American-based multi-national
corporations and financial institutions. With U.S.
hegemony, expansion and reforms of formal schooling
became means of promoting U.S. concepts of an 'efficient' and 'democratic' society.[33]

The intention to continue with a well established
tradition of socially orientated normal education has been
regarded by U.S. AID experts as a sign of 'inefficiency' and
'backwardness'. Furthermore, the well-established social
values and ideological orientation of the Escuela Normal are
considered by Washington policy makers as the expression of
'communist infiltration'. According to a Senate document
issued in 1964, and dealing with the theme of alleged
communist infiltration in the educational systems of various
Latin American countries, not even one normal school reported
was free from the so-called 'communist plot'. Measures
should be taken, the report claimed![34]
Such a political view has now pervaded the overall
decision-making style imposed at the Ministries of Education
of Latin America.
A reformulation of the priorities of the education of
elementary teachers in Latin America has been carried out,
according to A.G. Marquez, without consulting the trainees
or the practising teachers. The obvious and predictable
result is widespread anomie.
Almost throughout the region, progressive educationists
do not take part in the determination of educational
policies. These are agreed at the level of national political power and in accordance with the interests of the State
as perceived by the ruling elite. Teachers and other
educators are mere executants of a policy they are not in a
position to criticise or reform. At the present time it is
very clear that maestros are perceived as symbols of
'subversion' and supporters of the class struggle. Merely
to question the status quo is regarded as suspicious whereas
in former times a healthy criticism was the normal
environment.[35] One must be aware that such situations of
intervention in the educational schemes for teachers, can
produce, in the long run, profound attitudinal changes
towards conformism with the future generation of primary
school teachers. Yet one of the sources for the reproduction of the militant attitudes of primary school teachers
of Latin America, has been and still is the normal school
tradition in itself. Thus, when assessing the value of such
educational schemes one has to search and separate, the
explicit and 'officialized' pedagogical ideologies –

154

progressivism in the 1930s and 1940s, educational technology in the recent years - from the actual educational and corporate action of the maestros at the grass-root level.

However, the new educational technology reinforces the 'progressivist' myth of education as the tool for social change, where the maestro, the neutral apostle of non-conflictive reformism, is now portrayed as benign in terms of values and their infusion. The authorities see him as, and would like to ensure him to be, a mere technocrat.

If the normalistas then apparently underline their commitment to political radical militancy and union action, rather than seeking pedagogical solutions, it is basically because they have become increasingly aware of the fact that very little can be achieved from isolated educational action in the class-room. In Latin American societies at any rate, the grass-roots is firmly under political control - a clear example of dependency at work.

The use of new media and modular systems of literacy and numeracy, the so-called 'software' dimension of techno-logical change, have proved to be useful only at experimental level and within the range of externally financed, and therefore influenced, projects. According to the Bolivian educational agency INDICEP, such technological schemes have a tangential effect on those few teachers which are engaged in their development. Apparently they help to reinforce the naive, (in the sense of Freire), self-image of a technocrat solving strictly educational problems and freed from social and political engagement.[36] Such an effect would of course be more welcome to Latin American governments and American agencies alike.

Externally enforced priorities for the education of teachers upon the existing tradition in the decade of the 1970s need to be re-evaluated, mostly because a decline in the normal school tradition of social and national engage-ment can be clearly observed. Moreover, some important remarks should be added from the quantitative side. Since the introduction of U.S. orientated processes of "reform" of teacher education in Latin America, the growth in the supply of teachers has decreased from 7.3% p.a. between 1960 and 1965 to 6.8% p.a. during the remainder of the decade. This demonstrates that the claims of efficiency as a justification of the reform and the whole programme of modernisation should be re-assessed. If a decline in the rate of teacher supply is desirable, then what is the reasoning behind such a policy?

A new breed of international and 'internationalized' (on behalf of U.S. AID orientated scholarships) pedagogues, has been very influential in reducing the received conventional wisdom laboriously built up in the tradition of Latin American teacher education. This was for long, as we

155

have seen, a liberal tradition. In some cases these pedagogues have been integrated into elementary teacher training at the university level, so that the normal school tradition has been deprived of some of its basic values, values which gave force and a sense of pride to the teaching profession.. The social and vocational status and appeal of the normal school have been shattered in the name of modernisation. Although a symbolic university character has been conferred upon some future elementary school teachers, the teaching profession still lacks social prestige and is perceived by Academia as a bothersome newcomer. In fact, nothing has been offered in exchange and the results are increasingly disquieting. However, it is claimed that in-service state and university training has been increased as never before. In fact, this new scheme is basically orientated towards the mere description and transference of technical skills. The use of "Gagné gadgets" for curriculum development are presented as unique and scientific out-of-discussion panacea. However, this in-service project has been shown by Larrea and others[37], to be quite unsatisfactory.

It is now clear that an attempt to deprive the Latin American tradition of teacher education of its historical concern with social justice and national self-reliance, is under way. However, it is also clear that it is not possible to cover-up the real issues of Latin American educational underdevelopment with alleged "purely technical solutions".

In a UNESCO report about the present situation of the teachers of Latin America it is shown that the changes proposed by the Alliance for Progress[38] were not achieved and that the social condition of the teachers during the 1960s deteriorated markedly, and to the extent of:

> adversely affecting the teachers' efficiency, given the fact that apart from the discontent and impatience provoked, the teacher has been forced to excessive work in the private educational sector or in other sorts of activities alien to the teaching profession.[39]

Finally, if we consider the fact that in the last decade, the political scene of Latin America has been increasingly dominated by authoritarian governments of the conservative military type, where personal human rights are threatened, it should be said that education lacks open means for orientating itself towards the solution of the social and economic problems of Latin America.

It is within this framework that teacher education is compelled to give solutions. However, if the teacher steps out of his comfortable "educational technology", in order to improve his situation by canvassing in favour of the old unionism and normal school strategies, he is labelled as a

156

'communist'. This means his expulsion from the teaching profession, and in the extreme cases of military fascist regimes torture, exile or even assassination.

One may conclude therefore that while priorities for teacher education are certainly changing under the guise of "modernisation", such changes are not necessarily for the better.

NOTES

1.   In this aspect we follow Freire's view: 'Since cultural invasion is an act of conquest per se, it needs further conquest to sustain itself. Propaganda, slogans, myths are the instruments employed by the invader to achieve his objectives: to persuade those invaded that they must be objects of his action, that they must be docile prisoners of his conquest. Thus it is incumbent on the invader to destroy the character of the culture which has been invaded, nullify its form, and replace it with the by products of the invading culture', 'Extension or Communication' in Education the Practice of Freedom, London, Writers and Readers Publishing Co-operative, 1974, pp. 111-112.

2.   The term criollo refers to the white or mixed race descendants of the conquistadores.

3.   Harold Davies, The Latin American Thought: a historical introduction, New York, The Free Press, 1974.

4.   Roberto Koch, 'Education in the Americas: a Comparative Historical Review' in Eastern Regional Conference of the Comparative Education Society/OAS, Challenges and Achievements of Education in Latin America, Washington, O.A.S.-Pan American Union, 1964, p. 37.

5.   Webster Browning, 'Joseph Lancaster, James Thomson and the Lancasterian system of mutual instruction, with special reference to Hispanic America', Hispanic American Historical Review, (HAHR), Volume 4, number 1, 1921, p. 78.

6.   ibid., p. 84.

7.   ibid., p. 96.

8.   Cameron D. Ebaugh, Education in Chile, Washington, U.S. Office of Education, 1945, p. 7.

9.   As quoted in Cesar Godoy Urrutia, Educacion y Politica, Santiago, Ediciones Tierra y Escuela, 1959, p. 183, (writers' translation).

10.   Luis Reissig, 'The Argentine' in The Year Book of Education, London, Evans Brothers, 1953, p. 529.

11.   Carlos D. Valcarcel, Breve Historia de la Educacion Peruana, Lima, Editorial Educacion, 1975, pp. 163-164. Our translation.

12.   G.E.R. Burroughs, Education in Venezuela, London and Connecticut, Archon Books, 1974, p. 20.

13.   Ivan Illich, Celebration of Awareness, London,

Penguin Books, 1973, p. 92.

14.   Paul Monroe, Essays in Comparative Education, New York, Columbia University Teachers College, 1927.

15.   Gilberto Freyre, 'Brazil' in The Year Book of Education, London, Evans Brothers, 1953, p. 536.

16.   Amanda Labarca, Realidades y Problemas de Nuestra Ensenanza, Santiago, Ediciones de la Universidad de Chile, 1953.

17.   Georges Dale, Education in the Republic of Haiti, Washington, U.S. Department of Health, Education and Welfare, 1959.

18.   The term maestro is applied in Latin America to denote a primary school teacher.

19.   Agustin Nieto-Caballero, 'Colombia' in The Year Book of Education, London, Evans Brothers, 1953, p. 553.

20.   John A Britton, 'Teacher Unionization and Corporate State in Mexico, 1931-1945', HAHR, Volume 59, number 4, 1979, pp. 676-677.

21.   J.C. Mariategui, Temas de Educacion, Lima, Amauta, 1973, p. 48.

22.   ibid., pp. 68-69.

23.   Francisco Moran, 'El Salvador' in Educational Year Book of the International Institute of Teachers College, New York, Columbia University Teachers College, 1942, p. 203.

24.   As quoted in C. Godoy Urrutia, op. cit., p. 55.

25.   Hans Schmidt, The United States Occupation of Haiti 1915-1934, New Brunswick, Rutgers University Press, 1971, pp. 135, 146.

26.   As quoted by Louise Schoenhals, 'Mexico Experiments in Rural and Primary Education: 1921-1930', HAHR, Volume 44, 1964, p. 24.

27.   Various recent PhD dissertations have tackled the problem of Misiones Culturales in detail and should be considered as the best contributions in this field.
J.A. Barret, 'Adult Education in Mexico, (1920-1924)', unpublished PhD, The Florida State University, 1970.
Raymond Multerer, 'The Socialist Education Movement and its impact on Mexican Education, 1930-1948', unpublished doctoral dissertation, State University of New York at Buffalo, 1974.
D.L. Raby, 'Rural Teachers and Social and Political Conflict in Mexico 1921-1940', unpublished doctoral dissertation, University of Warwick, 1970.

28.   In relation to the developments of Warisata a good analysis in Andrew Pearse, 'Structural Problems of Education Systems in Latin America' in Richard Brown (ed), Knowledge, Education and Cultural Change, London, Tavistock Publications, 1973. Also, Toribio Claure, 'In Rural Bolivia Indians Take to School', Americas, Volume 8, 1965, and Juan Hohenstein, 'La busqueda de identidad: El desarrollo de la educacion rural an Bolivia', Estudios Andinos, Volume 2,

number 4, 1971.

29.   For the Guatemalan case see: Chester L. Jones, Guatemala: Past and Present, New York, Russell and Russell, 1966, and OEA, Campanas de Alfabetizacion en America Latina, Washington, O.A.S.-Pan American Union, 1965.

30.   F.S. Cespedes, 'The Contemporary Educational Scene in Latin America' in Eastern Regional Conference of the Comparative Education Society, op. cit., p. 47 (the emphasis is ours).

31.   Ernesto Schiefelbein and G.D. Russell, Development of Education Planning Models and Application in the Chilean School Reform, Lexington, Mass., Lexington Books, 1974, p. 120.

32.   Gabriel Betancour, 'Education: Backbone of the Alliance for Progress', Americas, Volume 15, number 10, 1963.

33.   Martin Carnoy, Education as Cultural Imperialism, New York, David McKay, 1974, p. 310.

34.   On educational 'witch hunting' in Latin America see: U.S. Congress, Foreign Affairs Division, Communist Infiltration in Latin American Educational Systems, Washington, Library of Congress, 1964.

35.   Angel Diego Marquez, 'The Education in the Latin American Context', Prospects, Volume 5, number 2, 1975.

36.   INDICEP, 'INDICEP y la educacion popular en America Latina - grandes corrientes ideologicas', Convergence, Volume 4, number 4, 1971; also C. Chadwick, 'Por que esta fracasando la Tecnologia Educativa?', Revista de Tecnologia Educativa, Volume 2, number 4, 1976.

37.   Julio Larrea, 'The Education and Training of Teachers in Latin America', in The Year Book of Education, London, Evans Brothers, 1963.

38.   Alliance for Progress: 1961 agreement between the U.S. and most Latin American States with the object of improving economic conditions in South America, partly through educational and security programmes. For a further discussion on these problems, see Vicente Lema and Angel D. Marquez, 'What Kind of Development and which Education?', Prospects, Volume 8, number 3, 1978.

39.   Carmen Lorenzo, Situacion del Personal Docente en America Latina, Santiago-Chile-Paris, UNESCO-OREALC, 1969, p. 318; also Angel Oliveros Alonso, La formacion de los profesores en America Latina, Barcelona, Promocion Cultural, 1975.

TRENDS IN THE PROFESSIONAL PREPARATION OF TEACHERS OF PHYSICAL EDUCATION

Michael Mawer

INTRODUCTION

Physical Education may be taught by a specialist teacher whose training may have been directed towards the elementary or secondary school, or by a 'generalist' or 'class teacher' whose training may include the study of all aspects of the school curriculum. In the developed countries of the world it is likely that a 'specialist' will teach physical education in the secondary school, and in some cases 'specialists' may be specifically trained for the elementary school. Generally speaking it is the 'class teacher' that teaches physical education in the elementary school.

In the emerging countries of the world specialists for the secondary school may not be available, or be in short supply, and teachers will either attend limited in-service courses in the teaching of physical education, or a 'generalist' will have to contend with a limited initial training course.

The last twenty years have seen changes in both the structure of initial training for specialist teachers of physical education and in the functions of training institutions. The expansion of knowledge in physical education and related areas of study, a greater interest in sports science research, and the coaching of elite athletes to international success, have been factors that may have led to these changes.

THE PROFESSIONAL PREPARATION OF THE SPECIALIST TEACHER OF PHYSICAL EDUCATION

The considerable expansion of areas of knowledge related to physical education in the last twenty years, largely as a result of research efforts in the developed countries, has led to the acceptance of physical education as an academically respectable area of study in many countries.

160

Consequently a three or four year degree course for the specialist physical education student may be common in many countries, with the subject enjoying comparative status with other subjects in institutions of higher education and universities. As Bennett, Howell and Simri suggested in 1975:

> Today the professional physical educator might assume as a starting point that the desirable standard of preparation for the specialist teacher of physical education is a four year curriculum at a university or college leading to a recognised degree. One also might assume that the students faculty, courses and facilities for physical education would have a status and support comparable to other subject areas within the institution.

The earlier survey by Bennett et al.[1] had shown that three or four year degree level courses for physical education specialists had existed for some time in the Soviet Union, Hungary, Czechoslovakia, East Germany, West Germany, Austria, U.S.A., Canada, Egypt, Great Britain and Japan.[2]

More recent evidence suggests that many of the socialist countries[3] and Canada[4] are putting into operation five year courses of study and that three or four year degree level courses at a recognised college or university are available in Norway, New Zealand, Italy, Australia, Denmark, France, Nigeria, Nicaragua, Ivory Coast, Ghana, India, Saudi Arabia, Thailand, Indonesia, Iran, Iraq, Belgium and Finland.[5] Equally effective courses appear to exist in Sweden, Holland and Switzerland, although they may only have 'diploma' status, and reasonably sound certificated courses for physical education specialists are being developed in several South American countries, notably Chile, Argentina and Uruguay.[6]

A good example of recent progress is France. Prior to 1975 the regional institutes of physical education and sport were attached to a school of medicine at a university, but since 1975 with the creation of the new Diploma of General University Studies in Sciences and Techniques of Physical Activities and Sport, the training of physical education and sports teachers has been taken over by the universities.[7] Only those fifteen universities having a regional institute of physical education and sport were in fact allowed to operate such courses. Students who pass their diploma can be admitted to a second tier of higher education, the professionally-oriented 'licence' in the Science of Physical Activities and Sport, and a final fourth year examination for recruitment to the profession.[8] As with the Belgian and

161

Italian situation, it is the 'diploma' or 'licence' which is achieved as a first qualification and not the actual degree.[9]

In the U.S.A. and Canada a three year (general) or four year (honours) degree course is the pattern for prospective physical education teachers, although this is now often taken in the form of a three or four year degree followed by a year of professional studies as in Canada.[10]

In Japan a total of forty-nine universities offer physical education as an undergraduate course of study in a faculty of physical education. These are four year courses and have as their prime objective the professional preparation of physical education teachers for the upper secondary school level.[11]

There are four teachers' colleges for the training of the specialist physical education teacher in Israel, of which the Zinman College at the Wingate Institute is possibly the most famous. It was established in 1944 in Tel Aviv, and besides serving as a training centre for most national sports teams, the Institute is home for the Department of Research and Sports Medicine, Department of Professional Publications, and the National Archives of P.E. and Sport.[12] In 1973 the first step towards the recognition of physical education as an academically respectable course of study leading to degree status was achieved. Until then students were awarded a diploma of the Ministry of Education and Culture (Dip. Phys. Ed.). In 1973 the three year course at the Wingate Institute was accepted as leading towards the B.A. degree of the universities of Tel Aviv and Haifa. This was a great step forward for the status of physical education as an area of academic study as Eldar has suggested:

> The special meaning of this development in Israel is not only the fact that a College of Education attained academicisation, but more important still, that physical education was recognised as an academic discipline with equal rights in the academic world of Israel.[13]

The basic qualification for specialist physical education teachers in Australia has been the diploma in physical education granted after three years' training at a state teachers' college. But now, the University of Sydney offers a four year B.P.Ed. degree and the Teachers' College of Western Australia has a four year B.Ed. degree.[14]

In New Zealand there is only one university offering courses in physical education and that is the University of Otego at Dunedin where there is a diploma and bachelor's degree in physical education.[15]

Although physical education has been studied since 1882 at the University of Helsinki, only recent developments at the new faculty of physical education at the University of

162

Jyvaskyla has brought the study programme of physical education students in line with other university students. The new study course is for a master of science in physical education instead of the earlier bachelor's degree, and is obtained through studies based on the new educational programme of physical and health education sciences.[16]

The training of the physical education specialist in Nigeria normally took place at the advanced teacher training colleges, of which five existed in 1965. The first university to have a physical education department and to award bachelor degrees in physical education was the University of Nigeria, Nsukka, and this was followed by the University of Ife in 1968, and more recently by Ahmadu Bello and Lagos universities. It would appear that physical education has successfully made the transition into academic respectability in the universities of Nigeria, although recent writers still consider that there is still some way to go in achieving equal status with other university students. For example, Adedeji comments:

> It is expected that within the next couple of years physical education shall not only be for social education, but also for academic existence when through the implementation of the UNESCO charter it becomes a WAEC subject. When physical education is granted this accord, it will break new ground which will demand a sharp distinction in the preparation of physical educators.[17]

The appointment of Dr. Klaas Rijsdorp in 1969 as Professor Extraordinarius to the Chair of Physical Education Sciences at the State University of Utrecht in Holland was a very important development for Dutch physical education. This appointment in some ways indicated that the scientific aspects of physical education were recognised in academic circles, and in turn led to further developments in university physical education. In 1971 the Minister of Education established an interfaculty of physical education at the Free University of Amsterdam, with the task of developing scientific knowledge in physical education and the aim of applying this knowledge to the practical situation. Programmes are offered in applied anatomy, exercise physiology, motor learning and movement education, and may lead to doctoral degrees.[18]

In certain countries, Switzerland for example, there may be two levels of professional preparation for the secondary school physical education teacher. A holder of the Swiss physical education diploma I will have completed four semesters of university study and he may teach pupils in the seven to nine age range. A holder of the physical

163

education diploma II will have completed eight semesters of university study and may teach in the superior secondary schools.[19]

Barriers to progress in the emerging nations

Other countries in the under-developed world have not managed to achieve standards of initial training equivalent to a three or four year degree course, and the lack of progress of physical education as an academically respectable area of study leading to degree status may be dependent upon a number of factors. Such factors may include inadequate government support and funding, and poor library and sports facilities, but very often physical education is simply not seen as a valuable subject in the curriculum.

The plight of Colombia may be a suitable example of such difficulties. There is one teacher training institution for physical education in Colombia, no graduate programme, and very poor facilities at the National Pedagogic University. Clay cites the opinions of the Rectora President of the National Pedagogic University on the problems of teacher preparation in physical education in comparison with other subjects:

> There is a lack of understanding of the physical educa-
> tion teachers' place in the community of scholars, and
> while many students seek to be teachers in other fields,
> few choose to become teachers of physical education:
> students choosing physical education as a profession
> tend to come from a lower social strata than those
> choosing other fields; except for those written in
> English there are few books available to support
> physical education as a field of merit: and the lack of
> physical plant or facilities that could indicate support
> for physical education as a field is a factor. Finally,
> the general lack of orientation to the importance of
> physical education at the secondary level.[20]

Similar problems exist in Ethiopia, El Salvador, Mali, Mauritania, Cyprus, Jordan and other emerging nations.[21]

In Jordan there appears to be a 'cultural bias' against sport, and although physical education was considered an integral part of the three year economic and social development plan of 1975 to 1978, the majority of the population do not have a favourable attitude toward sport and physical education as the recent I.C.H.P.E.R. survey revealed.

> The image society generalises of a sportsman is not
> favourable. Jordanians, who are on the whole a very
> serious and hardworking people, do not look with much

affection upon the young man who 'wastes' his time and
energies on things that do not really help to 'develop'
the Fatherland. Sportsmen, it is generally misconstrued,
are young men who exert themselves on 'nothing'. As
for young women who indulge, the picture is even
grimmer.[22]

A similar situation exists in many Asian countries
where taking part in sport during the school years is frowned
upon by both parents and teachers. In these countries
pressure is so great for students to achieve good academic
grades for admission to universities that the physical education programme is given less recognition in schools.[23]

On the other hand, Arab states like Kuwait seem to have
made considerable progress in the development of physical
education in schools and sport in the community. They have
an active Olympic Committee, every district has a multi-
sport club, and youth centres encourage participation in
sport.[24] In Saudi Arabia degree qualifications are required
for specialist teachers in schools with personnel being sent
overseas to study for their first degrees.[25]

Three other examples of recent progress are India,
Pakistan and Hong Kong. Although Johnson (1980) reported
that physical education had a low status in India as a
profession, the I.C.H.P.E.R. report of 1981 suggests that
the status of directors of physical education and sports
coaches had improved in that they are now paid more or less
the same salary as other teachers. Nevertheless, many of
India's fifty-three colleges training physical education
teachers to degree status, and the five universities
offering post-graduate courses in physical education are
ill-equipped, poorly staffed and limited in library facilities; research is scarce.[26]

In Pakistan, although the physical education teacher
has yet to achieve the salary status of the Indian teacher,
there is now greater importance placed on the school physical
education programme, whereas previously it was completely
ignored in the education system. Provision for health and
physical education as part of primary curricula was made in
the education policy of 1972 to 1980, and consequently
professional preparation of physical education teachers has
improved. Nevertheless, qualifications are at present at
junior and senior diploma level, and the duration of the
course is only one year. Sports facilities are also still
very poor and library facilities limited.[27]

The situation in Hong Kong is one of very gradual
progress in the face of many economic and social problems,
not least of which is the emphasis placed on children
working hard for examination success rather than playing
sport.[28] Although Hong Kong does not yet train specialist

physical education teachers to degree level, there are now three colleges of education which offer two year physical education elective courses, and one college that offers a three year full-time course for specialising in physical education at secondary level.[29]

Although there has been recent progress in the initial training of specialist physical education teachers in some countries, the situation is still rather bleak concerning certain emerging nations. In the 1981 I.C.H.P.E.R. survey eleven countries were still concerned about improving their training of physical education teachers, with some African nations having almost no trained physical educators, and four emerging nations suggested that substantial progress in physical education generally was being nearly impossible without international financial aid.[30]

Government support for physical education and sport

The progress of physical education into the realm of academic respectability and the training of specialist physical education teachers to degree level may reflect the value placed upon sport and physical education by the government of a country.

The motives underlying national government involvement in sport and physical education are complex and interwoven, although Semotiuk has attempted to clarify the issues involved.[31] He concluded that governments may be motivated to develop sports programmes for the following reasons:
- political indoctrination;
- increase labour productivity;
- success in international competition;
- social order and control;
- health and well-being of individuals;
- international goodwill;
- defence of the country;
- economic reasons;
- laws - maintenance of social order.[32]

In some cases governments may have recognised that a sound physical education programme in the nations' schools may lead to the development of sportsmen of international calibre and the resulting prestige of international sporting success. In fact certain African countries where there is a negative government attitude towards physical education have suggested that a change of terminology from physical education to 'sports education' may lead to more government support for physical education programmes.[33]

In communist countries such as the Soviet Union great importance is placed on a sound programme of physical education, which is seen as vital for 'labour and defence' and an important component of communist upbringing.[34] An

166

improved standard of physical education and sport is seen as meeting the cultural requirements of youth and working class people, and this is linked very much to the growth and well-being of the socialist personality. Marxist goals relating to recreation emphasise the provision of recreation for all and the need for the new Soviet man, the 'Builder of Communism', "to have every opportunity for harmoniously combining 'spiritual wealth, moral purity and perfect physique' - a healthy mind in a healthy body for everyone".[35]

Consequently, in the Soviet Union and other eastern bloc countries, the training of the specialist physical education teacher is a well-established process. In the Soviet Union in 1973 there were 220 secondary specialist and higher schools training 102,000 future specialists in physical education. This included 91 faculties of physical education attached to pedagogical institutes and universities with a total of 32,000 students, and 23 institutes for physical culture educating 38,000 students.[36]

An appreciation of the political value of sporting success through the promotion of elite sport, with a broad base of sport and recreation to serve either the top of the elite pyramid or to supply a physically fit and healthy populace for industrial expansion and defence is not the sole preserve of the Eastern European communist countries.[37]

France as much as any other European country has adopted an elitist approach since 1960. In 1975 the existing National Sports Institute (I.N.S.) and the top teacher training establishment (E.N.S.E.P.S.) combined to become a centre of excellence for the promotion of high level sport in France (I.N.S.E.P.S.). Also, under the 1975 law, the functions of this new establishment were not only to develop a high level of professional training for physical education teachers, coaches and administrators, but also to undertake scientific research in sport, coach national teams and train top level young athletes to international success.[38]

It does appear that recent government support for physical education and sport in certain countries has resulted in the training of more specialist teachers to degree level and the establishing of specialist training institutions with a wide range of functions. This is particularly the case in the Philippines and Korea.

After the Olympics in Germany in 1972, the national sports associations in the Philippines were heavily critic-ised by the press and the public to such an extent that in 1974, the President replaced the outmoded Philippine Amateur Athletic Federation with the Department of Youth and Sports Development which was directly under his control. A new programme of sports development for the nation's youth was instigated, and a centre to train sports specialists, physical educators and recreation teachers was established

167

at the Department of Physical Education at the University of the Philippines. In 1976, the Board of Regents of the University approved the elevation of the Department of Physical Education into a degree granting unit and called it the U.P. Institute of Sports, Physical Education and Recreation. One year later the President promised that the government would offer its full support to a nationwide sports programme.[39]

The Republic of Korea put into operation new educational policies in 1961 and placed a great deal of emphasis on health and physical education. A greater time allocation for physical education was offered in all schools and more physical educators were to be trained to help expand the programme. The objectives of the National Physical Education Promotion Law in 1963 related to fitness, social aspects of physical education, new facilities, more specialists and 'to provide for the proper guidance of outstanding athletes'. In 1970 the city government of Seoul established a junior and senior high school to educate and train young athletes. At the same time the National Physical Education Council was created by the government and the Prime Minister served as chairman. There are ten universities and six colleges now offering degree study in physical education, but as yet no doctoral programme.[40]

Although one of the main problems regarding inadequate government funds for the training of physical education teachers is that many developing countries experience a lack of academic and public recognition of physical education, many Asian countries have nonetheless incorporated physical education and sport into their development plans.[41]

Library facilities

Obviously, a sound programme of professional preparation to degree level is dependent upon good library facilities, and this was one of the greatest deficiencies found in some of the developing nations (Brazil, People's Republic of China, Ethiopia, India, Mexico, and Thailand) by Bennett, Howell and Simri in their study of thirty-five nations[42], and in some African countries including Nigeria.[43]

Research

The developing nations are also less likely to be able to fund research programmes in physical education or related areas of study. Emerging nations generally have more pressing and urgent problems to solve such as the elimination of poverty, literacy, and housing programmes, the eradication of disease, etc.[44] If research is done at all, it tends to be restricted to surveys of the physical education programmes

168

in schools and the fitness testing of school children.[45]

One might argue that research and training in research techniques are not an important issue in the training of a physical education teacher, but it is undoubtedly important in the development and academic recognition of physical education as an area of study at university level, as well as for the physical education profession as a whole.

In the Soviet Union and other eastern bloc countries, research in physical education and the sports sciences is state financed and well-established in post-graduate departments of physical culture universities and scientific research institutes.[46]

Research in physical education and the sports sciences is now playing a more important role in many teacher education institutions in most European countries, Japan, Canada, U.S.A., New Zealand and Australia.[47] In the Federal Republic of Germany, for example, former institutes of physical education have become scientific institutes of sports with chairs for science of sports.[48]

At a more modest level, India is pleased to report that the first step in the development of research in physical education may have been taken with recent fellowships having been introduced in several institutions for research work in the field of physical education, sports and medical aspects of sports.[49]

It could appear that the increase in research activity in physical education over the last fifteen years had led to the expansion of knowledge in fields of study related to physical education.

Originally, research in physical education has been identified with medical and physiological topics; hence in many cases any link with universities in the professional preparation of teachers in many countries has been with medical schools. Although these areas of research are still given priority in many institutions, the last fifteen years have seen considerable research into the social and behavioural aspects of sport and physical education. Such an expansion may be related to a general development in interest in the behavioural sciences over recent years. In addition, medical and physiological aspects have also seen a broadening of areas of research and such fields as biochemistry, biomechanics, ergonomics, exercise physiology have been added to research in the natural sciences related to physical education.

There appears to be different attitudes towards research in physical education and sport between western and communist countries. While in the west there is a more specialist approach, in communist countries there has been a more integrative approach with several departments working at a common project and with centralised research institutes

169

emphasising the need to link theory with practice.[50] Nevertheless, recent developments in many European countries suggest that there are institutions playing a more integrative role than before.[51]

A concerted effort to co-ordinate and encourage research in physical education and sport really started in 1959 when the International Council for Sport and Physical Education was initiated, having as one of its objectives

> to support research and to establish co-operation with arts and sciences related to sport and physical education.[52]

Since the mid-1960s many smaller organisations based on a particular study area have been established, and in turn such organisations have helped to expand the various areas of knowledge related to physical education. The International Society of Sports Psychology was established in 1964, the International Committee for Sport Sociology in 1966, and the Philosophical Society for the Study of Sport was founded in the U.S.A. in 1972. The development of these organisations led to publications such as the International Journal of Sports Psychology (1970), the International Review of Sport Sociology (1966), the Journal of Sport History (1974), the Journal of Biomechanics (1968); yet the most established research publication, the Research Quarterly, has been published by the American Association for Health, Physical Education, Recreation (and now 'Dance') in the U.S.A. since 1930.

The status and consequent funding of research in physical education and sport vary in the different countries. In communist countries and Japan there are a large number of full-time research scientists employed, whereas in many western nations lecturers may still have to combine research with their teaching duties, although research fellowships or assistantships are now more common. In 1975 approximately ten full-time researchers were found in each of Canada, France, Israel, New Zealand, South Africa and Switzerland and none in Holland, Nigeria, Norway, Taiwan and Uruguay.[53]

Opportunities for studying in Canada and the U.S.A. at master and doctoral level have existed for some time, and physical educationists from all over the world have improved their qualifications in this way when their own countries have not operated such programmes.[54]

The first doctoral degrees in physical education were largely in medical aspects of physical education but now, according to Pieron, one can obtain a doctorate in a variety of sub-disciplines allied to physical education in the U.S.A., West Germany, Austria, Belgium, Czechslovakia, Poland, Canada, South Africa, Finland, Australia, Great Britain,

170

Japan and the Netherlands.[55]

The expansion of theoretical work in initial training courses for physical education teachers

The expansion of research in physical education and the academic study of various areas of knowledge related to physical education in the last twenty years has resulted in a very broad curriculum for the professional preparation of physical education teachers.

As such courses have become more theoretical, they have become more acceptable in the academic world, as Bennett et al. have noted:

> One is tempted to make the generalisation that physical education is better accepted by the academic community in those countries where the greater part of the course work is theoretical.[56]

In fact, in the U.S.A. some courses in physical education seem to have become almost totally theoretical, and more recent changes in polytechnic and college courses in Great Britain since the James Report[57], and the call for diversification of college courses, has led to the development of highly theoretical courses in this country. Also the titles of such courses may have changed with 'Human Movement Studies', 'Sports Studies', 'Sports Science' etc. being more common titles.

Certainly there is the acceptance in some countries that the field of Sport and Physical Education can be studied as a discipline in its own right, as one might study mathematics or history. In such cases the student purely studies the academic content of the subject as well as research technique, and his courses will be designed to produce a student who may help develop the body of knowledge. The student may also decide to teach physical education and take a post-graduate qualification, although other career opportunities may be open to him.

As courses have become more theoretical, many feel that the balance between theory and practical work may have suffered, and consequently courses may have lost contact with the practical nature of the profession. In this respect, Seurin, commenting upon the training of French physical education teachers, gives two warnings

> against the dangers of excessive intellectualisation when too many teachers become scientific researchers, and against the powerful social influence of sports tending to the production of sports trainers rather than physical educators.[58]

171

In communist countries like East Germany[59] and Romania[60], although there is a greater importance now placed upon theoretical study of the sports sciences and research, there is still an important concentration on practical aspects of courses.

As a result of the third reform in higher education in East Germany in 1969, a scientific-productive curriculum was established for physical education specialists. After a uniform basic training for all students in East Germany and the Soviet Union, early specialisation is stressed, where students have to participate in intensive training in one sport. Soviet students also have to spend a period of time working as coach in their chosen event in an elite 'Sports School', learning how to select talented children, evaluate their performance and coach them to improve their performance.[61]

In Canada, U.S.A., Japan and Norway 75% or more of the curriculum was theoretical in 1975, as opposed to 70% in Finland and 40% in Austria.[62]

In France the Diploma in Sciences and Techniques of Physical Activities and Sport course at I.N.S.E.P. in Paris lasts two years and at least one-third of the total teaching time must be practical. Theory takes up the remainder of the time as Table 1 indicates.[63] As 40% theory was recorded as being fairly typical of French institutions in the early 1970s, it would appear that recent moves to university courses has emphasised a greater proportion of theoretical study as Seurin had suggested.[64]

But it has not been the ratio of theory and practical physical experience that has caused many physical educators to be dissatisfied with new courses - it is more the imbalance between college-based work and teaching practice. Such feelings have been noted by writers in both Finland and Israel.

Table 1: The Academic Year 1976-77: Subjects Selected by the Paris v University. Distribution of teaching time (1st + 2nd years)

Subjects	Teaching	Total Teaching Time	1st Year 700 hrs.	2nd Year 600 hrs.
	Modern Languages	65	65	
C O	General, historical and technological study of phys. act. and sport (1)	100	50	50

172

Table 1 (cont'd)

Subjects	Teaching	Total Teaching Time	1st Year 700 hrs.	2nd Year 600 hrs.
M P U L S O R Y	Evaluated/programmed phys.act. + sport, with other compulsory discipl. (2)	275	150	125
	Intro. to math, method, statistics + principles of mechanics (3)	100	50	50
60% min	Biological sciences: gen. biology, anatomy + hum.physiology (4)	175	125	50
(art.4)	Human sciences: princ. of psychology, socio-psychology + sociology (5)	175	75	100
CHOSEN BY THE UNIVERSITY	Biomechanics + physio. of human movement	50		50
	Education sciences	50	50	
20% max	Practical phys.act. + sports	200	100	100
CHOSEN BY THE 10% STUDENT min		130	55	75

After Villet, M. 'Training of PE/Sports teachers for secondary education', Paper presented at 2nd Anglo-French seminar,
INSEP, Paris, 1977, p. 56.

In his comments on the Wingate/Haifa University linked
degree course, Eldar has suggested:

Our opinion is that when we are concerned with teacher training, the specialisation in the sciences of movement and sport must be presented simultaneously and integrated with their educational implications, together with an in-depth study of the theory and practice of education. Separating the science of movement and its educational implications - or giving priority to only one of the two, will cause the desired target to be missed.[65]

In Finland, the weakness of earlier courses training specialist physical education teachers as well as other specialist teachers was the fact that academic education took place at universities and was followed by practical teaching which was totally separated from the university. As Telema points out when describing the new course at Jyraskyla University:

Theoretical elements and practice teaching should be inter-linked so that results of theoretical studies are from time to time applied in practice, and after some practice the students return to the faculty to supplement their theoretical competence on the basis of practical experience. This is the functional way of establishing fruitful interaction between theory and practice.[66]

In Japan, only four weeks' teaching practice is required, usually at the end of a three year theoretical degree programme.[67]

In the U.S.A., Canada and Great Britain special physical education teachers may have a one year professional programme at the end of a largely theoretical course. In some cases the earlier degree course may not actually be in physical education, but could be human movement studies, sports studies, etc. A degree course that does not have a qualification purely directed toward teaching may tend to offer a wider range of career opportunities. Consequently, students may prefer a one year teacher training qualification at the end of their degree course rather than the four year B.Ed. purely linked to the teaching profession.

Rather than have an imbalance between theory and practice, the socialist countries of Eastern Europe, while appreciating that the development of sports science in the 1970s means that a greater degree of background scientific knowledge is required on physical education courses, have very simply extended the period of training from four to five years.[68]

The development of institutions and courses that may educate
for a variety of career routes in physical education and
sport

Alongside the development and expansion of areas of knowledge
related to physical education has been the creation of
institutions that may offer career routes into occupations
outside teaching.

In communist and eastern bloc countries, higher
education institutions have for some time trained physical
education teachers, coaches, trainers and sports administrators alongside each other, although separate 'academies'
or 'schools' for coaches are now common.[69]

This is very different from the situation in North
America as Shneidman points out:

> In higher education, the main stress in North America
> is on the preparation of secondary schoolteachers.
> Soviet institutions of higher learning, however, also
> train highly qualified specialists in different sports.
> These specialists are later employed as coaches and
> administrators and also occupy top positions in clubs,
> sports societies, committees and federations.[70]

The Moscow Institute for Physical Culture, for example,
has pedagogical faculties which are mainly concerned with
the training of physical education teachers and instructors
for secondary specialised schools and institutes of higher
learning, while the sports faculties train coaches, trainers,
instructors and specialists in different areas of physical
education and sport.[71] A similar situation exists in
Bulgaria, the German Democratic Republic, Yugoslavia, Poland,
Czechoslovakia and Hungary, where separate courses of four
or five years' study may qualify the student either as a
physical education teacher, coach, or sports administrator.[72]

The National Sports Institute (I.N.S.E.P.) in Paris has
an education department that trains physical education
teachers, coaches, 'educateurs sportif' and sports administrators.[73] As an institution it is very similar to the
Wingate Institute in Israel[74] in that it also serves a
multitude of functions related to its initial brief of
being a centre 'par excellence' for the promotion of high
level sport in France. In this respect I.N.S.E.P. has
three other departments, a high level sport department for
elite athletes and coaches, a research department and a
medical department with physiological monitoring of elite
athletes as one of its functions.[75]

In certain countries, broad based courses may offer
students the opportunity to change the career route during
a course by choosing course modules or credits that direct

them into recreation management, leisure or sports administration, research, physiotherapy or coaching.

For example, in Finland, although the basic degree, the
master of science in physical education, is taken by all
students, and half of the studies are common to all students,
students may eventually specialise in teaching, physiotherapy,
administration, public health, or coaching, as Table 2
shows.[76]

Table 2: A Schematic Model of the Structure of the Educational Programme at the Faculty of Health and P.E.,
University of Jyvaskyla

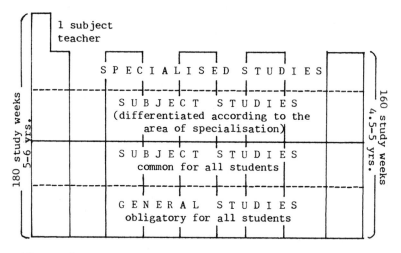

After Telema, R. 'The Training of Physical Education teachers
in Finland', International Journal of Physical Education,
Volume XVI, number 4, 1979, p. 12.

At the Wingate Institute in Israel, the physical
education sciences aspect of the course, particularly at the
advanced (third year) level, includes subjects that, in
addition to their contribution to the work of the teacher in
schools, are designed to prepare students for other occupations outside teaching. In following up the past graduates
of Wingate in 1979, it was found that 15% of them were
occupied in organisational or administrative work or were

instructors of physical education in local municipalities, university, community centres, or sports clubs.[77]

In Cuba students at the E.S.E.F. colleges (Escuala Provinciale de Educacion Fisica) must decide during the course whether they are going to specialise in teaching, coaching, therapeutic gymnastics or recreation management, but all students attend a similar basic course. This common basic course enables the physical education teacher in Cuba to become a 'community' physical educationist, as Hampson suggests:

> The essence of the training at the E.S.E.F. college is the creation of a new type of physical education specialist. This is the obvious parallel with the creation of the New Man. A P.E. specialist who would be capable of initiating research in the sports sciences, biological sciences and in teaching techniques. Such a specialist would be expected to work for the benefit of others in the general community, so that the general level of physical education and sport could be raised. Once again one can note the obvious parallel with Guevara's philosophy.[78]

In Romania a unified four year curriculum is offered by the Institute for Physical Culture in Bukarest. There is a common basic two year course with the opportunity to specialise as a 'coach' in the third and fourth years or become a secondary school physical education specialist.[79]

THE PROFESSIONAL PREPARATION IN THE TEACHING OF PHYSICAL EDUCATION OF ELEMENTARY SCHOOL TEACHERS

The professional preparation of the non-specialist teacher in the teaching of physical education continues to be unsatisfactory in many of the developed countries, to the extent that many children throughout the world may not be taught by a physical education specialist until the age of eleven years. But there are signs that this is changing. In the case of the emerging nations, the problems are more acute with the possibility of little organised physical education at all at elementary school level.[80]

The classroom teacher in the elementary school is considered to be an expert teacher of all subjects in the elementary school curriculum, yet physical education may have a very limited time allocation on professional courses[81], or be optional. In fact, physical education is not required as part of an elementary teacher's course in Denmark and West Germany, and Swedish teachers may choose between physical education and music.[82] In Great Britain a recent national survey[83] has shown that many college courses are now allotted much less than the recommended thirty hours[84], and at some colleges the course is optional. It was noticeable in the British survey that many physical education lecturers put the blame on the development of the B.Ed. degree for primary teachers, and that academic study appeared to have greater emphasis than curriculum method courses.

In many countries inadequate training of elementary school teachers in physical education has meant that physical education specialists, often having been trained specifically for the elementary school, either tour schools as advisory teachers[85] or are employed as 'curriculum leaders'.

In Israel, specialist teachers and 'expert' peripatetic physical education teachers are used to 'counter' the inadequate training of the classroom teacher through school-based in-service work.[86] A similar situation is in operation in Austria.[87]

Other countries like Finland and the German Democratic Republic devote more time to the training of elementary teachers in the teaching of physical education. Finland allocates at least 200 hours[88] and the German Democratic Republic 131 hours to training in physical education (although this is likely to be increased with a fourth year of training) as well as using specialist teachers in the elementary schools.[89] In fact the use of specialists in the elementary school is becoming more common practice.

In Uruguay primary teachers may supposedly specialise in physical education with a one year course, and in Argentina the same course is of two years' duration.[90]

Mongolia tends to use para-professional staff in the elementary school for teaching physical education[91] and in New Zealand 20% of primary teachers may have majored in physical education.[92]

Half of elementary school classes in the U.S.A. are now taught by specialist elementary school physical education teachers[93] and because of inadequate professional preparation of class teachers, physical education specialists are now employed in Dutch elementary schools.[94] There is also evidence that more specialist teachers will be used in the earlier grades of Soviet schools.[95]

It does appear that in certain countries of the world greater value is placed on the importance of specialist teaching of physical education in the elementary schools, or at least in having adequate professional training for the class teacher. In other developed countries previously sound professional training of class teachers may have been affected by a greater emphasis on more academic courses, with physical education course modules being optional[96], but also in certain countries, Great Britain being one, there is still considerable opposition to the physical education

178

specialist in the elementary school.

CONCLUSION

The considerable expansion of research and the areas of knowledge related to physical education and sports in the last twenty years have helped physical education become an academically respectable field of study in many developed countries. Institutions training specialist teachers of physical education have become more closely linked with universities or have become multi-purpose institutions training teachers, coaches, recreational managers, adminis- trators and research workers in a variety of sub-disciplines.

In certain cases the study of physical education and sport has become a discipline in its own right with students following courses in research techniques related to expanding the body of knowledge in such fields as exercise physiology, sports sociology, sports psychology, biomechanics, and the comparative and historical study of sport. In fact physical education as a course title may be less common, with human movement studies, sports education, sports studies, sports sciences, recreational studies and physical culture more the vogue.

The development of physical education as an academically respectable area of study may not necessarily be important for the development of a competent teacher, but it is vital for the maturation of physical education as a profession.

In the developing nations of the world, poor library and sports facilities, inadequate funding of research, and a lack of recognition of the value of physical education in the school curriculum continue to inhibit the development of physical education and the training of the specialist teacher to degree status. On the other hand emerging nations may see the training of a well-qualified physical education teacher as a necessary step in the development of sport in their country, with the ultimate aim of achieving possible recognition in the international sporting arena.

In the elementary school, although there is a trend towards the employment of specialist teachers in some countries, on the whole inadequate training in the teaching of physical education for the 'class teacher' has meant that the elementary school physical education curriculum continues to be an area of concern.

NOTES

1   B.L. Bennett, M.L. Howell and U. Simri, Compara- tive Physical Education and Sport, Philadelphia, Lea and Fabiger, 1975, p. 92.
    2.   ibid.

3. Z. Jaworski, "Study curriculum for physical education of the universities of the socialistic countries", International Journal of Physical Education, Volume XVI, number 3, 1979.

4. International Council on Health, Physical Education and Recreation, National Policies and Practices concerning the role of physical education and sport in the education of youth, London, UNESCO, 1980.

5. ibid.

6. ibid.

7. M. Villet, "Training of P.E./Sports Teachers for Secondary Education" in Comparative Study on the training of physical education teachers for secondary schools, Second Anglo-French Seminar I.N.S.E.P., Paris, 1977.

8. ibid., p. 60.

9. B.L. Bennett et al., op. cit.

10. G.A. Paton, "Sport and Physical Education in Canada" in W. Johnson (ed), Sport and Physical Education Around the World, Champaign, Illinois, Stipes Publishing Co., 1980.

11. T. Reilly, "The Background and Organisation of Physical Education in Japan", Physical Education Review, Volume 2, number 1, 1979.

12. D. Eldar, "P.E. in Israel - Teacher Training", British Journal of Physical Education, Volume 9, number 2, 1978.

13. D. Eldar, "The training of physical education teachers in Israel", Paper presented at the Second British-Israeli Seminar on Physical Education, Sports and Leisure, Warwick University, September 1980, P.E.A.

14. J.A. Daly, "Sport and Physical Education in Australia" in W. Johnson, op. cit., p. 13.

15. International Council on Health, Physical Education and Recreation, op. cit., p. 81.

16. R. Telema, "The Training of Physical Education Teachers in Finland", International Journal of Physical Education, Volume XVI, number 4, 1979.

17. J.A. Adedeji, "The Ascendancy of Physical Education, 1900-1960: A study of physical education as a teaching subject in Nigerian schools", International Journal of Physical Education, Volume XVII, number 3, 1980, p. 26.

18. J. Broekhoff, "Sport and Physical Education in the Netherlands" in W. Johnson, op. cit., p. 439.

19. International Council on Health, Physical Education and Recreation, op. cit., p. 102.

20. M.A. Clay, "Sport and Physical Education in Colombia" in W. Johnson, op. cit., p. 140.

21. International Council on Health, Physical Education and Recreation, op. cit.

N. Fox, "Trends and progress in physical education and sport in selected emerging nations", Bulletin of Physical Education, Volume XII, number 3, 1976.

22. International Council on Health, Physical Education and Recreation, op. cit., p. 69.

23. W.K. Low, "Problems in the development of sports in schools and in the community in Asian countries", F.I.E.P. Bulletin, Volume 50, number 3/4, 1980.

24. D.W.J. Anthony, "Oil rich Kuwait gives a boost to school sport", Times Educational Supplement, 14th April, 1975.

25. International Council on Health, Physical Education and Recreation, op. cit., p. 98.

26. W. Johnson, "Sport and Physical Education in India" in W. Johnson (ed), op. cit., pp. 309-11.
International Council on Health, Physical Education and Recreation, op. cit., p. 53.

27. International Council on Health, Physical Education and Recreation, op. cit., p. 89.

28. S.K. Wong, "A Comparative Study of Physical Education, Sports and Recreation in Hong Kong and Japan", unpublished M.A. dissertation, University of Hull, 1981.

29. W.K. Low, "The training of physical education teachers in Singapore and Hong Kong", F.I.E.P. Bulletin, Volume 47, number 3, 1977.

30. International Council on Health, Physical Education and Recreation, op. cit., p. 8.

31. D.M. Semotiuk, "Motives for national government involvement in sport", International Journal of Physical Education, Volume XVIII, number 1, 1981.

32. ibid., p. 25.

33. International Council on Health, Physical Education and Recreation, op. cit., p. 8.

34. N. Shneidman, The Soviet Road to Olympus: Theory and Practice of Soviet Physical Culture and Sport, London, Routledge and Kegan Paul, 1979, p. 2.

35. J. Riordan, "Physical culture in the Soviet Union", Physical Education Review, Volume 1, number 1, 1978, p. 10.

36. N. Shneidman, op. cit., p. 73.

37. J. Riordan (ed), Sport under Communism, London, C. Hurst and Co., 1978.
J. Riordan, "Provision for excellence in Sport - the U.S.S.R." Report of the British Universities Physical Education Association Biennial Conference, Heriot-Watt University, 1980.

38. M. Speak, "The Concept of Excellence in Sport in France and its implications for French Universities", Report of the British Universities Physical Education Association Biennial Conference, Heriot-Watt University, 1980.

39. J.J. Ruiz, "Sports and Physical Education in the Philippines", in W. Johnson, op. cit., pp. 489-509.

40. Kim Daeshik, "Sport and Physical Education in the

Republic of Korea" in W. Johnson, op. cit., pp. 383-98.

41. N. Fox, op. cit., p. 21.

42. B.L. Bennett et al., op. cit., p. 98.

43. Personal communication, S. Obasohan, Lecturer in Physical Education, Abraka College of Education, Bendel State, Nigeria.

44. N. Fox, op. cit., p. 19.
J C. Andrews, "Problems of Physical Education in the World", Paper presented as part of the 'Ciclo International de Conferencias Sobre Problemas de La Educatias Fisica en el Mundo', Vera Cruz, Mexico, 1981.

45. International Council on Health, Physical Education and Recreation, op. cit.

46. N. Shneidman, op. cit., p. 81.

47. International Council on Health, Physical Education and Recreation, op. cit.

48. ibid., p. 47.

49. ibid., p. 55.

50. N. Shneidman, op. cit., p. 83.

51. M. Speak, op. cit., p. 50.

52. B.L. Bennett et al., op. cit., p. 169.

53. ibid., p. 172.

54. T. Slack and G. Fishouse, "Physical Education Degree Opportunities in Canada", British Journal of Physical Education, Volume 10, number 3, 1979.
S. Ross, "P.E. and Sport in Canada - II", British Journal of Physical Education, Volume 7, number 4, 1976.

55. M. Pieron, "Structure et Organisation des Etudes de Doctorat en Education Physique", Gymnasion, Volume IX, number 9, 1972.

56. B.L. Bennett et al., op. cit., p. 95.

57. Teacher Education and Training (James Report), H.M.S.O., 1972.

58. P. Seurin, "The Training of Physical Education Teachers in Schools", Revue d'Education Physique, Volume XVIII, number 1, 1978.

59. Werner Kuhn, "Sport and Physical Education in the German Democratic Republic" in W. Johnson, op. cit., pp. 255-76.

60. J. Anderson, "P.E. in Romania", British Journal of Physical Education, Volume 6, number 6, 1975.

61. J. Hargreaves and D. Kingston, "From G.T.O. to Olympic Glory", Bulletin of Physical Education, Volume XV, number 1, 1979.

62. B.L. Bennett et al., op. cit., p. 95.

63. M. Villet, op. cit., p. 56.

64. P. Seurin, op. cit.

65. D. Eldar, op. cit., p. 8.

66. R. Telema, "The Training of Physical Education Teachers in Finland", International Journal of Physical

Education, Volume XVI, number 4, 1979, p. 14.
67.   T. Reilly, op. cit.
Matthew G. Maetozo, Kim Daeshik and Yang Boon Han, "Physical
Education and Sport in Japan", International Journal of
Physical Education, Volume XVIII, number 1, 1981.
68.   Z. Jaworski, op. cit., p. 39.
69.   N. Shneidman, op. cit.
70.   ibid., p. 86.
71.   ibid., p. 74.
72.   Z. Jaworski, op. cit.
73.   M. Speak, op. cit.
74.   S. Ross, "The Wingate Institute for Sport and
Physical Education", Canadian Association of Health, Physical
Education and Recreation Journal, Volume 44, number 6, 1978.
75.   M. Speak, op. cit.
76.   R. Telema, op. cit., p. 12.
77.   D. Eldar, op. cit.
78.   L. Hampson, "Socialism and the aims of physical
education in Cuba", Physical Education Review, Volume 3,
number 1, 1980, p. 80.
79.   Z. Jaworski, op. cit.
80.   International Council on Health, Physical Education
and Recreation, op. cit.
81.   G. Paton, "Sport and Physical Education in Canada"
in W. Johnson, op. cit., p. 96.
82.   B.L. Bennett et al., op. cit., p. 102.
83.   M.A. Mawer, "Professional courses in physical
education for non-specialist Primary and Middle School
teachers", British Journal of Physical Education, Volume 9,
number 6, 1978.
84.   British Association of Organisers and Lecturers in
Physical Education, Training in Physical Education for
Primary Teachers, 1974.
85.   K. Whitaker, "Co-operative approach to primary
physical education", British Journal of Physical Education,
Volume 11, number 3, 1980.
86.   Roches Ilana, "Professional Courses in Physical
Education for Class Teachers", Paper presented at the Second
British-Israeli Seminar on Physical Education, Sports and
Leisure, Warwick University, September 1980.
87.   N.J. Moolenijzer, "Sport and Physical Education in
Austria" in W. Johnson, op. cit., p. 30.
88.   Anna-Maija Kivimaki, "Finnish Objectives", British
Journal of Physical Education, Volume 8, number 2, 1977.
89.   Werner Kuhn, "Sport and Physical Education in the
German Democratic Republic" in W. Johnson, op. cit., p. 271.
90.   International Council on Health, Physical Education
and Recreation, op. cit., pp. 10 and 119.
91.   ibid., p. 79.
92.   ibid., p. 81.

93.   ibid., p. 117.
94.   J. Broekhoff, op. cit., p. 440.
95.   J. Hargreaves and D. Kingston, op. cit., p. 28.
96.   M.A. Mawer, op. cit.

THE TRAINING OF TEACHERS OF MODERN LANGUAGES IN ENGLAND AND FRANCE

Robert Weil

> After six or seven years of being taught a foreign
> language, 99% of pupils are incapable of forming an
> original sentence, of reading a newspaper article or
> of conversing with a foreign child of their own age
> in his language ... If parents imagine that their
> children learn a foreign language at school in order
> to be able to use it later in life they are totally
> mistaken.[1]

Language teachers may nod sagely as they hear this
indictment, couched in terms with which they have become
familiar through their perusal of many an official report.
If they have read these very words, either in The Guardian
of 9 June 1981 or The Sunday Telegraph of 26 July 1981,
they may recall that the quotation is a translation from an
article that appeared in Le Monde on 30 January this year.[2]
The headline of this article refers to the désastre of the
teaching of modern languages in France and to the ten
reforms proposed by Pierre Bertaux, Professor of German at
Paris III (Asnières-Sorbonne Nouvelle). Bertaux is the
official spokesman of the Council for the Dissemination of
Foreign Languages which was set up by Giscard d'Estaing in
1980. Although this body has not as yet published its
findings, these reported comments and recommendations, made
in the presence of the then Minister of Education, were
intended to cause maximum impact.

This is not the place to discuss the state of the
teaching of modern languages, either in France or this
country. No doubt, many teachers hold strong views on the
subject, as shown, for example, in the correspondence
columns of Le Monde of 11 March.[3] We must confine ourselves
to the report's implications for the training of teachers
of modern languages. Indeed, recommendations 4 and 5 specifically underline the need for changes in the initial
training of teachers and in-service training, the latter

185

paragraph using the very vivid term of recyclage which
seems to suggest that teachers could be recycled like so
much industrial waste!

Teacher trainers would have their work cut out if all
the other recommendations were to be implemented. Thus
they would have to enable their students to introduce a
modern language to a much younger age cohort than at
present. (If Professor Bertaux and his colleagues knew
about the experiment to teach French in primary schools in
England in the 'sixties and the unfavourable findings of the
Burstall Report in 1974[4], they chose to ignore it). They
would also have to show teachers how to give intensive
courses to the same group of pupils for eight periods a day
for two or three or four weeks at a time. Teachers would
also have to adjust themselves to the startling, if perhaps
not altogether unwelcome, principle enunciated by Professor
Bertaux that only those pupils should be taught languages
who wanted to learn them. The other suggestions, that
greater emphasis should be placed on reading in the foreign
language, that foreign assistants should be more closely
associated with the teaching of languages, and that teacher
and pupils exchanges with other European countries should
be encouraged, all have implications for teacher training.

For a country that until quite recently paid scant
attention to the professional training of secondary
teachers, France would seem to have come a long way. It is
less than ten years since the Joxe Commission was set up to
report on "the teaching function in secondary education".
After noting with approval the Ministry's earlier statement
that "l'enseignement était une profession complexe et
difficile à laquelle il faut se préparer longuement, tech-
niquement et psychologiquement"[5], the Commission in the
twelfth of its eighteen recommendations stressed the need
for much better provision for the initial and in-service
training of teachers. Incidentally, in the second last of
its recommendations, which is concerned with the role of the
inspectorate, the Joxe Report stressed the value of comparisons with other educational systems. Even if it was only
for the higher echelons of the educational pyramid that a
niche was to be found for comparative education, it is
pleasing to note this accolade. Comparative studies represent not only an academic discipline, they often have an
"applied" dimension which can help administrators and
teachers in their search for a solution to particularly
difficult problems which other countries have also had to
face.

Joxe may have proposed - so had James[6] at about the
same time - but it is quite a different matter to assess
how effectively those in control of teacher training have
disposed. Judging by Professor Bertaux's strictures and

Eric Hawkins' book on Modern Languages in the Curriculum[7],
changes in the training of teachers of modern languages,
though adumbrated for a decade or so, have yet to be put
into effect.

Among those who, already some time ago, saw the need
for a new approach not only in this country but also on the
Continent, was W.D. Halls whose book on Foreign Languages
and Education in Western Europe was published in 1970. He
records that in 1969 the European Ministers of Education
adopted a resolution which aimed at converting into reality
the slogan "a modern language for everybody by 1980".[8] He
traces this aim back to a conference of the Council of
Europe, held at Sèvres in 1959, and to subsequent meetings
at ministerial level when it was resolved that "the programme should include the opening of national documentation
and information centres on modern language teaching; the
extension by all European countries to pupils aged ten and
over of the teaching of a widely spoken European language;
the extension of language teaching later to pupils below
that age; the modernization of teaching programmes; the
expansion of study visits abroad and of exchanges; and the
development of teacher-training programmes which would
include courses on recent methodological findings, linguistics, and the use of educational technology".[9]

A check list on progress so far in England and France
would reveal some encouraging facts. Thus the Centre for
Information on Language Teaching and Research and its French
counterpart serve as very useful documentation and information centres. Most pupils over ten or eleven are, in fact,
taught a foreign language. As for extending the teaching
of modern languages to pupils in the primary school, we
have seen that, in spite of Halls' assertion that "there can
be no turning back"[10], the experiment has not been considered
a success in England and has been abandoned in many areas,
although it may yet be tried in France. In the intervening
years there has been an expansion of study visits and
exchanges abroad, but only an upturn in the economic
fortunes (of which, at present, there is little sign in
either country) will prevent retrenchment of such programmes.
This leaves us with teacher training linked to the modernization of teaching programmes.

In his book Halls stated that "the attainment of
bilingualism in Western Europe by 1980 will depend largely
on the quantity and quality of teachers available".[11] He
added that "although the problem of numbers now seems
nearer solution, we have perhaps as yet paid insufficient
attention to the quality of teacher training, the first
condition of which is the acquisition of linguistic
competence".[12] The problem of numbers has indeed been
solved in a way that, surprisingly, does not seem to have

been foreseen by demographers. Because of the falling
birthrate, even in France in spite of all the inducements
there to reverse the trend, there is apparently an embarras
de richesse as far as teacher numbers are concerned. As a
consequence, higher qualifications are now required of
future teachers. In the department where I teach we have
insisted, for the past few years, that future teachers of
modern languages must have spent at least one academic year
abroad, and I imagine that other institutions in the United
Kingdom and France now make similar stipulations. Of course,
a year abroad, even as assistant(e), does not, by itself,
constitute a guarantee of linguistic competence, but without
this experience it is much less likely that the teacher will
be sufficiently fluent in speaking, and thus teaching the
language. One of the main reasons for the disappointing
results of primary French was the lack of fluency, and hence
confidence of many of the primary teachers. But in the
secondary sector, because of the more stringent qualifications that are now required, we have the right to expect
new teachers of modern languages to have attained an
acceptable level not only of accuracy but also of fluency.
This can and must be a top priority in our selection
procedure.

Two further advantages for teacher training accrue if
the year abroad has been spent in a school. Successful
completion of a stint as assistant augurs well for the
student's ability to cope with teaching practice, which will
require all the stamina and ingenuity which he or she will
have shown in the other country. The student who has
successfully survived in a completely strange school in a
foreign environment is unlikely to be unduly dismayed by
whatever may be in store nearer at home. Secondly, such a
student almost automatically becomes a comparativist and,
as a recent field worker, has a great deal to contribute to
the discussion of comparative issues.

Dr. Halls had specifically referred to teacher training
programmes "which would include courses on recent methodological findings, linguistics, and the use of educational
technology".[13] For the latest and very informative and
cogently argued statement on these and other aspects of the
teaching of modern languages, we can turn to Eric Hawkins'
book to which reference has already been made. Indeed, it
is likely that Professor Bertaux and his colleagues are
familiar with some of Hawkins' views. Thus when Bertaux
castigates "la méthode du saupoudrage horaire"[14], it is
difficult not to think of Hawkins' condemnation of the
"drip feed" method. However, it is extremely doubtful
whether it will prove feasible, either in England or France,
to manipulate the school timetable (not to mention one's
Headteacher and colleagues!) in such a way as to allow the

concentrated teaching of modern languages envisaged by both men, and therefore training for such a hypothetical "immersion" treatment is unlikely to feature prominently in institutions in either country.

Concerning linguistics, it would be interesting to find out what priority it is given in the various education departments. The subject is not mentioned by Professor Bertaux. Hawkins, on the other hand, attaches great importance to it, but he also quotes Chomsky who admitted that he was "frankly rather sceptical about the significance for the teaching of languages of such insights and understanding as have been attained in linguistics and psychology".15 It may well be that colleagues in England and France are now less convinced of the strictly utilitarian value of linguistics. Unless Hawkins' advocacy of a new school subject called "Language", a bridging course between the mother tongue and foreign languages, were given official backing, which is unlikely, linguistics will hardly continue to feature prominently in teacher training programmes.

As for educational technology, Hawkins, although far from being an educational Luddite, has never been one to be blinded by it. He certainly recognizes the tremendous value of a tape or cassette recorder and of other machines, but they do not represent a panacea - least of all the so-called language laboratory. He maintains that the only true laboratory for the modern linguist is the country whose language he is studying. Bertaux would not dissent from this view. He advocates teacher and pupil exchange, but has nothing to say about educational technology. It will hardly be accorded as prominent a place in teacher training as in recent years, but, of course, we must continue to ensure that our students can use competently and confidently the various recorders and projectors that are available.

If neither recent methodological findings nor linguistics nor the use of educational technology are likely to be given top priority billing in teacher training, what are the most important issues? The basic problem to be faced by all teachers of modern languages in both countries is the survival of the subject in the curriculum. It may seem paradoxical, but in spite of, or perhaps because of the remarkable increase, during the past decade or two, in the number of pupils having a modern language on their timetable, the subject is in danger of disappearing from the curriculum. In the selective grammar school or the former lycée, the place of modern languages was secure enough, although even here the decline of Latin (not to mention Greek) which was not so long ago thought to be in an impregnable position, should have set the alarm bells ringing. But in the comprehensive school there is a very real risk of French being declared a subject non grata

because it is considered to be too difficult, not to say
"élitist". The position of English in the <u>collège d'enseign-</u>
<u>ment secondaire</u> may be less vulnerable. This is not because
teachers there are more successful in teaching the foreign
language (according to Bertaux they clearly are not), but
because English is "in", because it is "chic" to know some
English, the language of cop and pop. However, even if
there is less pupil resistance in France to the learning of
a foreign language, the opposition may come from the
teachers. Professor Bertaux, looking at the problem from
the point of view of an academic, believes that the attempt
to teach a foreign language to every pupil, in the name of
a mistaken view of egalitarianism, represents an enormous
waste of time, money and effort. The subject should be
restricted to those who want to learn, and what they want
to learn would have to conform to the traditional and time-
honoured syllabus.

Hawkins takes a very different view. He believes that
equity demands that every pupil should be given the
opportunity to learn a modern language, and that it is
especially the child from a deprived background who must be
given the chance of making a new start in a neutral medium
to help him overcome deficiencies in his own language. If
we accept Hawkins' thesis - and Bertaux is not the only one
who would have to be persuaded - it follows that the top
priority of any teacher training course must be the
realisation that teachers will have to cater for an all-
ability range. This, of course, does not imply that pupils
must be taught in mixed-ability classes. Indeed, after the
first year or so, this would be as unwise as to match heavy-
weights with lightweights, or to have undifferentiated
("unstreamed") football teams.

The Council of Europe with its work on the "threshold"[16]
and "waystage" levels, and the many working parties throughout the United Kingdom which are in the process of devising
"graded" tests in French and other languages point the way
to more realistic and clearly defined aims. It is worth
remembering that in music it has long been established that
pupils proceed from one grade to another as they acquire
additional skills.

Within the framework of a common curriculum, to which
both countries now seem committed, teacher trainers will
have to devise different teaching strategies to suit
different groups of pupils. "In der Beschränkung zeigt sich
erst der Meister" - Goethe's "Meister" does not, of course,
refer to the school master, but the dictum that the true
master is the one who is aware of the limitations imposed
on him and is determined to see them not as an insurmountable obstacle but as a positive aid to greater achievement,
might well encourage us and our students as we face the

190

problem and challenge of teaching the entire ability range without alienating the great majority of pupils. A realistic limitation of aims does not necessarily imply the abandonment of whole areas of language studies, as has sometimes happened. Thus, in the past, it has been considered fashionable to jettison grammar. Yet Professor Bertaux is surely right when he maintains that "la grammaire n'a pas dit son dernier mot"[17] (grammar has not said its last word). One suspects that Professor Hawkins would not dissent from this view, provided that grammar was taught in a meaningful manner.

The value of written language in the classroom has also been questioned, and some teacher trainers have looked askance at their students using readers in their lessons or even writing foreign words on the blackboard. They may be surprised to read in Hawkins' book that we actually deprive pupils if we do not allow them to learn a language by eye as well as by ear. Both he and Bertaux include reading as one of the desirable skills and achievements. There is nowadays so much varied reading material available that it would be folly to exclude it from the potential aids at our disposal.

The emphasis in our language teaching may in future concentrate on the receptive rather than the productive skills, because success, the key to further progress, is more likely to be achieved in comprehending the foreign language than in actually using it. But here, too, we should avoid being dogmatic, because pupils can be quite keen to express themselves in the other language, if sufficiently provoked! It need not be our task as teacher trainers to devise yet another method for language teachers (Hawkins lists forty-four differently named methods!)[18]: we should look for those elements, to be found in most methods, that will help us in our task.

In the United Kingdom and France, language teachers are probably, on the whole, less successful than their colleagues elsewhere in Europe. The main reason is that English speaking pupils and, to a lesser extent, French speaking pupils are less motivated to learn other languages. Meetings with our colleagues in other countries might well help us and the French, in a comparative setting, to pool ideas in order to disprove the statement made to the Select Committee on Education and reported in the TES that "teaching modern languages in secondary schools is a waste of time and money"[19], the very words used in France by Professor Bertaux.

One hundred years ago (in 1882) Viëtor proclaimed: "Der Sprachunterricht muss umkehren".[20] A former Minister of Education is not the only one to dislike U-turns. Learning from our own experience and that of our colleagues elsewhere

191

in Europe, and eschewing commitment to any one panacea, it must be possible to ensure that teaching a modern language makes a positive contribution to the education of the great majority of pupils. This must be our priority.

NOTES

1.   The Guardian, 9 June 1981, p. 11.
2.   Le Monde, 30 January 1981, p. 11.
3.   Le Monde, 11 March 1981, p. 14.
4.   C. Burstall, M. Jamieson, S. Cohen and M. Hargreaves, Primary French in the Balance, N.F.E.R., London, 1974.
5.   "Rapport de la commission d'études sur la fonction enseignante dans le second degré". La Documentation Française, Paris, 1972, p. 103.
6.   Teacher Education and Training. Report of a Committee of Inquiry appointed by the Secretary of State for Education and Science. H.M.S.O., London, 1972.
7.   Eric Hawkins, Modern Languages in the Curriculum, Cambridge University Press, Cambridge, 1981.
8.   W.D. Halls, Foreign Languages and Education in Western Europe, Harrap, London, 1970, p. 6.
9.   ibid., p. 20.
10.   ibid., p. 21.
11.   ibid., p. 94.
12.   ibid., p. 95.
13.   ibid., p. 20.
14.   Le Monde, 30 January 1981, p. 11.
15.   Eric Hawkins, op. cit., p. 179.
16.   J.A. van Ek, The Threshold Level for Modern Language Learning in Schools, Longman, London, 1976.
17.   Le Monde, 30 January 1981, p. 11.
18.   Eric Hawkins, op. cit., pp. 307-308.
19.   The Times Educational Supplement, 7 August 1981, p. 5.
20.   W. Viëtor, Der Sprachunterricht muss umkehren, published by the author, Heilbronn, 1882.

COMPARATIVE EDUCATION IN BRITISH TEACHER EDUCATION

Keith Watson

Sadly, it must be stated at the outset, the tenor of much of
this paper is depressing. In spite of Britain's political
and economic ties with the European Economic Community; in
spite of the stress placed in the Brandt Commission Report
on the need for "schools all over the world to pay more
attention to international problems"[1] and for children and
adults to be made more aware of the growing interdependence
of the world; and in spite of the Rampton Report's emphasis
on teachers as "the central figures in the education process"
regarding the education of ethnic minority children and the
development of a multi-cultural approach to teaching[2], the
British teacher educational institutions are in danger of
turning in upon themselves and, like the politicians and
Treasury Mandarins of Whitehall, of valuing a subject only
according to its immediate usefulness or cost effectiveness.
The truth is that although Comparative Education is alive in
British teacher education institutions, its state of health
gives considerable cause for concern.

   After the cutbacks in teacher education during the
1970s and the closure of about one third of all colleges of
education, with the merger of a further third into polytechnic institutes offering courses under CNAA validation, it
was inevitable that there would be some reduction in the
teaching of Comparative Education. However, not only is
there a measure of hostility towards Comparative Education as
a subject that should be taught in teacher education institutions because it is regarded (by some) as irrelevant,
impractical and unnecessary but there is also a marked decline
in the importance attached to comparative studies even in the
existing institutions which still continue to teach it. The
result is that the number of students who undertake some form
of comparative studies is in the minority. In many cases the
subject has been dropped altogether or has been relegated to
the level of an optional subject while in some university
departments of education there is a growing danger that

comparative education will become a thing of the past, when it ceases to be taught on the retirement of the existing staff member or members who teach it since, under present circumstances, the likelihood of their being replaced is, to say the least, in most cases remote.

THE DEVELOPMENT OF COMPARATIVE STUDIES IN EDUCATION

The 1960s saw a rapid growth in comparative education studies both in the USA and in Europe. The Comparative Education Society in Europe (CESE) formally began in 1961[3] with sixty founding members who came from Japan, the USA and Canada as well as from Europe. Other sections of this parent organis- ation also sprang up during the 1960s.[4] Amongst these was a British section, subsequently renamed the British Comparative Education Society (BCES)[5], which had its initial meeting at a conference held at Reading University in September 1965. This was mainly attended by university academics with an interest in overseas education systems, especially in Europe and North America, who had overseas connections or with contacts with international organisations. Shortly after- wards, in November 1965, a letter was sent out by Paul Mercier, the acting information officer of the embryonic society, then based at the Institute of Education at Reading University, to all the colleges of education informing them of the proposal to create a CESE (British Section) as from a second comparative education conference to be held at Reading University in September 1966 and inviting potential members to join the society. At the same time a questionnaire was sent out seeking to ascertain how many colleges were actually involved in teaching Comparative Education or aspects of comparative studies. One hundred colleges replied, forty-nine of which indicated that some Comparative Education was taught, five at PGCE level, forty-four at certificate or proposed BEd level. Twenty of the courses were options and only twenty-eight offered more than twelve lectures devoted to aspects of comparative education during the entire course. All the colleges except two arranged for some kind of over- seas visit or staff exchange while twenty-five of them had overseas visitors or students attending courses at the college. Indeed there was an exceptionally wide range of interest shown in overseas education which was extremely refreshing. Apart from the usual study of European education systems, both East and West, the USA and the Soviet Union, there were also courses on Cameroon, Israel, Jordan, Pakistan and Thailand, presumably because of a specific interest of certain members of staff. The response of these colleges came at the beginning of the period of rapid expansion of teacher education in the UK, when colleges of education were upgraded to colleges of higher education, four year BEd

194

courses were introduced and student numbers on initial
training courses doubled from 60,000 (1963/4) to over 120,000
by 1971/2.

Looking back, the 1960s were ripe for the growth of
interest in Comparative Education. Not only was there
growing debate about the purpose, scope and methodology in
Comparative Education but there was a sense of optimism and
expectancy in educational circles generally.[6] There was a
spate of literature on Comparative Education themes. Some of
the major works on methodology appeared during the 1960s.[7]
UNESCO launched its massive study of the world's education
systems in its World Survey volumes. It also launched the
journal International Review of Education in 1955 from the
International Institute of Education in Hamburg while
Comparative Education was launched in 1964. Comparative
Education Review, begun by George Bereday in 1957 as a journal
designed to help teachers in training as well as those already
in the classroom, was already showing the need for an understanding of education systems and issues across the world.
The World Yearbooks of Education produced jointly by the
University of London Institute of Education and Columbia
Teachers' College, New York began to examine contemporary
issues from a comparative perspective and showed that
Comparative Education as a discipline had a significant role
to play in analysing problems such as church and state,
teacher education, educational planning, the educational
explosion, education within industry and education in cities.

The 1960s was the age of educational expansion in both
rich countries and poor countries alike. Louis Cros described
the results of this rapid expansion in his famous book,
L'Explosion Scolaire[8], a term that became widely used in
government and educational circles. Numerous national and
international reports advocated the need for investment in
and the expansion of educational provision, especially at
secondary and tertiary level, in the interests of economic
growth. The Robbins Report of 1963 for example made considerable use of comparative data in its arguments favouring
the expansion of higher education in the UK. There were
dozens of educational experiments: new structures such as
open-plan primary schools, middle schools, comprehensive
secondary schools, polytechnics, colleges of higher education,
open access institutions and teachers' centres as well as
curriculum development centres and projects. Similar developments took place throughout the industrialised world. The
names given to them may have differed but the concepts were
remarkably similar. In the developing countries there was a
widespread belief in the importance of education as a factor
in national development[9] especially as many former colonial
territories, particularly in Africa, gained their independence
at this time. The UNESCO Regional conferences that were held

in Karachi (1960), Addis Ababa (1961), and Santiago (1962) established regional plans and national targets for educational expansion during the period up to 1980 in the main geographic regions of the Third World and encouraged numerous educational experiments.[10] Considerable faith was placed in the role of educational planning, and institutions such as the International Institute of Educational Planning (Paris, 1968) were established with the intention of acting as training centres for educational planners from around the world as well as international centres for research into educational planning. Notes of caution were introduced by Anderson[11] and Coombs[12] but at the time few heeded them as report after report came out in favour of educational growth, new forms of education, lifelong education, nonformal education and numerous other approaches.[13] Inevitably in such exciting times this was a period of growth for many subdisciplines within the field of education and Comparative Education laid claim, with considerable justification, to being of major importance. As Vernon Mallinson pointed out in the preface to his major work on the subject: "The study of Comparative Education is still in its infancy, and though we are in the midst of a critical phase of one of the most momentous expansions of educational effort in the world's history, too few people recognise the relevance and importance - I might also add <u>the vital necessity</u> - of such a study".[14]

Since the early 1970s however there has been a crisis of confidence concerning education's role in socio-economic development in both the advanced and the developing countries. Doubts about education's ability to bring about social amelioration, let alone lead to improved economic growth, have been widely expressed. As Torsten Husén has observed, everywhere, but in the industrial world in particular, schooling is being questioned.[15] Inflation and financial constraints have led to cutbacks in investment in education. The falling birth rate and the resultant decline in demand for teachers in schools[16] has inevitably led to a period of dramatic and unprecedented decline in teacher education provision which in this country has led to closures and the merger of many teacher training institutions during the 1970s.

During this period of contraction comparative studies in education have also suffered. The dramatic increase in fees in universities and to a lesser extent in polytechnics has led to a noticeable downturn in the number of overseas students, themselves a valuable source of information on international educational affairs as well as being attracted to courses in comparative education.[17] Moreover there has been a crisis of confidence in the value of Comparative Education as well as to its place in educational institutions. While there has undoubtedly been much valuable research work

196

undertaken during the 1970s[18] there was a considerable sense of gloom and despondency in the "state of the art" issue of <u>Comparative Education</u> in June 1977[19], largely because of cutbacks in funding for research and travel, both essential ingredients for the furtherance of practical and realistic studies in Comparative Education, but partly also because of the fear that in a period of contraction the major concern of teachers is for survival while that of educational administrators is for preserving only those courses with an obvious practical relevance for the classroom situation. For far too many teachers and administrators Comparative Education is regarded as an interesting luxury, a "frill", but an unnecessary ingredient for a common core teacher education curriculum. The result has been a growing mood of introspection and a withdrawal of interest in or concern for the wider issues of international education.[20] Similar anxieties have been expressed with regard to the situation in the USA.[21]

Ironically it is during a period of uncertainty, especially when many countries are faced with very similar common problems and issues (e.g. falling birth rates and school enrolments, the need for examination reform, multi-ethnic provision, a common curriculum, better vocational training, provision for unemployed school leavers, etc.) that an international awareness is needed more than ever to show that the difficulties faced in one country are at least shared by others while the solutions to particular problems may differ in degree but may be worth studying for the lessons that can be learnt. Several scholars have recently argued the case for more, not less, comparative and international studies in education precisely because the 1980s are likely to prove so uncertain.[22] Unfortunately, the reality is that these are siren voices which are unlikely to be heard or acted upon by policy makers and administrators and above all by directors of teacher education institutions facing staff cutbacks and financial constraints.

It is precisely because the circumstances at the beginning of the 1980s are so fundamentally different from those in the middle of the 1960s and because the state of the art of Comparative Education at institutional level was unknown as a result of contraction and the development of new award-bearing courses recognised by the Council for National Academic Awards (CNAA) rather than by the University Departments of Education, that it was thought useful to ascertain what the current position is regarding the teaching of Comparative Education in British teacher education institutions. The task of ascertaining this position was undertaken by the author using a questionnaire approach and the remainder of this paper is a discussion of his findings.

197

The Survey

A detailed questionnaire was drawn up at Reading University School of Education during the summer of 1980. It was checked and modified by members of the Executive Committee of the British Comparative Education Society before being sent out, together with a covering letter, to all the principals and/or departmental heads of teacher education institutions throughout the UK during the spring term of 1981. The initial response to the letter and questionnaire was mixed. About 50% of the institutions contacted bothered to reply. As a result a follow-up letter was sent during the summer term of 1981. The response to the second letter resulted in a steady trickle of completed questionnaires although four of the leading UDEs, where it is known that Comparative Education is taught, did not respond to either of the letters.[23] Their lack of response, however, does not invalidate the major thrust of the report on the survey findings that follows.

Letters and questionnaires were sent to 134 institutions. Replies were received from 106 of them, making a response of 79.10%. For purposes of analysis and comparability these were broken down into different levels and types of institution as can be seen from Table 1.

Table 1: Replies to the Survey

	Number of Institutions Approached	Number of Institutions Replying	% Response	Nil Returns
Colleges of Education	24	14	58.3	1
Colleges/ Institutes of Higher Education	42	37	88.0	1
Polytechnics	25	18	72.0	-
Universities	43	37	86.0	6
	134	106	79.10	8

The number of University departments included two at the London University Institute of Education (Comparative Education and Education in Developing Countries), two at Sussex (the Education Area and the Institute of Development

198

Studies), the constituent university colleges making up the University of Wales, and the Open University, which, while not specifically a university in the traditional sense, nor preparing students for teaching, nevertheless offers many courses with some comparative dimensions.

The nil returns were received from the universities of East Anglia, Edinburgh (though some comparative work is undertaken through the Centre for African Studies), Lancaster, Stirling, Strathclyde (no UDE) and Sussex (Education Area); from Buckinghamshire College of Higher Education and from Bishop Grossteste College.

It was apparent that certain institutions were hazy with regard to what constitutes Comparative Education. This is a not uncommon situation since every major book on the subject sets out to define the areas of concern before proceeding to considerations of methodology or the inter-pretation of different countries' education systems. However although the questionnaire was couched in sufficiently broad terms to cover international education, overseas education, urban education, multi-racial education, education in developing countries and development education a few respondents saw the words Comparative Education on the first page of the questionnaire, decided it was not taught as such and never turned to the second page to see if some compara-tive aspects might have been covered under educational studies or social aspects of education! Fortunately, the number of respondents fitting into this category amounted to no more than half a dozen.

Where Comparative Education is taught

Of those 106 institutions replying to the survey it will be seen from Table 2 that Comparative Education or aspects of education which have a clearly definable comparative component in them are taught in only 68 of them, i.e. in 64.15% of the teacher education institutions involved. The majority are Colleges of Higher Education or UDEs. While 58 teach Comparative Education as such, 23 examine aspects of Compar-ative Education under social aspects of education, while 15 have special courses on education in developing countries, 16 on multi-racial education and 10 on urban education.

Comparative Education is also examined in 13 specialist courses which range from overseas science education and rural education to ideologies, international perspectives and comparative sociology. A disturbing feature, however, in the light of the current social class and ethnic conflicts in our own society and the growing interest in problems of economic development is how few courses are devoted to urban or multi-racial education or how few (15) have a specifically Third World emphasis. This is discussed in more detail later.

Table 2: Where Comparative Education is studied

	C. Ed. Taught	C. Ed. Not Taught	C. Ed. Dropped/about to be dropped	Comp. Ed.	Internal Ed.	Ed. Abroad	Social Aspects	Administration	Urban Ed.	Development Ed.	EDC	Multi-racial Ed.	Others (eg rural education, ideologies, international perspectives, area studies)
								C. Ed. taught as					
Colleges of Ed.	8	6	2	6	1	2	2	-	-	-	-	1	7
Colleges of Higher Ed.	25	12	12 (Maybe start in 4)	24	3	1	9	1	4	3	9	7	3
Polytechnics	5	13	9	5	2	1	8	3	3	2	1	4	3
Universities	30	7	7 (Out of existing 30)	23	3	3	4	2	3	3	5	4	-
Totals	68	38	30	58	9	7	23	6	10	8	15	16	13

Undoubtedly the most disturbing feature of the whole survey however, is the fact that Comparative Education as such has been dropped during the past few years or is about to be dropped as staff leave and are not replaced at 80 different institutions (2 colleges, 12 colleges of higher education, 9 polytechnics and 7 university departments of education. While one polytechnic and four colleges of higher education are considering developing courses in international education this is small consolation if it is realised that fifteen years ago over one hundred institutions would have been teaching the subject.

The reasons given for dropping Comparative Education as a component in teacher education courses vary, though there are several recurring reasons given   such as overcrowding of the timetable, constraints of time, lack of specialist staff that were given by all types of training institution. Since the overall impression given by the respondents to the survey is a gloomy one and since positive action to remedy the position can only be taken if the reasons for its decline are understood, it appears sensible to list some of the comments that were given.

The colleges of education expressed views that there were staff shortages; lack of demand; time constraints because of too many existing options; that Comparative Education could not be justified at a time of contraction; and that it was not essential for initial training. Other comments included:-
"a desirable area of study but not essential and in the present climate of opinion and thinking, like History of Education, it is highly suspect",
"because comparative studies are included in the 'integrated courses' there is no need to treat Comparative Education as a separate subject",
"apart from one lecture of a very general nature Comparative Education topics are all too infrequent. I always hope things will change but there is no immediate prospect of this",
"unfortunately cutbacks in terms of staff, books and general facilities present problems that at this point of time cannot be overcome".

Colleges of higher education referred to staff shortages; financial cutbacks; lack of student demand; lack of immediate practical relevance, etc., but most blamed the mergers with other colleges or institutions, rationalisation of courses and lack of co-operation on the part of the CNAA, for the demise of Comparative Education. One college respondent said that "under the rigorous selection for CNAA approval Comparative Education had to be dropped", while another said it had been abolished after ten years, in spite of its undoubted popularity, "because of the decline in the number of teachers in training and the end of university validation". Others

201

spoke of the question of priorities whereby such courses as the teaching of reading and coping with mixed ability classes had prior claims, though one college tutor believed that a knowledge of multi-ethnic problems in different contexts is essential for all teachers and another stressed that, while formally Comparative Education had been abolished, attempts were made to introduce a comparative dimension "where relevant" and "where possible" into the educational foundation course. Perhaps the saddest comment of all was: "It would not be surprising if Comparative Education were to be removed from the list of options available to BEd students partly because of falling BEd rolls and partly because optional courses should be directly and practically relevant to teaching".

Similar views were expressed in polytechnic departments of education where staff shortages, course rationalisation as a result of institutional mergers, lack of relevance at initial teacher training level, more pressing demands, and stress on highly structured and practically focussed courses were given as reasons for dropping Comparative Education. One polytechnic respondent ruefully commented, "In pre-service training we have so concentrated on curriculum/classroom issues as to make international education marginally important and very difficult to get across ... As a result at in-service level there is no regional demand except for liaison with the local Council for Race Relations". Another respondent pointed out that Comparative Education was dropped because of the changing nature of teacher education and not because of a rejection of an international perspective.

Several respondents from polytechnics, however, fairly and squarely put the blame for the diminution of the teaching of Comparative Education on CNAA rejection. One wrote, "It was sadly pushed out by the sociologists in the new CNAA validations", while another bitterly commented, "Although Comparative Education courses always proved extremely popular no provision has been made for comparative studies in the new CNAA degree (1981) due to CNAA policy", and he put in a plea that pressure might be brought to bear upon the CNAA that they might adopt a more broadminded and tolerant approach towards validation of courses. Another respondent observed that "only a minority of students opt for Comparative Education and hence with reduced initial training numbers and pressures to teach within ever tighter CNAA regulations it may not continue to be possible to offer it even as an option". It is worth observing that the BCES Executive Committee did make representations to the CNAA several years ago over this very issue, asking for representation on their education validating committees. Regretably, such is the standing with which Comparative Education is regarded in certain education circles, that these representations were

202

rebuffed. On the other hand it is worth pointing out that one polytechnic (Oxford) is not only developing development education courses but has been expanding courses in Comparative Education since 1975 in the belief that they are essential for helping students to combine education with languages.

University staff also made the point that in an overcrowded timetable Comparative Education tends to get pushed out, especially at the PGCE level where time is too short to teach any subject adequately. One university staff member observed that Comparative Education is probably more adversely affected by cuts than any other subject especially because rising costs make overseas visits increasingly difficult. Several respondents commented on the difficulties of concentrating expertise in one or two staff members since on their retirement there would be little, if any, chance of their replacement, with the result that the subject would disappear from the list of offerings available. Overcommitment of staff in other directions, leaving them with little real opportunity to concentrate on Comparative Education, was also commented on and one lecturer bitterly observed that in his institution, "There has been a persistent refusal to staff the department adequately so that because of overcommitment the chances of any single-minded commitment to teaching and research in Comparative Education is impossible".

It is quite obvious from many of the replies, particularly from those involved in teacher education in the polytechnics and UDEs, that the current state of affairs is viewed with a mixture of sadness and bitterness. Only in the colleges and in some colleges of higher education is there any general feeling that Comparative Education ought to be restricted to advanced study and not made available to all those in teacher training.

As can be seen from Table 3, the bulk of Comparative Education teaching takes place at BA/BEd level at colleges of higher education and at polytechnics (60 courses), at PGCE level, mainly in the UDEs (18 courses) and at in-service level. As is to be expected the majority of teaching at university level takes place at MA/MEd or at MPhil/PhD levels. However these figures hide enormous variations in offering, since while post UDE courses below advanced degree level run for at least two terms and offer between 20 and 40 hours of tuition, one college of education offers one lecture only at the PGCE level and two lectures at the in-service level, while the majority of the courses mentioned consist of only a few lectures which range from between 2 and 10 hours of tuition for the entire course.

While courses at colleges of education and polytechnics are almost evenly divided between compulsory and optional (Table 4) at the colleges of higher education and even more

Table 3: Levels of Teaching

	Initial Cert.	BEd./BA	PGCE	Dip./In-service	Spec. Courses eg O/seas,Admin.	Advanced Dip.	MA/MEd.	MPhil., etc.
Colleges of Ed.	6	9	4	6	2	–	–	–
Colleges of Higher Ed.	3	25	9	9	–	1	1	–
Polytechnics	3	13	4	4	–	1	1	–
Universities	–	13	18	6	3	8	19	11
Totals	12	60	35	25	5	10	19	11

Table 4: Compulsory or Optional Courses (By Level)

	Colleges Compulsory/Option		Colleges Comp/Opt.		Poly-technics Comp/Opt.		UDEs Comp/Opt.	
Initial Certificate	3	4	2	1	3	3	–	–
BA/BEd (Dip. HE)	3	6	13	22	7	8	5	7
PGCE	3	2	5	7	3	1	3	15
Dip./In-service	2	1	8	5	1	3	3	4
Advanced Dip.	1	1	–	1	–	–	4	6
MA/MEd	–	–	1	2	–	–	3	15
Totals	12	14	29	38	14	15	18	47

noticeably at university level Comparative Education courses are predominantly electives/optional. At only three UDEs are courses compulsory at the PGCE level (and this number will drop to two at the beginning of 1982/3) and at only three are they compulsory components of the MA/MEd levels. This is ironical when one considers that in spite of one respondent arguing that teaching comparative or international education at PGCE level was extremely difficult because of the political ignorance and lack of awareness of other societies on the part of the majority of students embarking on initial training many argued that they believed that all students, whether at initial or in-service levels, should have some knowledge of education overseas if for no other reason than that their mental horizons are widened and they are made to realise that the complexities of the education process are not necessarily nation- or culture-bound. It is also ironical when one consistently receives comments such as "Comparative Education is by far the most popular course", "Comparative Education courses have proved very popular and have always held up well against other courses", or "Comparative perspectives as part of any course designed for a multi-cultural society are essential ... All main studies (e.g. geography, English, history) fail to appreciate this even more than the education department - though even here it is not always easy to persuade colleagues that Comparative Education is essential rather than an extra".

Numbers on different courses

In the light of the above remarks it is not surprising to find that the majority of Comparative Education courses or courses with some comparative element are attended by relatively small numbers. At the college level the majority of courses offered at initial certificate level, BA/BEd, PGCE, or in-service levels are in the range 0-20 (13), 20-50 (9) or 50-100 (9). Only one course numbers between 100 and 120 (at initial certificate level), while two (one at initial certificate and one at PGCE level) number between 120 and 150 plus. With the ending of the initial certificate course numbers attending comparative courses will henceforth be overwhelmingly less than a hundred. The same picture is true of colleges of higher education where 30 of the courses offered in the range initial certificate, BA/BEd, PGCE or in-service are attended by less than 20 students, 20 courses are attended by 20-50 students and 11 are attended by between 50 and 100. Four BA/BEd courses are, however, attended by between 120 and 150 plus students. With the exception of one BA/BEd course and one PGCE course attended by over 200 students the majority of polytechnic courses are in the 20-50 range (15), 0-20 range (11), or the 50-100 range (3). One

Table 5: Numbers on Courses

	Colleges of Education					Colleges of Higher Education				
	0–20	20–50	50–100	100–120	120–150	0–20	20–50	50–100	100–120	120–150
Initial Cert.	4	3	3	1	1	1		1	1	
BA/BEd.	9	4	4			16	12	6		4
PGCE		2			1	4	5	3		
Dip./In-service		-	2			7	3	1		
Adv. Dip.						2				
MA/MEd.										
Totals	13	9	9	1	2	30	20	11	1	4

	Polytechnics					Universities				
	0–20	20–50	50–100	100–120	120–150	0–20	20–50	50–100	100–120	120–150
Initial Cert.	4	2	1					1	1	
BA/BEd.	4	11	2		1	7	3	1	2	1
PGCE		2			1	7	9		1	
Dip./In-service	1					2	1			
Adv. Dip.						6	1	2		
MA/MEd.	2					8	4			
Totals	11	15	3		2	30	18	4	4	1

university in-service diploma and one university PGCE course attract between 120 and 150 students though the latter is being scrapped at the end of academic year 1981/2. Three courses attract between 100 and 120 (2 at PGCE and 1 at BA/BEd), 4 attract between 50 and 100 (2 advanced diploma, 1 at PGCE and 1 at BA/BEd level). The remainder of the 47 courses which range from BA/BEd to MA/MEd all attract less than 50 students. With the decline in numbers attending university based PGCE courses as from 1982/3 and with the drop in the number of teachers being released for in-service training, numbers are bound to fall even further. Teaching at advanced level - i.e. at MA/MEd, MPhil or PhD levels - is understandably overwhelmingly undertaken in the UDEs where 8 courses have between 0 and 20 students and 4 have between 20 and 50. Surprisingly only two polytechnic courses at this level have been noted. (See Table 5).

Course content and value

Respondents were asked to rank in order of importance on a 1-5 scale the teaching content of the different courses. The results of their replies have been analysed and condensed to a rank order out of ten but the resulting table (6) is only a crude assessment of the true weighting of courses since some institutions give equal weighting to all areas of study. Some of the replies gave no indication as to the real order of importance and some only ticked a few of the squares. However, it is possible to draw certain general conclusions.

The first general conclusion is not unduly surprising in the light of the remarks already made in this paper, namely that most courses are concerned with general descriptions of different education systems or with thematic comparisons rather than with methodology or theoretical considerations. Major consideration is given to other West European education systems, to the Soviet Union and the communist bloc, to North America and to the Third World in that order. Some attention is paid to China and Japan though only two institutions highlighted an interest in these two fascinating and distinctive education systems.

A second general conclusion is that concern for methodology and theoretical approaches to Comparative Education are mainly the province of the universities and the polytechnics where master's level work and above is undertaken. Surprisingly very little advanced Comparative Education work is undertaken in the polytechnics and surprisingly some of the colleges claim to devote time to methodology, although it is more likely that reference is made to different approaches to the subject than to the implementation of any particular method.[24] One institution, the University of London Institute of Education, devotes a considerable amount of time at

Table 6: Course Content at different levels (ranked out of 10)

	Initial Certificate				BA/BEd				PGCE				Diploma/In-service				Advanced Diploma			MA/MEd		MPhil/PhD
	Colleges of Education	Colleges of Higher Ed.	Polytechnics	UDEs	Colleges of Education	Colleges of Higher Ed.	Polytechnics	UDEs	Colleges of Education	Colleges of Higher Ed.	Polytechnics	UDEs	Colleges of Education	Colleges of Higher Ed.	Polytechnics	UDEs	Colleges of Higher Ed.	Polytechnics	UDEs	Polytechnics	UDEs	UDEs
Methodology/Theory	5.3	-	-		4.4	3.2	2.3	0.7	5.0	-	5.0	2.2	3.3	-	-	-	5.0	10.0	1.2	10.0	4.7	5.4
Systematic Comparison	6.6	3.3	-		4.4	4.8	6.1	1.5	7.5	4.4	5.0	3.8	3.3	4.4	2.5	5.0	10.0	10.0	6.2	10.0	6.8	3.6
Western Europe	8.3	6.6	3.3		8.8	8.4	6.9	5.3	10.0	5.5	7.5	8.3	5.0	6.6	-	6.6	5.0	10.0	8.7	-	10.0	
North America	10.0	6.6	3.3		6.6	6.0	3.8	3.8	7.5	5.5	2.5	8.3	5.0	3.3	-	6.6	5.0	10.0	7.5	-	9.4	
Soviet Union/Communist bloc	10.0	6.6	6.6		7.7	7.6	6.1	4.6	10.0	5.5	5.0	10.0	5.0	5.5	-	6.6	5.0	10.0	7.5	-	10.0	
Third World	5.3	6.6	3.3		3.3	6.0	3.8	3.0	5.0	3.3	2.5	6.1	3.3	3.3	-	5.0	5.0	10.0	8.7	-	10.0	
Other	1.1	6.6	-		-	-	0.7	-	-	-	-	-	-	-	-	-	-	-	-	-	-	

the advanced levels to a discussion of methodology.

Inevitably the more advanced the course work undertaken the more specialised is the area of study. Raggatt[25] has examined research work in Comparative Education during the 1970s and has shown that after ULIE only a handful of other institutions - e.g. Leeds, Reading, Manchester, Hull and Liverpool - have concentrated on Comparative Education research. The findings of the present survey would tend to substantiate Raggatt's findings.

Since implicit in the questionnaire was a belief that there are many very good reasons for studying Comparative Education, particularly in times of difficulty and uncertainty, respondents were asked four further questions, one relating to overseas visits or educational study tours and three relating to value judgements about the value of comparative studies in education.

One of Bereday's arguments was that students of Comparative Education should have the opportunity to experience foreign education systems at first hand[26] and the present writer's experience is that many students especially at PGCE level are initially attracted to Comparative Education studies in the hope that there might be an opportunity to undertake an educational study tour during the course of their period of training. Yet while the results of the survey would indicate that there are still a considerable number of overseas visits/study tours these are on the decline, mainly because of costs and the subsequent fall in demand. Two colleges of higher education, for example, have dropped overseas educational visits during the past four years on these grounds. The majority of colleges of higher education and polytechnic visits are BEd exchange schemes or specialist foreign language exchange schemes, while ten out of the twelve UDE visits are for specialist groups. The remaining two, organised by ULIE to the Soviet Union and jointly by Reading and Durham to France, are open to all-comers.

Table 7: Study tours and/or exchanges

	Yes	No	
Colleges of Education	4	8	2 nil returns
Colleges of Higher Education	22	15	
Polytechnics	9	8	
Universities	12	18	
	47	49	

The first of the value judgement questions asked respondents to rank the value of Comparative Education courses at initial training and at in-service training levels as essential, desirable, useful, marginal and irrelevant. The responses are given in Table 8.

It is clear from the replies that it is generally regarded as desirable or useful in colleges of higher education, polytechnics and UDEs, that there is little evidence of any strongly held views in the colleges and that some UDEs and colleges of higher education consider a knowledge of Comparative Education as essential at both levels of training. Perhaps most disturbing are the numbers in colleges and UDEs who regard Comparative Education as irrelevant.

The second and third value judgement questions sought to elicit a response about the professional value and the purposes in studying Comparative Education at whatever level. Respondents were asked to rank the "major benefit for students of undertaking comparative studies in education" and "the professional usefulness of an international/comparative dimension in education". Taking the latter question first it is quite apparent that a considerable number of staff in colleges and colleges of higher education regard comparative studies in education as of no professional value or of little professional value. The majority fit into the category of considering Comparative Education as useful but little more. On this evidence it would appear to be incumbent upon the BCES and those dedicated to the teaching of Comparative Education to sell the subject and to draw to the attention of professional colleagues, administrators and policy makers that there really are professional advantages in developing a less ethnocentric approach to teacher education.

Concerning the question about the major benefits accruing to students from comparative studies in education, respondents overwhelmingly believed that these lay in the provision of a deeper insight into the students' own education system and the identification of common problems and issues. The ranking can be seen in Table 10. Numerous attempts have been made to highlight the value of studying issues comparatively[27] and it is interesting to list some of the many other justifications for teaching Comparative Education that resulted from the survey. These ranged from the Beredayian arguments of "intellectual excitement", "the academic rigour of Comparative Education for its own sake", "fun and enjoyment", "sheer interest", and "the realisation that other societies actually have children" to "the development of global awareness", "the development of an understanding of development problems", and the development of a "European consciousness" or of an "awareness of the wider international world". One respondent was concerned that students should acquire an understanding of educational principles rather than simply acquire data about other countries and that they should appreciate how people in one culture think in a particular paradigm. Others took up similar themes. One argued that it is important to

210

Table 8: Value of Comparative Education courses at different levels

Training Level:	Colleges of Ed.		Colleges of Higher Ed.		Polytechnics		Universities	
	Initial	Inservice	Initial	Inservice	Initial	Inservice	Initial	Inservice
Essential	7	6	17	11	5	5	11	10
Desirable	8	8	22	18	8	10	18	16
Useful	7	9	17	17	7	5	16	16
Marginal	6	6	13	10	5	4	11	8
Irrelevant	7	6	6	7	3	3	6	7

Table 9: Professional Value of Studying Comparative Education (in ranking order 1-5, as a %)

	1				2				3				4				5			
	Colleges of Education	Colleges of Higher Ed.	Polytechnics	Universities	Colleges of Education	Colleges of Higher Ed.	Polytechnics	Universities	Colleges of Education	Colleges of Higher Ed.	Polytechnics	Universities	Colleges of Education	Colleges of Higher Ed.	Polytechnics	Universities	Colleges of Education	Colleges of Higher Ed.	Polytechnics	Universities
Extremely useful	38.5	28.6	25.0	23.1	11.2	4.2	-	-	11.1	34.8	33.3	35.3	-	-	-	-	16.7	4.8	25.	14.3
Very useful	7.7	35.7	31.2	23.1	55.5	54.2	60.0	70.6	22.2	4.4	8.4	23.5	-	5.0	11.1	-	-	-	-	-
Useful	30.8	32.1	37.5	50.0	11.1	29.1	10.0	17.6	66.7	47.8	41.6	29.4	25.0	15.0	11.1	16.7	-	-	-	-
Of little use	7.7	3.6	-	3.8	22.2	8.3	30.0	11.8	-	13.0	8.3	11.8	75.0	80.0	66.7	75.0	-	-	-	-
Of no use	15.3	-	6.3	-	-	4.2	-	-	-	-	8.3	-	-	-	11.1	8.3	83.3	95.2	75.	85.7
Totals	100	100	100	100	100	100	100	100	100	100	100	100	100	100	100	100	100	100	100	100

Table 10: The Major Benefits of Undertaking Comparative Studies in Education (in ranking order 1-5, as a %)

	1				2				3				4				5			
	Colleges of Education	Colleges of Higher Ed.	Polytechnics	Universities	Colleges of Education	Colleges of Higher Ed.	Polytechnics	Universities	Colleges of Education	Colleges of Higher Ed.	Polytechnics	Universities	Colleges of Education	Colleges of Higher Ed.	Polytechnics	Universities	Colleges of Education	Colleges of Higher Ed.	Polytechnics	Universities
Broaden the mind	7.1	14.6	5.5	16.2	27.3	20.0	6.25	17.3	20.0	40.0	21.4	13.0	100	34.6	-	-	83.3	49.0	-	-
To provide a deeper insight into own ed. system	57.2	48.8	50.0	35.5	9.0	20.0	11.25	37.9	20.0	13.3	21.4	21.8	-	11.5	-	-	-	-	-	-
To identify common problems/issues	28.6	29.3	27.8	38.7	45.5	37.5	43.5	20.7	40.0	26.1	27.2	30.7	-	19.3	-	28.6	-	51.0	-	-
To break down ethno-centricism	7.1	7.3	16.7	9.7	18.2	22.5	39.1	24.1	20.0	20.7	30.0	34.5	-	34.6	-	71.4	16.7	-	-	-
Totals	100	100	100	100	100	100	100	100	100	100	100	100	100	100	100	100	100	100	100	100

develop an understanding of the meaning of education, others were concerned that while educational innovations should be seen in a particular cultural context, students should be encouraged to believe that their own system could be changed and should be made aware of how educational policy and provision are interlinked. Others argued that the development of broader professional horizons beyond "a narrow domestic patch" could only be beneficial for future educational leaders who had to consider issues and problems such as curriculum development, vocational education and the problems of minority groups in inner-city schools. One writer pointed out that "analysis of functional problems of other societies provides a critical platform for analysing one's own suppositions" and another suggested that parents and members of education committees should be made aware of the European dimension over such issues as staff promotion, punishments and sanctions and staff training, including that of head teachers. An interesting distinction between international education and comparative education was drawn by one head of department of a college of higher education. The purpose of the former he sees as encouraging young people to develop understanding internationally through teachers, study tours, discussions and exchanges; the purposes of the latter are to deepen an understanding of international educational issues and to develop the cross-fertilization of ideas. In his own particular institution both Comparative and International Education are pursued.

While the majority of comments outlined above are mainly extensions of the original reasons suggested as justifications for the study of Comparative Education it can be seen that, far from there being a dearth of opinion regarding the worth of comparative studies in education, the opposite would appear to be the case. Given the wealth of reasons favouring Comparative Education, the low status of the subject in professional teacher educational institutions is a matter of some concern. Can professional studies, curriculum development, sociology of education or philosophy of education provide the breadth of experience, interest and thought development that is possible through Comparative Education? The answer must surely be in the negative. Yet the strength of the aforementioned topics lies in their strong professional base. One of the challenges facing comparative educators must be how best they can develop stronger professional inputs and an organizational structure during the 1980s.

Multi-racial education, interdependence and development education

Although not strictly in the fields of Comparative or International education, the questionnaire also sought to elicit information on the teaching of multi-racial education, development education and whether or not it was considered important that all students should be made aware of global interdependence. The reasoning behind the questions was that Comparative Education has a major part to play in all three areas and if they are believed to be of growing importance on the part of institutional respondents who might not be particularly in favour of the traditional approaches to Comparative Education this might form an entrée for comparative studies.

While a sizeable majority believe that a knowledge of multi-racial education is important or even essential (47.60%) and a few (18.08%) see it as unnecessary the overwhelming consensus of opinion is that multi-racial education is inadequately catered for. Sixty-eight institutions believe that multi-racial provision is unsatisfactory against 28 that believe arrangements are satisfactory. One respondent admitted that he had never thought about the question before, one (from Scotland) argued that it was not very relevant in Scotland while several from English colleges pointed out that as there are no multi-racial problems in their area it is hardly relevant to their teacher education curriculum.

Such a picture is very far from satisfactory. The Commission for Racial Equality (CRE) has been campaigning for years that all teachers in initial training should be made aware of the multi-racial aspects of British society.[28] The Green Paper of 1977 stressed the need for an awareness of the needs of ethnic minorities on the part of all teachers.[29] Advocates of a multi-racial curriculum[30] have argued that changes must take place in teacher education institutions if there is to be any hope of real change in the classroom. The findings of the present survey do little more than substantiate the gloomy observations of the Rampton Report when it stated that:

> The evidence we have received from all sources, including schools and teachers, LEAs, students and parents, presents an overwhelming picture of the failure of teacher training institutions to prepare teachers for their role in a multi-racial society. In very few institutions is a grounding given to all students in how to appreciate and understand the experiences and cultures of ethnic minority pupils or of how to help ethnic minority parents who may not have much personal experience of this education system ... No teacher training institution appears to have succeeded in providing a satisfactory grounding in multi-cultural education for all its students ... The great majority of students are thus entering teaching having received little or no guidance on how to adopt a broadly based approach to education which takes full account of the presence of

214

ethnic minorities in our society.[31]

Rampton stresses the urgent need for in-service training and urges "the governing bodies and maintaining authorities of all teacher training institutions in the public sector and university departments of education to institute a fundamental reappraisal of their policy towards multi-cultural education".[32]

Most courses/studies on multi-cultural education are related directly to the ethnic minorities in a given area and to teaching in local UK schools. Most are in those areas where there is a high concentration of ethnic minorities (e.g. Leicester, Leeds, Liverpool, etc.). Where there is general satisfaction regarding the course provision this comes because multi-racial education is covered in some form as part of the compulsory course but overwhelmingly courses are optional and thus only attract those already committed psychologically. Only four institutions, all UDEs, replying to this survey look at multi-racial education in any way comparatively. One reason may be the dearth of books which look at multi-cultural/racial education across cultures though this situation is changing rapidly.[33] I would suggest that the real reason, however, is the ethnocentricism that permeates so much of teacher education and the rejection of the need to look at important issues such as ethnic minorities comparatively.

In three of the colleges multi-racial education is covered as part of sociology, in two it is covered incidentally as part of the main course on educational studies, in five it is optional and in two it is referred to under social psychology or urban education. In eleven colleges of higher education which feel satisfied with the handling of the multi-racial issue a variety of titles are given to courses revealing the different emphases given to the topic: education in a multi-cultural society, multi-ethnic education in an urban context, the teaching of ethnic minority groups, race relations, immigrant education, race and prejudice, RE in a pluralist context, teaching English as a second language. One college specialises in Asian Studies and Carribbean studies, while several suggest that multi-racial education is "suffused throughout the whole course". However, perhaps the saddest comment on the college of higher education scene was the reply "the tutor concerned with multi-racial education is due to leave at the end of this academic year (1980/1). He is unlikely to be replaced". What hope is there for the Rampton Report's recommendation in that institution? In the seven polytechnics satisfied with multi-racial education provision the topic is covered under teaching in a multi-cultural society (2), multi-ethnic education (2), the multi-cultural classroom (1), the city and

215

new minorities/urban education (2). It is also referred to
incidentally under education of the disadvantaged (1) and
politics of education (1). There is one university centre
especially devoted to multi-racial education (at the London
Institute of Education) and three others which run special
courses on multi-racial education. Other university offerings
range from none, the odd lecture or two, incidentally in
seminars, to optional courses which might look at ethical
issues in education, contemporary issues, urban education,
the school in a multi-cultural context, religious studies and
TESL. However, it must be stressed that comparative offerings in this field are minimal. Several comparativists have
stressed the need to provide a lead in this field[34] and the
1980s provide an opportunity for comparativists to take the
initiative in the field of multi-racial, multi-cultural
education. It would be a pity if they let the opportunity
pass by because of shortage of funds.

There was considerable confusion over the second area
of general inquiry, that of development education. About a
dozen respondents, especially from colleges and universities,
admitted that they had never heard of the expression and a
number admitted that although they had heard the expression
they did not know what was meant by it. Essentially it is
any course that helps to explain the causes and features of
underdevelopment in Third World countries. Several scholars
have written about the field[35] but the best definition is
probably that given by the Ministry of Overseas Development
when it launched its special development education fund of
£215,000 in 1978:

> We use the term development education to describe those
> processes of thought and action which increase under-
> standing of the worldwide social, economic and political
> conditions, particularly those which relate to, and are
> responsible for underdevelopment. Its purpose is to
> encourage widespread involvement in action for improve-
> ment.[36]

Unfortunately finance was withdrawn from the best known
project on development education (at ULIE) by the Ministry
of Overseas Development as part of the present government's
cuts, but Oxfordshire is currently pioneering development
education in its schools and Oxford Polytechnic is monitoring
the programme. Many organisations, such as OXFAM, the World
Development Group, Christian Aid and TEAR Fund, have produced
materials in this field. It was felt to be important,
therefore, to see what provision is made in teacher training
institutions to draw the attention of their students to
aspects of development problems in the Third World, especially
since the government's view in 1978 was that "the need to

promote development education in schools is urgent".[37]

ODA's findings on "Attitudes to Overseas Development" showed a growing gap between public knowledge and concern and the needs of the developing world and which pointed out that

> Two-thirds of the nation have parochial and introverted attitudes, unsympathetic to a world perspective, clinging to the past and untutored to approach the future constructively. Attitudes towards the under-developed countries in particular are confused by stereotyped images, post-colonial guilt, racial and cultural prejudices, limited unbalanced knowledge, concern about future domestic employment, belief that overseas development is synonymous only with aid and that aid is motivated only by charity ...[38]

In view of this it is not surprising that there is such a low profile in teacher education institutions. Only three colleges, eight colleges of higher education, five poly-technics and eight UDEs felt that development education was adequately covered. Only 24 institutions out of a total of 106 replying to the survey (22.64%) examine the topic in any serious way. This is hardly likely to encourage the promo-tion of development education in schools while the present cutbacks in the aid budget will further hamper developments in this field and only increase the sense of apathy. It is not without significance that those countries which are most concerned with promoting an awareness of development problems in their schools, Sweden, the Netherlands and Norway, spend most on official aid as a percentage of their GNP.[39]

Where development is encouraged it is covered under such topics as Third World studies, education in developing countries, development studies, international understanding, geography, environmental education, urban education and overseas administration courses. Perhaps the most disturbing feature of the replies was not that development is not widely taught - this was to be expected in the light of the ODA findings - but that a considerable number of respondents regard the whole area of development education as unnecessary or of marginal interest. (See Table 11.2).

In the light of the above two areas of inquiry it seemed logical to introduce a third area, that of "a knowledge of our interdependence with other nations". The Green Paper of 1977, already referred to, had stated that "nor are our young people sufficiently aware of the international inter-dependence of modern countries. Many of our pressing problems can only be solved internationally, so our children need to be educated in international understanding as well", and went on to stress the need for an understanding of global interdependence to be taught in all schools. Unfortunately,

217

Table 11: Professional rating of the need for students to have a knowledge of multi-racial education, development education and global interdependence (as a %)

Legend for column groups (1–5), each split into four institution types:
CE = Colleges of Education · CHE = Colleges of Higher Ed. · P = Polytechnics · U = Universities

Table 11.1: Multi-racial Education

	1				2				3				4				5			
	CE	CHE	P	U	CE	CHE	P	U	CE	CHE	P	U	CE	CHE	P	U	CE	CHE	P	U
Essential	42.9	66.6	76.4	32.1	16.0	8.0	12.5	6.25	4.5	40.0	33.3	37.5	12.5	13.1	–	7.1	–	4.5	–	14.2
Important	57.1	19.6	23.6	53.6	68.0	48.0	62.5	18.75	4.6	60.0	–	6.25	–	4.3	–	–	–	–	–	–
Useful	–	11.1	–	14.3	–	28.0	–	18.75	86.4	–	44.5	50.0	–	–	–	85.8	–	–	–	–
Marginal	–	–	–	–	8.0	8.0	12.5	25.0	4.5	–	22.2	6.25	–	–	–	–	–	–	10	–
Unnecessary	–	2.7	–	–	8.0	8.0	12.5	31.25	–	–	–	–	87.5	82.6	100	7.1	–	95.5	90.0	85.8
Totals	100	100	100	100	100	100	100	100	100	100	100	100	100	100	100	100	100	100	100	100

Table 11.2: Development Education

	1				2				3				4				5			
	CE	CHE	P	U	CE	CHE	P	U	CE	CHE	P	U	CE	CHE	P	U	CE	CHE	P	U
Essential	21.2	7.1	–	16.7	8.0	12.5	6.25	33.3	25.0	25.0	33.4	6.25	25.0	33.3	25.0	12.5	–	14.3	–	37.5
Important	36.4	28.6	21.7	33.3	48.0	62.5	18.75	16.7	4.2	11.1	31.25	12.5	15.0	–	12.5	12.5	–	–	–	–
Useful	30.3	42.9	69.6	33.3	28.0	12.5	50.0	16.7	50.0	50.0	22.2	66.7	60.0	66.7	62.5	62.5	100	85.7	–	62.5
Marginal	6.1	21.4	8.7	16.7	16.0	12.5	25.0	20.8	22.2	20.8	11.1	6.25	–	–	–	–	–	–	–	–
Unnecessary	6.1	–	–	–	–	–	–	11.1	–	–	–	6.25	–	–	–	12.5	–	–	–	–
Totals	100	100	100	100	100	100	100	100	100	100	100	100	100	100	100	100	100	100	100	100

Table 11.3: Global Interdependence

	1				2				3				4				5			
	CE	CHE	P	U	CE	CHE	P	U	CE	CHE	P	U	CE	CHE	P	U	CE	CHE	P	U
Essential	8.3	37.1	25.0	18.5	12.5	20.0	28.6	16.7	25.0	18.2	26.7	12.5	9.6	11.4	42.8	28.6	8.3	7.1	–	–
Important	50.0	34.3	50.0	44.5	25.0	56.0	42.8	33.3	12.5	–	25.0	–	9.6	11.1	–	–	–	–	–	–
Useful	25.0	20.0	16.7	29.6	50.0	20.0	14.3	16.7	25.0	72.8	62.5	33.3	62.5	77.8	–	50.0	–	–	–	–
Marginal	16.7	5.7	8.3	7.4	12.5	4.0	–	33.3	33.3	4.5	–	4.5	–	–	7.2	–	–	–	–	–
Unnecessary	–	2.9	–	–	–	–	14.3	–	4.5	4.5	10.8	50.0	80.8	–	50.0	71.4	91.7	92.9	100	100
Totals	100	100	100	100	100	100	100	100	100	100	100	100	100	100	100	100	100	100	100	100

views have changed since the recent DES documentation on the core curriculum has tended to play down this element in the curriculum.[40] But the Brandt Commission also took up the cudgels in favour of a knowledge of global interdependence:

> We are convinced of the great role education has to play: a better knowledge of international, and not least North-South affairs will widen our views and foster concern for the fate of other nations, even distant ones, and for problems of common interest. The commission feels that schools all over the world should pay more attention to international problems so that young people will see more clearly the dangers they are facing, their own responsibilities and the opportunities of co-operation ...[41]

It went on to say that "increased attention should be paid to educating public opinion and the younger generation regarding the importance of international co-operation".[42]

Yet what really is the position in our teacher education institutions concerning the development of a wider understanding of international affairs? Only 17 institutions (3 colleges, 4 colleges of higher education, 2 polytechnics and 8 universities) or 16.5% of those answering the survey feel that they try to cover this aspect adequately under such topics as geography, international understanding, politics of education, or the occasional lecture on the Brandt Report or North-South relations. There is only one course (at Glasgow University) which specifically deals with the issues of interdependence. At the author's own institution (Reading) not only was considerable ignorance shown concerning Brandt during the last academic session but there appears to be a high degree of apathy amongst the majority of PGCE students towards North-South issues. Yet the Brandt Report has been Britain's best seller during 1980 and 1981, and meetings on and off campuses have been packed, though usually not by teachers. This is perhaps not at all surprising when so many staff within teacher education institutions regard such an aspect of their work as teaching about interdependence as of marginal professional value or even unnecessary. Two college of higher education respondents even refused to answer the question on the grounds that they regarded it as contentious!

General comments

One of the most interesting aspects of the whole exercise has been the unsolicited general comments of many of the respondents over and above the ones already cited. Although the comments are obviously personal a few are mentioned here

since there appears to be a general feeling that the traditional approach to teaching Comparative Education and even the
very name Comparative Education may be inadequate for dealing
with the issues of the 1980s. There is a very clear divide
between those who see Comparative Education as an academic,
intellectual discipline and those who want it to be and only
believe it can be of value if it has a very practical application. If it could be made more practical it would then be
made more readily available for all students.

Several comments highlight the first point of view:
- "Comparative Education is inadequate to examine the issues
of the 1980s. International studies is a much better concept
because it gives broader scope at both theoretical and
practical levels and because it can cover professional staff
development";
- "Comparative Education will presently be replaced by International Education drawn up by geography and history tutors";
- "Comparative Education is too discipline-centred. We need
to move away from a disciplined approach to a problem-centred
approach which means that comparative issues are thus taught
incidentally rather than as a separate subject";
- "I believe in a European perspective and value a comparative perspective in the preparation of all teachers but I
believe that this is best covered as an integrated part of
other topics and not as a separate subject, "Comparative
Education" ... I believe the widening of perspectives in
comprehensive reorganisation, multi-cultural/multi-ethnic
education, the organisation of higher education, teacher
education, curriculum development, etc. is the way forward
rather than the creation of distinct courses in 'Comparative
Education'";
- "It is a mistake to teach Comparative Education as a
separate subject in an Education Department. Education is so
much part of the fabric of society that it should be taught
in the department whose subject the teacher is going to
teach. Education apart from language, history and institutions is an artificial thing".

Some of the reasons why it is not taught widely below
degree level were given as "the need for students to have a
degree of academic maturity", the difficulties in obtaining
up-to-date primary and secondary source material, the need to
be analytical of problems and issues rather than merely
descriptive. On the other hand one polytechnic head of
department wryly observed that "the reason why Comparative
Education is taught at such a low level in teacher education
courses in the UK is the fear that alternative paradigms
threaten the existence of the dominant power structure in our
own society!". It would appear that whatever happens one
cannot win!

The greatest pleas, however, came from those who argued

that students needed "practical nuts and bolts" courses, not theoretical ones and not abstractions about methodology. One reply put the point in general terms when it was suggested that Comparative Education would be more readily acceptable and eagerly taught if it could "strive to cover practical issues, i.e. those issues that relate to the professional preparation of teachers. Comparative educationists must ask themselves how can an international dimension in education be of practical "use" to the student teacher?" While the majority of comparativists since Michael Sadler's famous speech at Guildford in 1900 have had little difficulty in showing the practical usefulness of Comparative Education[43] the modernists would see the practical usefulness in showing how different ethnic groups are treated in schools in different societies, how teachers manage classroom discipline, what is taught in different school curricula, etc. Herein lies food for thought.

Conclusions

Although there were certain weaknesses with the survey in so far as some respondents found the ranking of questions difficult or did not understand topics such as 'development education' and not all the questions were completed in the same detail - nevertheless certain lessons can be learnt which have implications for the British Comparative Education Society.

While Comparative Education continues to be a popular subject where it is taught, whether as an option or as a compulsory component of a course, it is increasingly studied by a minority of students in small groups or in elective classes. There is undoubtedly some opposition to the subject as irrelevant and unnecessary because of its apparently theoretical nature and its lack of clear practical goals for students in training. It is not highly ranked in many institutions and hence is regarded as peripheral to the "real", empirically based, subjects such as sociology and psychology. Because of financial cutbacks courses have been dropped or are under threat of being dropped because of the non-replacement of staff with a Comparative Education interest. On new courses or in newer institutions especially, Comparative Education is increasingly seen not as a separate subject but as a dimension of integrated courses which examine specific topics such as urban education or multi-cultural education though in the latter instance a comparative perspective is more in theory than in reality.

Should Comparative Education only be for theorists and those taking higher degrees or does it also have an application for policy makers and administrators and does it have a practical role for the teacher whether on initial training

221

or on in-service training? Should it seek to make a greater contribution to other disciplines such as sociology, administration and politics than has hitherto been the case? These are very real questions that must be honestly faced by Comparative Educationists as well as by the BCES during the 1980s for one clear result from the survey is that unless there is greater concern to develop practical biases to comparative studies and there is less concern for debates about theoretical models and methodologies of approach in the current financial and academic climate, Comparative Education could be reduced to becoming an academically respectable subject undertaken by a few students at higher degree level only. The need for a comparative and international dimension to the study of educational issues is possibly greater in times of contraction than in times of expansion but the voices of those involved in the field need to be heard more clearly than hitherto. There are many achievements in the field and there is much to be proud of. The need is to continue to make contributions to national and local debates on educational issues wherever and whenever possible and to fire the enthusiasm of younger teachers as they train for their chosen profession. As Philip Altbach observed in an editorial on "Whither Comparative Education?":

> Comparative education must seek to make itself increasingly relevant to the problems and concerns of education in our own countries, on broader policy and research issues, and to its constituency - teacher educators and professionals in the field of education. Our field has advocated relevance for a long time and there are concrete examples of research efforts in this direction. For example studies on the comparative evaluation of educational policy, on the problem of multi-ethnic education and multi-cultural education, on the means of providing equal educational opportunity, and other such issues can provide useful insights to policy makers and scholars concerned mainly with national problems and issues ...[44]

There is the challenge for the 1980s. It must not be ignored.

NOTES

1. The Brandt Commission Report, North-South: A Programme for Survival, London, Pan Books, 1980.
2. H.M.S.O., West Indian Children in Our Schools (The Rampton Report), London, H.M.S.O., 1981.
3. R. Plancke, 'The Comparative Education Society in Europe: Ten years of Meetings', Paedagogica Historica, Volume XIII, number 2, 1973.

4.   R. Cowen, 'Comparative Education in Europe: a note', <u>Comparative Education Review</u>, Volume 24, number 1, 1980.
5.   The British Section of the Comparative Education Society in Europe voted at its Fourteenth Annual Conference in Bath in September 1979 to form a separate British Comparative Education Society. Since then it has been known under this title.
6.   H. Weiler, 'Education and Development: from the age of innocence to the age of scepticism', <u>Comparative Education</u>, Volume 14, number 3, 1978.
7.   G.Z.F. Bereday, <u>Comparative Method in Education</u>, New York, Holt Rinehart and Winston, 1964; B. Holmes, <u>Problems in Education</u>, London, Routledge and Kegan Paul, 1965; E.J. King, <u>Comparative Studies and Educational Decision</u>, London, Methuen, 1968; V. Mallinson, <u>An Introduction to the Study of Comparative Education</u>, London, Heinemann, 1964; H.J. Noah and M.A. Eckstein, <u>Towards a Science of Comparative Education</u>, London, Macmillan, 1969.
8.   Louis Cros, <u>L'Explosion Scolaire</u>, Paris, Spelman, 1967.
9.   D. Adams and R.M. Bjork, <u>Education in Developing Areas</u>, New York, David McKay, 1969; J.S. Coleman, <u>Education and Political Development</u>, Princeton, Princeton U.P., 1965; F.H. Harbison and C.A. Myers, <u>Education, Manpower and Economic Growth</u>, New York, McGraw Hill, 1964; J.K.P. Watson, 'Education as a Factor in Development: Past, Present and Future', <u>Compare</u>, Volume 4, number 2, 1974.
10.   See <u>International Journal of Educational Development</u>, Volume 1, number 1, 1981, for a series of papers discussing the effects of the UNESCO Regional Plans on educational development.
11.   C.A. Anderson and M.J. Bowman (eds), <u>Education and Economic Development</u>, Chicago, Aldine, 1969.
12.   P.H. Coombs, <u>The World Educational Crisis - A Systems Analysis</u>, London, Oxford U.P., 1968.
13.   For example: E. Faure, <u>Learning to Be</u>, Paris/London, UNESCO/Harrap, 1972; P. Lengrand, <u>Lifelong Education</u>, Paris, UNESCO, 1969; P.H. Coombs, R.C. Prosser and M. Ahmed, <u>New Paths to Learning for Rural Children and Youth</u>, Essex, Connecticut, International Council for Educational Development, 1973.
14.   V. Mallinson, op. cit.
15.   T. Husen, <u>The School in Question</u>, London, Oxford U.P., 1979.
16.   J.K.P. Watson, 'Education for Uncertainty - Issues facing Educational Administrators in the 1980s', <u>Educational Administration</u>, Volume 8, number 2, 1980; J.K.P. Watson, 'Coping with Change - Pressures on Educational Administrators in England and Wales', <u>Canadian Administrator</u>, Volume XX, 1981.

17.   P.R.C. Williams (ed), The Overseas Student Question, London, Heineman, 1981.

18.   P. Raggatt, Research in Comparative Education in the 1970s, (forthcoming).

19.   See especially the paper by W.D. Halls.

20.   An exception is the British Educational Management and Administration Society which recently formed a European Forum and which has arranged several study tours during recent years.

21.   P. Altbach, 'Whither Comparative Education?', Comparative Education Review, Volume 24, number 2, 1980.

22.   J.K.P. Watson, 'The Importance of Comparative Studies in Education', Didactica, Volume 13, number 1, 1980; W.K. Kay and J.K.P. Watson, 'Comparative Education: the Need for Dangerous Ambition', Educational Research, Volume 24, number 2, 1982; E.J. King, Education for Uncertainty, Inaugural Lecture at King's College, University of London, 1977.

23.   Cambridge, Kent at Canterbury, Leeds and Oxford.

24.   P.E. Jones, Comparative Education: Purpose and Method, Brisbane, University of Queensland Press, 1971; G.W. Parkyn, 'The particular and the general: towards a synthesis', Compare, Volume 5, number 3, 1976; A.R. Trethewey, Introducing Comparative Education, Oxford, Pergamon, 1976.

25.   P. Raggatt, op. cit.

26.   G.Z.F. Bereday, op. cit.

27.   A.R. Trethewey, op. cit.; E.J. King, Other Schools and Ours, London, Holt Rinehart and Winston, 5th edn., 1979; E.J. King, C.H. Moor and J.A. Mundy, Post-Compulsory Education: A New Analysis in Western Europe, Volume 1, London, Sage, 1974.

28.   Commission for Racial Equality, Teacher Education for a Multicultural Society, London, C.R.E., 1974.

29.   Department of Education and Science, Education in Schools: A Consultative Document, Cmnd. 6869, London, H.M.S.O., 1977.

30.   R. Jeffcoate, Positive Image: Towards a Multi-racial Curriculum, London, Chameleon Books, 1979; A.N. Little, Educational Policies for Multiracial Areas, Inaugural Lecture, Goldsmith's College, University of London, 1978; A.N. Little and R. Willey, Multi-Ethnic Education: The Way Forward, Schools Council Pamphlet 18, London, Schools Council, 1981.

31.   Rampton Report, op. cit., pp. 60-61.

32.   ibid., p. 64.

33.   See for example: B. Bullivant, The Pluralist Dilemma in Education, Hemel Hempstead, George Allen and Unwin, 1981; J. Bhatnegar (ed), Educating Immigrants, London, Croom Helm, 1981; World Yearbook of Education 1981, Education of Minorities, London, Kogan Page, 1981.
224

34.   N.D.C. Grant, 'Educational Policy and Cultural
Pluralism: a Task for Comparative Education', Comparative
Education, Volume 13, number 2, 1977; R.G. Paulston,
'Ethnicity and Educational Change: a priority for Comparative
Education', Comparative Education Review, Volume 20, number
3, 1976; J.K.P. Watson, 'Educational Policies in Multi-
cultural Societies', Comparative Education, Volume 15, number
1, 1979.

35.   R. Burns, 'Development Education', I.Y.C. issues,
number 4, 1979, Sidney, UNICEF, 'The Development of Development Studies', Papers presented to 36th A.N.Z. Ass. Congress,
Canberra, January 1975.

36.   Ministry of Overseas Development, Development
Education, Report and recommendations by the Working Party
of the Advisory Committee on Development Education, Overseas
Development Paper No. 14, London, H.M.S.O., 1978.

37.   ibid.

38.   ibid.

39.   Official aid in Sweden accounts for 0.82% of GNP,
in the Netherlands 0.75% and in Norway 0.66%. The figure
for the UK is 0.38%.

40.   Department of Education and Science, A Framework
for the Curriculum, London, H.M.S.O., 1980, and The School
Curriculum, London, H.M.S.O., 1981.

41.   The Brandt Report, op. cit., p. 11.

42.   ibid., p. 292.

43.   M. Sadler, 'How far can we learn anything of
practical value from the study of foreign systems of education?', Lecture delivered at Guildford, 20 October 1900 and
reprinted in J.H. Higginson, Selections from Michael Sadler,
Liverpool, Dejall and Meyorre, 1980, and Comparative Education Review, Volume 7, number 3, 1963-64.

44.   P. Altbach, op. cit., p. 154.

LIST OF CONTRIBUTORS

PILAR AGUILAR

is a Research Student at the University of Hull Institute of Education

ROBIN BURNS

is Senior Lecturer at the Centre for Comparative and International Studies in Education at La Trobe University, Australia

MICHAEL BYRAM

is Lecturer in the School of Education, University of Durham

LINDA DOVE

is Lecturer in the Department of Education in Developing Countries, University of London Institute of Education

SERVICE FARRANT

is Education Officer, Education Division of the Commonwealth Secretariat, London

RICHARD GOODINGS

is Senior Lecturer in the School of Education, University of Durham

NIGEL GRANT

is Professor of Education in the University of Glasgow

EDMUND KING

is Emeritus Professor of Education in the University of London

ANNE MacLAUGHLIN

is Assistant Professor in the School of Physical Education, University of Victoria, Canada

MICHAEL McPARTLAND   is Lecturer in the School of
                       Education, University of Durham

MICHAEL MAWER   is Lecturer in the Department of
                       Educational Studies, University
                       of Hull

PETER MURPHY   is Assistant Professor in the
                       Department of Communication and
                       Social Foundations, University
                       of Victoria, Canada

JOHN OWEN   was formerly Senior Lecturer in
                       Comparative Education at
                       Buckinghamshire College of Higher
                       Education

GONZALO RETAMAL   is a Research Student at the
                       University of Hull Department of
                       Adult Education

WILLIAM TAYLOR   is Director of the University of
                       London Institute of Education

KEITH WATSON   is Lecturer in Comparative
                       Education, University of Reading

ROBERT WEIL   is Lecturer in the Department of
                       Education, The Queen's University,
                       Belfast, N. Ireland

227

DATE DUE